THE DIVORCE AND SEPARATION OF ALIENS IN FRANCE

THE DIVORCE AND SEPARATION OF ALIENS IN FRANCE

BY

LINDELL THEODORE BATES
Doctor of Laws
(Universities of Paris, Madrid and New York)
Member of the Bars of the United States, England and Spain
Commander with Star of the Royal Spanish Order of Isabella

NEW YORK
COLUMBIA UNIVERSITY PRESS
1929

Published November, 1929

Printed in the United States of America
THE AD PRESS, LTD., NEW YORK

DEDICATED

TO THE MEMORY OF MY FATHER

LINDON WALLACE BATES

who died in Chantilly, France, April 21, 1924

and

TO THE MEMORY OF MY BROTHER

LINDON BATES, JUNIOR

who died on the Steamship *Lusitania,* May 7, 1915

PREFACE

This book is intended to serve as a manual upon the French law of the divorce of aliens. It has been prepared in a form such as will enable American and British lawyers to understand this law and competently to advise their clients in view of it. It is hoped that it will assist toward judgments having a better chance of extraterritorial recognition than some of those now rendered. If the book produces even a measure of such social service, the labor of writing will have been repaid and its purpose fulfilled.

The author has avoided as far as possible theoretical discussion of the many debatable legal questions involved in the French law of divorce. He has endeavored to set forth the weight of authority and current practice, with a summary indication only of the conflicting views. He has been obliged to pioneer somewhat in the subject, for no other detailed treatise upon it has yet been written in English, nor is there a textbook in French devoted especially to the divorce of aliens. The author wishes to place it on record that he is not a partisan of easy divorce. On the contrary, he considers that marriage should be indissoluble save under very exceptional circumstances.

This occasion is taken to thank Judge Samuel G. Archibald, of the Canadian Bar, located in Paris, for the author's privilege of learning at first hand French divorce practice; and M. Henri Gadd, his able associate, for pleasant and useful discussions of French law while the author was practicing in Paris. *Maître* Jacques Scheftel, of the French and Imperial Russian Bars, has been so kind as to read the manuscript of this book. *Maître* Guillaumin, *Bâtonnier* of the *Ordre des Avocats* of Paris, placed the facilities of the Library of the Paris Bar at the author's disposal and thereby made it possible to verify certain citations found in reports not elsewhere available. The author wishes also to express his appreciation to the officers of the Columbia University Press, in particular to Messrs. Frederick Coykendall and Charles G. Proffitt, for their helpful attitude in relation to the publication of this book.

LINDELL T. BATES

August 1, 1929

55 East 65th Street
New York City

CONTENTS

Chapter I

NATURE OF DIVORCE AND SEPARATION

According to Justinian, the Latin word *divortium* was formed from the two words *diversitas* and *mentium*. Whatever its origin, the word divorce has come to signify a particular consequence of mental diversity or incompatibility, namely, the termination of marriage. Article 227 of the French Civil Code says:

> Marriage is dissolved: 1st, by the death of one of the spouses. 2nd, by divorce lawfully pronounced.

By divorce is meant in French law "The dissolution of the marital bond judically pronounced during the lives of the two spouses." (Carpentier, *Divorce et séparation de corps,* 1889, vol. 1, sec. 1.) The institution resembles the *divortium a vinculo matrimonii* of the Romans.

Divorce puts an end to the marriage relation. It is to be distinguished, however, from an annulment of marriage, which latter also dissolves the marriage. Divorce is pronounced for cause occurring after marriage, annulment for cause occurring before it. A divorce terminates the relation as of a date after the marriage solemnization, a marriage having existed or being assumed to have existed in the interval. An annulment operates retroactively to the date of solemnization of the marriage, the judgment declaring in effect that no marriage ever existed. The grounds for divorce are not the same as those for annulment. A voidable marriage may either be annulled or be treated as binding and ended by divorce, if there are the corresponding distinct grounds. Even a void marriage may be ended by divorce if it is ostensible and prima facie valid and the validity is not placed in issue.

A divorce is also to be distinguished from a separation. The French *séparation de corps* is a separation of the persons from bed and board. It involves of necessity therewith under article 311 of the Civil Code a *séparation de biens,* namely, a separation of the property of one spouse from that of the other. Separation in French law is the *divortium a mensa et thoro* of Canon law, a mere relaxation of the marital relation. Separation excuses the couple from performance of certain matrimonial duties and deprives them of certain rights, leaving nevertheless a subsisting bond or marriage status.

In the law of France there is no such thing as a qualified, temporary or partial judicial separation, save a possible six months' *délai d'épreuve,* a test period, based on the hope of reconciliation, ordered occasionally by a court before it will pronounce divorce, and save a separation *pendente lite,* during the proceedings of a divorce or a separation action. Apart from these two exceptions, a separation is always complete and potentially permanent. Nevertheless, it may be converted into or be superseded by a divorce, or be ended by a reconciliation.

A separation, like a divorce, must necessarily be a judicial act in order to be lawful. *Séparation de corps* is more than the mere living apart or *de facto* separation of the couple. The law admits of no contractual or voluntary separation, even to regulate a physical separation already existing in fact. Article 307 of the Civil Code expressly forbids separation by mutual consent. This is construed to forbid any separation not based upon a judgment. While there is no corresponding provision applicable to divorce, nevertheless the prohibition is deemed to exist *a fortiori,* by implication, the articles of the Civil

Code allowing divorce by mutual consent having been abrogated in 1816 and never having been reënacted.

In French law there is a legal remedy called a *séparation de biens* (separation of property) without a *séparation de corps.* A word of explanation concerning it is necessary. It is the practice in France for parties intending to marry to enter into a notarial contract in which their property rights during marriage are set forth. Thus a partnership or association of the spouses is formed. A general or limited community regime may be selected, or the *dotal* (dowery) regime or the regime of separation of property. In the absence of a written contract the law indicates that the regime shall be that of general community as to personalty and future acquisitions. During the marriage the husband administers community property, *dotal* property and in most cases even the separate property of the wife. This management may be so inefficient as to warrant intervention by the court. Under such circumstances an action lies at the instance of either party to change the original matrimonial regime into that of separation of property. *Séparation de biens* may accordingly be pronounced without affecting the personal relations of the spouses. Since a mere *séparation de biens* without a divorce or separation of the persons leaves untouched the marriage and the marital rights and duties in so far as the persons are concerned, the subject will not be dealt with in this book. An explanation of the French law of *séparation de biens* belongs in a treatise on marriage contracts and on the property rights of married women, not in a study, such as this, on divorce and separation.

The above definitions and distinctions are faithfully observed by French authors and law courts. Separation is never, in France, called divorce, as it is even today in Spain, Italy and various other countries in which the

DIVORCE AND SEPARATION

Canon law of the Catholic Church still has influence. The word divorce in France is not modified by any adjective, as it is on occasion in Great Britain and in the United States, where by limited divorce is meant judicial separation and by absolute divorce is meant dissolution of the marriage by divorce.

Chapter II

HISTORY

The major influences which have molded the laws and institutions of France are the laws of Rome, of the Germanic tribes, of the Catholic Church, of the French Revolution, and of Napoleon. They have each in turn affected the law of divorce and separation.

As Voltaire facetiously remarks, divorce is but a few weeks younger in the world than marriage. The laws of Moses allowed divorce. In the Roman Republic the general legal principle theoretically existed that marriage could be dissolved as it was contracted, that is to say, with entire liberty. Such, says Montesquieu, was the law of the Twelve Tables. Custom and religion, however, were even then opposed to divorce in Rome and elsewhere in the pagan world. Rome, indeed, counted five centuries before her first known divorce took place. In the year 447 of the Foundation of the City (236 B. C.) Lucius Antonius is said to have been expelled from the senate for having repudiated his wife without previously consulting his friends. In a single year in the same century, one hundred and seventy Roman matrons were convicted of poisoning their husbands! Divorce, which at that time was difficult for husbands to achieve, was practically impossible for wives. Wives were unable in fact if not in law to repudiate their husbands and this practical disability lasted until the time of Domitian.

The Roman Empire was far less strict morally than the Republic and as time passed divorces became more and more frequent. Seneca says that in his day wives counted the years by the number of their husbands. Juvenal caustically remarks that a good wife is rarer than a white crow! Divorce was rampant at the opening of the Christian era not alone at Rome, but in the Provinces. Gaul was no exception.

Divorce in Roman law took place either by mutual consent, *i. e., bona gratia,* or by the repudiation of one party by the other. Divorce by mutual consent seems never to have required the observance of any particular formalities, but repudiation, which in the days of Cicero could take place expressly or through implication, had, by the *lex Julia de adulteriis*, to be declared before seven adult citizens. No particular legislative purpose existed at this time to restrict divorce; only to render notorious the change in marital condition. So custom even after the *lex Julia* still recognized repudiation evidenced by the handing over of the household keys or by the delivery of a notice. Divorce by repudiation was indeed under some circumstances legally obligatory. A husband must cast from him an adulterous wife. Agreements not to divorce or to forfeit a penalty in case of divorce were void. Legal restrictions upon the practice of divorcing began only when the abuse of the institution attained such proportions that public morals were gravely threatened and the orderly succession to property was disturbed.

Christianity came, and among the reforms advocated by the Christian sect was that of domestic morality. Christianity urged a return to the purity and simplicity of bygone days. It sponsored the indissolubility of marriage. Biblical passages of St. Matthew (xix, 6, 9), St. Mark (x, 11, 12) and St. Luke (xvi, 18) are principally invoked in support of this doctrine. Saint Matthew's words are these:

HISTORY

What therefor God hath joined, let not man put asunder. (Chapter xix, verse 6.)

I say unto you, whomsoever shall put away his wife except for fornication and marries another, committeth adultery, and he that marrieth her when she is put away committeth adultery. (Chapter xix, verse 9.)

Prior to the fall of the Western Empire (376 A. D.), Christianity had not materially modified the law or practice of divorce. In fact, the attitude of the Church itself was for a long time unsettled. The Council of Arles (352 A. D.) did not succeed in dissipating the uncertainty concerning the true meaning of the verses of St. Matthew, for it is indeed difficult to reconcile the words "except for fornication" of verse 9 with the absolute terms of verse 6. Clerical opinion finally inclined to consider the exception in verse 9 in the light of an error inconsistent with verse 6. The latter sets forth the doctrine of the indissolubility of marriage without qualification and is the basis for the view of marriage as a sacrament. Milton says the priest, not God, forbade divorce.

In the chaos of laws in the Dark Ages among the barbarians in Gaul, it is difficult to distinguish the parts played respectively by the customs of the conquerors, the Roman law and the canonical regulations. It is well known that the invaders of the Western Empire recognized and practiced divorce with great freedom. Nevertheless, they gradually came under the influence of the Roman Church, and in the Frankish Monarchy traces are visible of obedience to the Church in this relation. The Church in France gradually attained exclusive cognizance of matrimonial causes.

The later Roman law influenced law in France indirectly and chiefly through the Church regulations until the revival of Roman law in the Middle Ages. By the time of the great codification of Justinian, clerical influence at the seat of government in Constantinople had become strong. At this period divorce *bona gratia* was limited to cases in which both parties wished to live thereafter in continence, *propter castitatem*. Divorce by repudiation was authorized only for certain enumerated causes. Repudiation without cause was severely punished. When the grounds were inadequate the repudiating spouse was not allowed to remarry either during a given period or during life. Later, divorce by consent was abolished altogether and divorce by repudiation gradually became obsolete. After the twelfth century a consummated marriage could no longer be ended by any form of divorce. Separation, temporary or permanent, was the only practical relief, unless annulment could be attained. Nevertheless, divorce existed and the attitude of the Church toward divorce was not entirely fixed until the sixteenth century.

At the Council of Trent, November 12, 1560 a great debate was held concerning the dissolubility or indissolubility of marriage. The indissolubility doctrine won. Divorce was categorically forbidden. The Church thenceforth prohibited a second marriage during the lifetime of the spouses save in two cases, namely, when one spouse became Catholic while the other remained non-Catholic, and when one spouse entered a convent or monastery while the other remained in the world. In these cases, a dispensation to remarry, rather than a divorce, was accorded to the Catholic or lay spouse respectively. When both parties were Catholic and continued to live in the outer world, a *divortium quoad thorum et mensam,* a permanent separation from bed and board, was available, but not a *divortium a vinculo matrimonii*. At this Council, the Church emphasized the sacramental aspect of marriage and its superiority to the civil contractual aspect. Marriage preserved this religious character in the dominions of the

Most Christian King of France and Navarre through the Middle Ages and until the French Revolution.

The eighteenth century witnessed in France the birth and growth of a powerful sentiment for moral reform, economic emancipation and political liberty. This climaxed in the Revolution. The movement in France to reform society and government and to attain freedom of thought reached fruition in 1789. The dominance of nobles and Church then ended. Marriage was deeply affected by the new current of ideas. The Revolution remade of this institution a purely civil contract, eliminating the aspect of sacrament and abolishing the jurisdiction of the Church in matrimonial causes. It went even further. On September 20, 1792, the first day of the sitting of the National Convention and the day before the proclamation of the Republic, a divorce law was enacted.

The law of 1792 reflected the complete victory of the civil over the ecclesiastical theories of marriage, of contract over sacrament. The law authorized divorce for various causes by judgment of a family tribunal. It went to the extreme of reviving divorce *bona gratia,* by mutual consent, without a judgment. It abolished altogether judicial separation, temporary as well as permanent.

As a result of the complete reversal of law, the divorce situation in France rapidly came to resemble that of imperial Rome at its worst. Couples unhappily married rushed to take advantage of the new liberty. In Paris, in the year VI of the Republic (1798) the number of divorces exceeded that of the marriages! A reaction was inevitable. This began under the Consulate. Napoleon, in 1801, remarked: "An honorable man never decides upon divorce unless his wife has been unfaithful to him and unless the divorce can be obtained without scandal. These principles are ingrained in the French soul."

HISTORY

The French Civil Code of 1803, called the Code Napoléon after 1807, abrogated the law of 1792 and the maze of supplemental executive regulations and decrees of the Revolutionary period.* It authorized divorce and permanent separation for adultery, condemnation to a degrading and corporal punishment, violence, cruelty and gross insults. Divorce for cause was of frequent occurrence under the French Empire, but far less so than had been the case under the Republic. Divorce by mutual consent was also recognized by the Code, but to be effectual it had to be approved by a judgment. The attainment of this was surrounded by such formalities that Napoleon's own divorce from Josephine is said to be the only known instance of such divorce under the Civil Code. In fact, however, Napoleon's divorce bore but slight resemblance to the type of divorce by mutual consent established by the Code. It was really a politico-legal event, *sui generis.* A declaration of consent to divorce was signed by the imperial couple and by various distinguished witnesses. It was then recorded with the senate and proclaimed by the sovereign.

Clerical ascendancy returned for a time in France with the Bourbons, at the fall of the Empire. By law of May 8, 1816, the divorce articles of the Code Napoléon were repealed and only the separation articles remained. In fact, the Code Napoléon soon thereafter lost its name and became again the Civil Code, which it has since been popularly called, although a decree reëstablishing the Napoleonic name was published in 1852, during the Second Empire.

Repeated efforts were made in the years following 1816 to reinstate divorce. Political liberalism gained ground steadily in France after 1830, particularly after

*Decrees in France are executive, not judicial acts; they resemble executive regulations in America, orders in council in England.

1848. Even the encyclical of Pope Leo XIII, of February 10, 1880, severely condemning divorce, was powerless to stem the tide and on July 27, 1884, most of the divorce articles of the Civil Code were reënacted. Those articles permitting divorce by mutual consent remained, however, abrogated. For a few years following the enactment of the law of 1884 the Catholic Church made efforts to obtain its repeal, or at least to bring about its restrictive interpretation. In vain was considerable pressure brought to bear upon bench and bar to apply the law in a manner which would not violate Canon law. Nevertheless, since 1884 divorce and separation have coexisted in France, and divorce as an institution is now firmly entrenched. On occasion even today opposition to divorce is manifested. For instance, in 1923 the mayor and municipal councillors of the small provincial town of Ploughne resigned rather than officiate at the remarriage of a divorced person.

Procedure in divorce and separation actions was changed in important respects by the law of April 18, 1886. Various other amendments to the substantive and adjective law have been made since then. For ten years the French rules on the conflict of laws were codified by the Hague Convention of June 10, 1902. This was ratified June 1, 1904, and denounced on December 13, 1913, to take effect June 1, 1914. The Convention applied between France and the leading European countries only. Neither the United States, Great Britain, Spain nor the Latin-American Republics ratified or adhered thereto. Nationals of the latter countries were, nevertheless, given by the French courts the benefit of similar rules, even in matters in which the Convention had departed from the earlier French law. By law of June 6, 1908 conversion of separation into divorce after three years was changed from permissive to mandatory at the petition of either party. Apart from these enactments, the texts of law in France in relation to divorce and separation have remained substantially the same during the last forty years.

Aside from Napoleon's divorce, legislative or executive divorce or separation has never been known in France. Ecclesiastical separations lost civil effect at the Revolution. Contractual divorce by consent without judicial intervention was possible for a few years during the Revolution, but not since then. Since those days divorce and separation have been purely judicial and strictly civil in character. The former British and American practice of private acts of parliament or legislature granting divorce has never existed in France, nor indeed the present Scandinavian practice of divorce or separation by royal decree.

Chapter III

STATISTICS

Divorce is now frequent in the French Republic, even among Catholics. In 1885 there were recorded 4,277 divorces; in 1913, 15,372; in 1921, 21,033. Today, the figure is nearly thirty thousand. Separations are but a quarter as numerous. About 20 percent of the judgments rendered are not recorded and hence remain inoperative. During 1922, the ratio of divorce in France was 70.4 per hundred thousand inhabitants, which may be compared with 135.4 in America, 59.6 in Germany, and 6.8 in England. (Rosenberg, *Ehescheidung und Eheanfechtung,* 1926, p. 121.) About 85 percent of the divorce petitions in France are granted, and only 15 percent are refused. (Planiol, *Traité élémentaire de Droit Civil,* 2d Ed., 1903, Vol. III, p. 160.) Of separation applications 75 percent eventuate. In 90 percent of the actions the ground for divorce or separation is "gross insults." The wife is plaintiff in 65 percent of the divorce, and in 80 percent of the separation, actions.

In 1926, there were in France 2,498,230 aliens in a total population of 40,743,851. These foreigners are mostly Italians, Spaniards, Belgians and Swiss, but there are also large colonies of British and Americans. The "British and American Paris Directory, 1926" lists about twelve thousand names. "Americans in France, A Directory 1927-1928" mentions roundly four and a half thousand. This is but the fixed British and American population of a certain social or business prominence, the large number of tourists, transients, students, etc., being omitted. In 1928 there were 26,187 United States citizens "permanently domiciled" in the Department of the Seine (Paris and suburbs).

Concerning the divorce and separation of aliens in France, there are no statistics. Separations of Italians and Spaniards amount probably to over two hundred a year. Divorces of British subjects are estimated at less than a dozen per annum, and there are only a few separations. Before the War, there were comparatively few divorces of Americans, but from 1919 to 1927, the rate increased enormously. The mark of a hundred was passed in 1922, and that of three hundred was reached in 1926. In 1927 the American papers published a list of United States citizens who had been divorced in France during the preceding year. The names created a sensation in both countries. A reaction set in and in 1927 the number of American divorces in France fell. Probably fewer than two hundred eventuated in that year. In Paris there were about one hundred and seventy, of which over one hundred and forty came before the 3d chamber of the Tribunal of the Seine. It is doubtful whether ever again the excessive figure of 1926 will be reached.

The number of divorces and separations among aliens in France is out of proportion to the fixed foreign population. It is far too high in the case of Americans, and indicates extensive migration for divorce from America to France. Of the three hundred or so American couples divorced in France in 1926, more than half had been married in New York! France has become indeed the divorce Mecca for aliens, particularly for fashionable Americans. The Gould, Valentino, Vanderbilt and Salm cases have focussed attention upon this fact. Established in Paris are some forty American lawyers, a dozen British solicitors, and representatives of the legal profession of practically every other foreign country. Divorce plays a part in the practice of many, if not most, of these.

STATISTICS

Recent events have shed light upon the so-called American "divorce mill" in France. The Ministry of Justice completed in June, 1928 an investigation into the matter. It apparently found irregularities in procedure and petty grafting. The principal irregularities consisted in improper evidence of domicile submitted to the courts, in non-observance of the requisite time intervals for performance of legal formalities, etc. Possibly also erroneous or misleading certificates of custom (expert evidence) on American law were used in some cases. The matter came up before the French disciplinary authorities in such judicial affairs, namely, the Court of Cassation, which imposed certain penalties. In consequence, the number of divorces granted to Americans in 1928 was even lower than in 1927. Practice has become stricter but no change in the French statutory law of divorce has been made in view of this episode.

Chapter IV

CELEBRATED CASES

Before entering upon a consideration of the details of French law in relation to the divorce and separation of aliens,* it may be of interest to recount a few of the famous or notorious cases. The details herein given are all derived from published reports or public records of the various cases. The author disclaims any intent to defame anyone or to do anything else than comment fairly upon matters of public interest. A brief outline will acquaint the reader with the manner in which matrimonial controversies are presented to and solved by the French courts. So many interesting cases are found in the reports that one is embarrassed in selecting a few only for special study.

1. The Affaires† Martinez del Campo

The Count of San Antonio, a Spaniard living in Barcelona, son of the Marshal Serrano, dictator of Spain, married in Paris on October 11, 1880, the wealthy heiress of the Spanish family Martinez del Campo. The marriage ceremony was the necessary civil one, as required by French law. It was followed by a religious solemnization

*The terms "aliens," "foreigners," and "abroad" are used from the point of view of France, except in the chapters on the recognition of French judgments in other countries, in which chapters these terms are used from the viewpoint of such countries.

†French judgments set forth the opinion as well as the award. Cases are cited by the name of the court, date judgment was rendered, name of the report, etc. Important cases are popularly referred to as the "*affaire*" —mentioning the name of a party.

at a Catholic Church in Paris. The marriage did not turn out well; owing, so the wife said, to her husband's impotency. In 1881 the Countess sued before the Tribunal of the Seine to annul the marriage on this ground. The husband contested the French jurisdiction and by judgment of December 27, 1881, the Tribunal declined to entertain the suit, saying the Spanish ecclesiastical courts should take cognizance. In the case of Catholics in Spain, matrimonial causes come before the ecclesiastical courts and an appeal from their judgments lies to the Roman Rota. Instead of bringing an action for annulment before the Church court in Barcelona, the Countess applied directly to the Pope for an annulment of her marriage. A rescript delegated the Bishop of Paris to carry out in that city the preparatory procedure and the taking of testimony necessary for a decision upon her petition. While the ecclesiastical action was in course, the Countess applied to the Tribunal of the Seine for alimony and suit-money. By judgment of January 13, 1883 (*Journal Clunet** 1883, p. 169) both were refused her for the reason that the husband was only temporarily sojourning in France during the time in which the Bishop was trying the annulment action. On September 2, 1885, the Sacred Congregation of the Holy Office granted the wife an annulment for non-consummation of the marriage. In view of this judgment, she considered herself thereafter unmarried and took no steps to obtain *exequatur* (domestic confirmatory judgment) of the Roman judgment in France or in Spain.

Shortly thereafter Miss Martinez del Campo fell in love with a Frenchman named Mielvaque. Her family opposed the match, so the lovers or lover staged a kidnapping. One day when the young lady and her chaperon

*The reference is to the *Journal de Droit International Privé*, by E. Clunet.

were driving in the *Bois de Boulogne,* a group of equestrians approached the carriage. The duenna was induced to descend and was engaged in conversation. The young people took advantage of this to drive away in the carriage.

No mayor of any borough (*arrondissement*) in Paris could be found who would marry them, since the lady's French civil status record showed no trace of any annulment, the Roman judgment not having been recorded in France or the civil marriage record corrected. The couple accordingly fled to Belgium, hotly pursued by the lady's brother. The police of Brussels refused to separate the elopers, as both were of age and the lady had been kidnapped with her consent if not indeed with her connivance. Nevertheless the Belgian authorities would not go so far as to marry them. The couple sailed for England. On landing at Dover, they very nearly succeeded in inducing the local registrar to issue a marriage license, but he communicated with the central registry in London and the registrar-general advised him not to permit the marriage. Consequently the young people went on to London.

Meanwhile the confidential agent of the Martinez del Campo family reached London and filed a *caveat* at the central registry to prevent the issuance of a license. The family contended in this instrument that the Papal annulment was void and that the girl was still married to the Count of San Antonio. In view of this attitude, the central registry after a hearing definitely refused a license. It is not stated in the reports and articles dealing with the case what fate eventually befell the parties, but much ink flowed concerning the possible solutions for the marital difficulties. On the facts of the case, no action could be brought by the wife in France for annulment, divorce, separation, or provisional remedies. (*Enlèvement de femme majeure, Journal Clunet,* 1887, p. 451.)

2. THE Affaires GOULD

Frank J. Gould, an American, married in Scotland a British subject, Edith Kelly. She became thereby a United States citizen. For a number of years before the marriage the husband had lived in Paris, but he still had a house at Tarrytown, New York, and in his will he stated that he was domiciled in New York State. After the marriage the couple lived for a time in New York, and thereafter resided in Versailles, where Mr. Gould owned a palatial home.

Mrs. Gould started the matrimonial litigation by bringing an action for divorce before the Tribunal of Versailles, making in her petition serious allegations of immorality against Mr. Gould. She apparently also caused the police to raid his house at Versailles to confirm the charge that he had a mistress living there with him. The two were not caught in adultery *flagrante delicto.* Mr. Gould defaulted at the preliminary "conciliation" hearing and the president of the Tribunal accordingly gave Mrs. Gould leave to sue for divorce and awarded her temporary alimony. She failed to serve the *assignation* (*i. e.,* writ of summons and bill of complaint) within twenty days of the president's order, nor did she serve it at all. Consequently the accessory relief lapsed, but the action still remained pending and she could have served process at any time.

While Mrs. Gould's action was at this stage, Mr. Gould ascertained that his wife was living in Paris with Mr. "C.", said in reports to have been an American army officer. The police were asked to verify the fact and a raid took place upon a residence at Paris in which Mrs. Gould and "C." were reported found in adultery *flagrante delicto.* The husband thereupon in turn brought suit for divorce before the Tribunal of Versailles. Mrs. Gould defaulted at *conciliation,* and Mr. Gould promptly served his summons and complaint upon her and on April 16, 1919 obtained judgment of divorce by default for her adultery. The wife seasonably entered "opposition" to the judgment, thereby opening the default. In her notice of *opposition* she objected to the jurisdiction on the ground that she was a "British" subject, domiciled in New York. She also denied the adultery and recriminated that Mr. Gould had himself committed adultery, as shown by the police report of the raid first above mentioned.

Mrs. Gould did not apply for a court order for the taking of testimony by an *enquète* (inquiry) to supplement her police report and to prove the husband's adultery on other occasions, nor did she ask a stay in order to bring special falsification proceedings of *inscription de faux* to impeach the veracity of the husband's police report against her. The case came on for trial (*audience*) before the Tribunal of Versailles simply on the pleadings and two respective police reports. Mrs. Gould did not proceed with her own co-pending action, nor apply to consolidate the two actions, nor counterclaim in her husband's action. The trial consisted therefore simply in an oral argument by counsel on the above papers.

The Tribuntal of Versailles, on December 9, 1919,* held that the wife had waived objection to the jurisdiction by not appealing from the order of the president at "conciliation" giving the husband leave to sue, that she was estopped from objecting to the jurisdiction since she had herself sued in France and her action was still pending. The Tribunal found as a fact that Mr. Gould's domicile was New York, but that the couple had long resided in France where adultery had taken place by the wife. The Tribunal recognized that recrimination was a defense

*The text of the judgment may be found in the printed record of Gould-Gould, 235 N. Y. 14, on file in the Library of the Bar Association of the City of New York.

in New York law, but nevertheless said it was *"pas concluante,"* that is to say, it was insufficient in French law. For these reasons the default judgment was confirmed.

The defendant wife took an appeal to the Court of Appeal of Paris, but here again she refrained from asking an inquiry to take testimony and did not counterclaim or go on with her own case. It is only fair to say, however, that had she sought such affirmative relief, her objection to the jurisdiction would surely have been deemed waived. The Court of Appeal rendered an *arrêt* (judgment) of divorce on July 7, 1920, by reason of the wife's adultery. At the hearing of the appeal the only serious debate was upon the question of jurisdiction, for the wife's bare denial of adultery was considered insufficient to overcome the husband's police report, which enjoyed public authenticity by operation of law. The court sustained the jurisdiction, not alone for the reasons given by the Tribunal of Versailles, but also because adultery had been committed in France and because recrimination, a plea to the merits, had been combined with a plea to the jurisdiction. The court said "the attitude taken by the lady contradicts the conclusions by which she declined the jurisdiction of the French judges."

Pourvoi (petition for review) to the Court of Cassation was filed, but again the only legal point in issue was jurisdiction. On December 8, 1920, the judgment of the Court of Appeal was affirmed. The highest court said that the residence of the couple in France and the commission of the adultery there were sufficient reasons for asserting jurisdiction, particularly since the defendant had herself brought suit in the country. The Court of Cassation did not mention the waivers relied upon by the lower courts to sustain the jurisdiction. (Paris, July 7, 1919; Cassation, December 8, 1920; *Journal Clunet,* 1921, p. 518.)

At this stage in the litigation the scene was temporarily shifted to New York, where Mrs. Gould brought suit for divorce. Her action was defeated there and the French divorce was considered *res judicata*. The American action is described in Chapter XXXIII, on the recognition of French divorce judgments in the United States.

Subsequently, litigation between the ex-spouses was renewed in France. The ex-wife went upon the Paris vaudeville stage under the name "Edith Kelly Gould." The ex-husband sued to restrain the use by her of his family name. The tribunal handed down a judgment forbidding Mrs. Gould to use the Gould name, with exemplary damages for every day during which she persisted in so doing. This was effective.

While the former Mrs. Gould never attempted to continue her own divorce action started at Versailles, which she could have done at any time before the New York decision, nevertheless she sued her husband again at Versailles in relation to property matters. She asked for liquidation and partition of community property and sale at auction of the real estate in France. She claimed to have married under the French regimen of general community (*communauté légale*) and hence to be entitled to half of her ex-husband's property, particularly of his extensive realty in France. The Tribunal of Versailles, May 15, 1924 (*Dalloz hebdomadaire,* 1924, p. 448) deciding against her, held that Americans married in Scotland without ante-nuptial contract and simply resident in France are governed as to property by their national regime, namely, separation of property; that the husband's realty in France is indeed governed by French law under article 3 of the Civil Code, but not in all relations; that article 1393 C.C., concerning the application of general community in the absence of written ante-nuptial marriage contract, applies to French citizens married in France, not to aliens married abroad, and finally that the principle of the immutability during marriage and indivisibility of the matrimonial regime prevents the application of a different law to the realty of the spouses from that which applies to their personalty. Mrs. Gould lost all her French and American actions.

3. The Affaire Countess Zamoyska

An Austrian wife sued her husband for divorce in France. He objected to the jurisdiction for the reasons that he was an Austrian domiciled in Galicia, Austrian Poland, that he was immune from suit as a deputy in the Austrian Parliament, and that actions brought by him for the restitution of conjugal rights were then pending both in France and in Austria. The Tribunal of the Seine, July 16, 1886 (*Journal Clunet,* 1886, p. 707) consolidated the two French actions, stayed for six months the husband's action for restitution of conjugal rights and dismissed for lack of jurisdiction the wife's action for divorce. The stay was granted so that the wife might sue in Austria. The unusual reason given for declining jurisdiction for the divorce was that Austrian law would have to be applied by the French court, that this law does not allow Catholics to divorce and that a French court could not apply the prohibitions of Austrian law to them since such a religious restriction is opposed to French policy. The only way out of the difficulty seemed to be to decline jurisdiction, which the court did. The Court of Appeal of Paris, February 26, 1891 (*Journal Clunet,* 1891, p. 1189) reversed this decision and asserted divorce jurisdiction because the husband had attended at *conciliation* and at a hearing to settle provisional remedies in each case without objecting to the jurisdiction, also because *compétence ratione personae* (jurisdiction) over aliens is discretional and permissive, not mandatory. In the exercise of its discretion and to avoid a possible denial of justice, the court held that it would take jurisdiction in view of the long residence of the couple in France and the uncertainty as to where the husband really was domiciled. The case consequently was remanded to the Tribunal for trial on the merits.

4. The Affaires Garlet

A Frenchwoman married a Belgian and thereby became a Belgian subject. The couple were domiciled in France. The wife sued for divorce in Paris and the husband seasonably objected to the jurisdiction on the ground of his alienage. The Tribunal of the Seine, January 5, 1887 (*Journal Clunet,* 1889, p. 812) accordingly dismissed the complaint. Thereupon, the wife started suit in Belgium. The husband this time objected to the Belgian jurisdiction, alleging that he was domiciled in France. The wife was non-suited because by Belgian law the courts of the domicile, not of the allegiance, have jurisdiction. The Court of Appeal of Brussels held the same view. The wife then started suit for separation in France, lack of jurisdiction for divorce being *res judicata* in that country. On July 29, 1889 (*Journal Clunet,* 1889, p. 712) the Tribunal of the Seine again declined to take cognizance, saying it did not have "to concern itself with the interpretation of law by a foreign jurisdiction." In other words, the refusal of the Belgian courts to adjudicate did not oblige the French courts to act. Fortunately the Court of Appeal of Paris felt otherwise. On August 8, 1890, it asserted jurisdiction so that "a person wronged may find somewhere a remedy" (*Journal Clunet,* 1890, p. 890).

5. The Affaire Count Menabrea

Count and Countess Menabrea were Italian subjects. The husband obtained on December 8, 1891, a presidential decree admitting him to French citizenship. He promptly —over-promptly—followed this on January 22, 1892 by a suit for divorce against his wife, who had remained Italian. The presidential decree of naturalization was published in the *Journal Officiel* on February 9, 1892. The wife objected to the divorce jurisdiction on the ground that the husband was still an alien when the divorce suit was started. The Tribunal of the Seine, November 9, 1892 (*Journal Clunet,* 1892, p. 1155) asserted jurisdiction on the theory that the husband became French on the date of the decree itself and a Frenchman can always sue an alien under article 14, C.C. in a matter of contract, which term includes a marriage. The Court of Appeal of Paris decided in the same sense on May 12, 1893 (*Journal Clunet,* 1893, p. 847). The Court of Cassation, July 16, 1894 (*Journal Clunet,* 1894, p. 1023) quashed the judgment of the Court of Appeal and sent the case back for retrial to the Court of Appeal of Orleans. The view of the Court of Cassation was that the French citizenship dated only from February 9, 1892, the date of publication, hence the husband was not entitled to invoke article 14, C.C. when suit was brought.

The situation then was that the judgment of the Tribunal of the Seine asserting jurisdiction was pending on appeal before the Court of Appeal of Orleans. If this court should follow the indication of the Court of Cassation it would render a judgment denying jurisdiction, replacing that of the Tribunal asserting it. Since the plaintiff was not entitled to invoke article 14 C.C., neither could he lawfully ask divorce, for an Italian lacks divorcing capacity. Count Menabrea therefore desired to discontinue his action, doubtless in order to start all over again, inasmuch as in a new action he could claim the benefit of French citizenship both as to jurisdiction and capacity to divorce. He accordingly served notice upon his wife that he renounced the benefit of the judgment of the Tribunal asserting jurisdiction and that he discontinued his action. The Countess endeavored to defeat the discontinuance by not assenting thereto. The Court of Appeal of Orleans, May 30, 1895 (*Journal Clunet,* 1895, p. 1063) held that the judgment of the Tribunal was only on jurisdiction, not on the status itself, hence article 249, C.C., prohibiting acquiescence in judgments of divorce, did not apply; consequently the plaintiff could renounce the benefit of the judgment and also discontinue the action without defendant's consent, for issue on the merits had not yet been joined.

6. The Affaire Valentino

Rodolfo Guglielmi (alias Valentino) an Italian, married Dorothy Hudnut in Indiana. The marriage took place after the enactment of the Cabel Act of September 22, 1922, and in American law the wife remained American. The couple came to France, their intention of divorcing being an open secret. As grounds for divorce the wife produced a letter in which Valentino declared that he had left her and that his decision to cease all relations with her was definite. The Tribunal of the Seine, January 18, 1926 (*Journal Clunet,* 1926, p. 663) pronounced divorce for "gross insults," the letter being considered to constitute this. No objection was taken to the jurisdiction. The Tribunal decided that the wife retained the rights and prerogatives of an American citizen and could invoke her national law as to her status and capacity, particularly that of Indiana, which allows divorce for adultery, impotency, desertion and "gross insults" (!) and which refers, for the divorce of citizens married in the state, to the laws of the domicile of the parties, in this case to French law. The parties admitted being domiciled in France and the judgment recites "that the spouses have established their domicile in France."

7. The Affaire Princess de Wrede

A Frenchwoman was married to an Austrian in Vienna with the usual Catholic ceremonies indicated by the local law. The wife thereby became Austrian. The husband later obtained Russian naturalization and conversion to the Orthodox Greek faith. The Russian ecclesiastical authorities then rendered a judgment pronouncing the marriage void unless the parties should within two months obtain an Orthodox blessing. This blessing was not procured, so the annulment became absolute. Thereupon the wife in turn became Orthodox. She then married Prince de Wrede, a Russian, in Paris. A civil marriage was solemnized at the borough hall, followed by an Orthodox blessing at the Russian Embassy.

The Prince de Wrede subsequently became a naturalized German subject and sued in Munich for annulment of his marriage on the ground that the wife's Austrian marriage still subsisted when he married her, because the Russian judgment annulling it was void. The wife appeared and contested the Bavarian action, but the decision went against her. The Prince thereupon applied for *exequatur* in France of the Bavarian judgment. During the pendency of this action he prevailed upon the French civil registry officials to mention the judgment of annulment on the French marriage record. This rectification enabled him to present a bachelor's certificate to the marriage officials in Switzerland and he promptly married another woman there. The Princess, his first wife, caused bigamy proceedings to be instituted against him in France.

Having achieved his purpose of amending the marriage record, the Prince wished to discontinue the French *exequatur* action. He accordingly served upon the defendant a notice of discontinuance, which she declined to accept. The Tribunal of the Seine, February 4, 1897, upheld the validity of the discontinuance notwithstanding her non-assent. The Court of Appeal of Paris, June 23, 1898 (*Journal Clunet,* 1898, p. 912) reversed this and not only disallowed the discontinuance, but forced the Prince to go to trial. At trial the court denied his prayer for *exequatur* and pronounced the Bavarian annulment judgment void. In other words the German annulment was considered void, the Russian annulment lawful, yet the latter had annulled a valid Austrian marriage. The Court of Cassation, May 9, 1900 (*Journal Clunet,* 1900, p. 613) affirmed the judgment of the Court of Appeal.

Later the Princess de Wrede was restored to French nationality by decree (Seine, March 12, 1912; *Revue Lapradelle,** 1918, p. 116, note). Probably she thereupon sued for divorce.

8. THE Affaire PRINCESS DE BEAUFFREMONT

The Prince and Princess de Beauffremont were French citizens married and domiciled in Paris. After three attempts the Princess obtained a separation and custody of the children. Thereafter she decided to marry Prince Bibesco. No divorce law existed in France at this time, so she could not achieve this purpose in her own country. She accordingly went to the Duchy of Anhalt in Germany

*The reference is to the *Revue de Droit International Privé,* by G. de Lapradelle.

and became naturalized there without her husband's knowledge and consent. In Prussian law, in force in Anhalt, there is a provision that a permanent separation between Catholics shall be deemed the equivalent of a divorce. It is highly doubtful if this law has any application to aliens or to foreign separations, but nevertheless the Princess managed to induce the civil authorities to marry her to Prince Bibesco.

Great was the scandal and indignation in France that a French woman should become a German and remarry in violation of the French separation judgment. The Prince de Beauffremont took immediate steps to contest the German marriage and to gain custody of the children. Protracted litigation took place in France and Belgium and there are several reported decisions in both countries. The vital issue was whether or not a French wife judicially separated from her husband could become naturalized abroad without her husband's consent. If she could, then the German divorce secured by operation of law might be valid by application to her of her new *lex nationalis*. The French courts held that the German naturalization was void since the husband had not consented thereto, that the German marriage was effected in deliberate fraud of the French law, and was bigamous and void. The custody of the children was taken from the wife and given to the husband, and surrender was enforced by an award of heavy damages for every day's delay in obedience. (Cassation, March 18, 1878; *Sirey,* 1878. 1.193.)

Chapter V

NATIONALITY

Since this book treats of the divorce and separation of aliens in France, it is necessary to state at the outset who are considered foreigners in the Republic.

The French Civil Code defines with care who are French citizens but it does not say who are aliens. The determination of who are aliens is therefore a problem of elimination. The Code was amended in essential particulars by the law of June 26, 1889 and the law of August 10, 1927. Concerning the effect of marriage upon nationality, the date of the marriage determines what law applies, whereas in relation to nationality of origin the date of majority, not of birth, determines the law. Thus, the 1927 law governs persons who had not completed their twenty-first year at the date of promulgation. (*Instructions aux préfets et aux parquets relative à la loi du 10 août 1927 sur la nationalité*. Par. 1.) A doctrine of French law is that nationality is not vested at birth but only at majority. The law of August 10, 1927 consequently operates retroactively as to persons still minors at the time it took effect. It does so notwithstanding the fact that article 2 of the Civil Code states that laws do not operate retroactively, since this provision of the Code does not apply to laws of public order, such as laws on nationality. Consequently, to determine the nationality of a husband or wife in France, it will be necessary to solve a conflict of laws in respect of time, as also a conflict in respect of legislative authority.

NATIONALITY

In reference to French nationality of origin, it is not now useful to consider the state of the law before 1889, but it is still necessary to consider the situation under the law of that year, since the law of 1889 applies to some persons still of divorcing age, and that of 1927 to many. Article 8 of the Civil Code, as amended by the law of June 26, 1889, granted a person French nationality *jure sanguinis* by reason of a French father, wherever the person was born. Le Maistre, a distinguished jurist of pre-revolutionary days, aptly said of a child: "The father is natural to him, the place is strange. In the one case it is the blood that is French, in the other it is only the air that is of France." French law has always laid especial emphasis upon allegiance *jure sanguinis*. But allegiance *jure soli* also plays some part. French nationality *jure soli* was conceded by virtue of birth in France, but only to a person one of whose parents was also born in France and with the right of the person to decline French citizenship at his majority if that parent were the mother. French nationality *jure soli* was likewise established regardless of the birthplace of the parents, if the person was domiciled in France at his majority, but with the right on his part to decline the citizenship. The law of August 10, 1927 repealed article 8 of the Civil Code as amended in 1889. The provisions concerning nationality *jure sanguinis* were reënacted by the new law, but nationality *jure soli* was extended. A person reaching majority after the date of the 1927 law is French *jure soli* provided his father was born in France or his mother is French. A person is also French but with the option of declining the nationality, if he was born in France of an alien mother who was herself born in France.

It is to be noted that in French law citizenship *jure sanguinis* is imposed; there is no option to elect a foreign nationality of the place of birth. French citizenship *jure soli* is also imposed in most cases. France, however, has never gone so far as to fasten her citizenship upon all persons born in France; or to give all such persons the right to claim it, as does the Fourteenth Amendment to the United States Constitution. Nor has France imposed her nationality by legislation upon classes of aliens *en bloc,* as was done by Brazil in 1889 where, upon the proclamation of the Republic, all aliens then domiciled in Brazil were declared to be Brazilians.

In regard to change of nationality by reason of marriage, article 12 of the Civil Code declared an alien woman marrying a Frenchman to be French. Article 19 declared alien a French woman marrying a foreigner, but not in case she failed to obtain his citizenship under his national law. The law of 1927 abrogated both these articles. A Frenchwoman thereafter marrying an alien remains French unless upon marriage she declares her intention of taking her husband's nationality. Nevertheless she loses French nationality if she acquires his nationality under his own law and the spouses establish their first matrimonial domicile outside France. An alien woman marrying a Frenchman after August 10, 1927 remains alien unless she elects French nationality at marriage or unless she loses her foreign nationality by her national law. Until the enactment of the 1927 law, France was a partisan of unity of nationality within the family. She is this no longer, but has followed the lead of the United States and Great Britain in allowing women marrying men of another country to preserve their own allegiance. France nevertheless still gives a certain preëminence to the husband's law and surrenders claim to her women when they follow their alien husbands abroad.

Consider now French citizenship by naturalization. By article 12 of the Civil Code the naturalization of a husband in France did not *ipso facto* extend to the wife, but it did to the minor children. The latter, nevertheless were allowed at majority to decline the change. The 1927 law retains the old rule as to the wife, but imposes citizenship upon the children, a right of election being denied them.

By article 18 of the Civil Code any person formerly French could be restored to French nationality by presidential decree provided he resided in France. Article 19 of the Civil Code also allowed the citizenship of widows and divorcées to be so restored. It was considered for many years that a married woman could not be restored to French nationality under article 18 C. C., only an ex-married woman under article 19 C. C. During the war, however, the practice grew up of allowing foreign married women, formerly French, to become French again without their alien husband's consent. On August 5, 1919, the Minister of Justice informed the Chamber of Deputies that the practice was then well established; although the civil courts had repeatedly declared it to be illegal. He suggested, indeed, that this was a way in which French girls unhappily married to American soldiers could give the French courts jurisdiction to divorce them. (Pillet and Niboyet, *Manuel de Droit International Privé,* 1925, p. 187.) The law of August 10, 1927, gave legal sanction to this practice. An alien wife, formerly French, can now regain French nationality by decree, even against her husband's wishes, provided the spouses have been separated *de facto* for more than a year or an action for divorce or separation is pending between them.

French nationality may be lost in a variety of ways, e.g., by naturalization abroad, provided the person is not in default in respect of military service. *Quaere,* whether or not so far as France is concerned, a French woman can become validly naturalized abroad without her husband's consent? The French courts some years ago emphatically declined to recognize any right in a French woman to become alien by naturalization abroad without leave of her French husband or court even when the couple were judicially separated. This is the decision in the Princess de Beauffremont case, decided by the Court of Cassation, March 18, 1876 (*Sirey,* 1878.1.193). Weiss considers that the law of February 6, 1893, restoring full capacity to women separated from their husbands, has changed the rule of the *affaire* de Beauffremont. (Weiss, *Manuel de Droit International Privé,* 5th ed. 1909, p. 132.) Perhaps the French courts would now, as a matter of reciprocity, concede to French wives of alien origin the absolute right of foreign naturalization, the law of 1927 allowing alien married women formerly French to reacquire French nationality without the intervention of their husbands. The answer to the question is still uncertain.

Mention should be made here that French law recognizes a condition or status of total absence of any nationality. A person may be *apatride* (*i.e.,* without nationality). Such in France is the position of an individual who has lost German nationality of origin by residence in France for over ten years, but who has never become naturalized in the Republic. (Seine, May 12, 1892; *Journal Clunet,* 1892, p. 937.) This is also the condition of Russian *émigrés* who have lost Russian nationality by the Soviet decrees of December 12, 1921 and October 29, 1924. This abnormal status is indeed today so well-known in France that persons without nationality but resident in the Republic are expressly subjected by the law of April 1, 1923, to compulsory military service.

Conflicts of nationality frequently arise before the authorities in France. Indeed, today there are a dozen or more citizenship cases in dispute between the United States State Department and the French Ministry of Foreign Affairs. They relate chiefly to the induction into the French Army of young men born in France of American fathers themselves born in France and of young men born in America of French fathers. In an endeavor to solve conflicts of nationality, France made special treaties with Switzerland in 1879, Belgium in 1891 and 1921, and Monaco in 1918. No treaty of this sort exists with the United States or with the other Powers.

Needless to say, a conflict between nationalities involving French nationality arising before a French court is decided in harmony with the views of French, not of foreign, law. *Lex fori* applies to nationality for reasons of sovereignty and public policy. (Weiss, *Traité théorique et pratique de Droit International Privé,* 1909-13, 2d ed., vol. 1, p. 305.) Nationality is a matter of public law rather than of private law, although written in the Civil Code, and the rules of this public law are supreme in France over those of the American Constitution. (Cassation, February 2, 1921; *Sirey,* 1921.1.113.)

When French nationality is not involved, as will be the case when the conflict is between two alien nationalities, the French *lex fori* is not necessarily alone applied. To determine an alien's nationality of origin, the French courts will probably consult the national law of his father. In case of a conflict between the imperative laws of two foreign countries equally to be respected by the court, the nationality claimed by the litigant will be favored. (Seine, January 4, 1910; *Journal Clunet,* 1911, p. 1265.)

The Valentino and Salm divorce cases strikingly illustrate the recent breakdown in France of the rule of unity of nationality within the family and of the predominance of husband's law. The Tribunal of the Seine, January 19, 1926 (*Journal Clunet,* 1926, p. 663) recognized the American nationality of the wife, a United States citizen married to an Italian (Valentino) in the state of Indiana after passage of the Cabel Act of September 22, 1922.

By Italian law the wife was Italian, by American law she remained a United States citizen. France treated her as American and allowed her to divorce. Had she been considered Italian she could have been awarded only separation, since Italian law forbids the divorce of her nationals and France respects the prohibition. The same principle was applied in the Salm case; the wife (Millicent Rogers) being American, the husband (Count Salm) Austrian. (Seine, April 11, 1927, unreported.)

Serious complications arise in relation to foreign naturalizations. Laurent-Bailly says that when two foreign nations claim the same person, the one by origin, the other by naturalization, French law will prefer the country to which the alien first belonged. (Laurent-Bailly, *Le Divorce et la séparation de corps en France et à l'étranger,* 1910, p. 42.) A person of German origin who became a naturalized Brazilian, but who secretly recorded with the imperial authorities under the law Delbrück his intention to retain German nationality, was considered to be still German in France, the naturalization being deemed inoperative and fraudulent. (Cassation, June 21, 1922; *Revue Lapradelle,* 1923, p. 313.)

It is still unsettled under what circumstances an alleged loss of alien nationality will be considered in French litigation. The Tribunal of the Seine remarked on May 10, 1890 (cited by Laurent-Bailly, p. 64): "The loss of nationality of origin by aliens under the laws of their own country must be without influence upon their situation vis-à-vis French law." Consequently, since the German authorities had not actually pronounced loss of German nationality to have taken place, the Tribunal would not do so. The same court shortly thereafter decided a divorce case on the basis of total lack of nationality on the part of the wife, who had ceased to be Italian in Italian law when her husband became naturalized in

France, but who had not become French by his naturalization. (Seine, November 9, 1892, cited by Laurent-Bailly, p. 41.) The judgment of the Tribunal of the Seine, May 12, 1892, already mentioned, passed upon an alleged loss of German nationality, found the loss to be a fact and decided the case accordingly. An alleged loss of Portuguese nationality, raised only incidentally in a divorce action, has been inquired into and no loss found according to Portugese law. (Seine, December 6, 1887; *Gazette du Palais,* December 7, 1887.) It would seem, therefore, that French courts will entertain an issue of an alleged loss of foreign nationality provided French citizenship is not involved and the litigation relates merely to private affairs, such as divorce and separation.

Chapter VI

DOMICILE AND RESIDENCE

It is necessary also to consider the law of domicile and residence in France in relation to aliens, for these matters have a bearing upon jurisdiction, service of process and eventual extraterritorial recognition of French judgments.

The word domicile is sometimes loosely used in France, just as it is in other countries. Aliens arriving in France are required to register with the prefect of police within a certain time, regardless of how long they intend to remain. The declaration is accompanied by a *certificat de domicile* signed by the *concierge* (janitor) of the hotel or apartment house in which the foreigner is stopping. The expression "domicile" used therein does not necessarily mean domicile in the strict legal sense, but simply dwelling place. The declaration ought not to be considered as evidence of a change of domicile to France, because transients are required to make it as well as permanent residents. Nor could it properly be treated as an election of a fictitious domicile equivalent to the indication of an address for service of process within the jurisdiction. The term "residence" in French is not synonymous with "domicile," as it usually is in divorce statutes in the United States and Great Britain.

Pothier, one of France's greatest legal authorities of the *aucien régime,* defines domicile as "the place where a person has established the principal seat of his habitation and of his affairs." (Pothier, *Introduction à la coutume d'Orleans, Oeuvres de Pothier,* by Bugret, 1861, section 8, p. 3.) Article 102 of the Civil

Code says that every "Frenchman" has his domicile for "civil" purposes "where he has his principal establishment." In order to change domicile, a person must actually reside in another place and have the intention of fixing there his principal establishment. (Article 103, C. C.) To establish intent in relation to a change of domicile, article 104 C. C. provides for the filing of a notice at the borough hall of the municipality which the person leaves and that of the *commune* to which he goes. A declaration made only at the latter is insufficient to establish intent. (Agen, April 10, 1900; *Dalloz,* 1900.2.430.) This would be true also of a declaration filed only at the former. Both declarations unaccompanied by actual removal would be inoperative. A change of domicile to be operative must be to a precise place. Consequently the Tribunal of the Seine, May 17, 1905 (*Journal Clunet,* 1906, p. 396) disregarded Jacques Lebaudy's purported removal to the "Sahara" and his election of a fictitious domicile at the "Embassy of the Empire of the Sahara in Brussels." The use of the word "principal" in articles 102 and 103 shows that there can be but one domicile. The principle of singleness of domicile, nevertheless, does not prevent in French law the coëxistence with the real domicile of one or more so-called "fictitious domiciles" (*domiciles fictifs*) independent of the real domicile. Such fictitious domiciles may be selected for forensic or other purposes; they are merely addresses for service of process or notices. Such domiciles are also called "elected domiciles" (*domiciles élus*). By fictitious or elected is here meant constructive, not false or fraudulent. The election of a constructive domicile does not involve the intent of article 103 C. C. A fictitious domicile is not the equivalent of a real domicile for all purposes.

While there is considerable authority in French law for the opinion that every person is necessarily domiciled somewhere, yet the courts have recognized the possibility of total absence thereof. For instance, the Tribunal of the Seine, February 3, 1897, (*Journal Clunet,* 1897, p. 331) found an Australian to have no domicile anywhere, neither in France, England nor Australia, although he had resided in France for the last two years.

Domicile is either voluntary or involuntary, *i.e.,* by operation of law. Persons who are under control of a *tuteur* (guardian) are necessarily domiciled with him. It is a principle of French law that a wife can have no other domicile than that of her husband, unless she is judicially separated from him. Article 108 of the Civil Code says a wife "has no domicile other than that of her husband." By article 214, C. C., a wife must follow her husband wherever he deems it advisable to live. In other words, a wife's domicile is fixed by operation of law. No such thing obtains as a present matrimonial domicile distinct from that of the husband. Nevertheless, a husband's domicile is deemed to continue where it was (so far as a wife is concerned) when she is not informed by the husband of a change of his domicile, although she is aware of the fact of his departure from France. (Dax, January 16, 1908; *Journal Clunet,* 1909, p. 154.) Similarly, the husband's domicile will be considered unchanged in relation to the wife, when he has deserted her and has set up a separate domicile elsewhere without giving her an opportunity to join him there. A wife cannot have a separate domicile in virtue of agreement with her husband. (Article 1388, C. C.) By article 108 of the Civil Code as amended by law of February 6, 1893 a wife judicially separated from her husband now has a domicile separate from his. But no matter what the provocation or circumstances, a wife cannot by French law leave her husband without a judicial separation and set up her own domicile elsewhere. A married woman in trade may have a fictitious separate domicile for business purposes, but this has no relation to divorce or separation.

Residence may be defined as "the place where a person fixes for a time his habitation." (Planiol, *Traité élémentaire de Droit Civil,* 2d ed., 1901, vol. 1, p. 219.) A person may have any number of residences. A wife suing for divorce or separation is always granted a separate residence *pendente lite* by order of the president of the tribunal. (Article 238, C. C.)

The rules of law above indicated are stated by the Civil Code to apply to French citizens. (Article 102 C. C.) The Code does not say they apply to aliens in France. Consequently very grave problems are presented concerning which law, French or foreign, on domicile and residence applies to foreigners. According to Pillet and Niboyet *lex fori* governs domicile and French law is to be applied to determine whether or not an alien is domiciled in the Republic. (Pillet and Niboyet, *Manuel de Droit International Privé,* 1925, section 447, p. 533.) Weiss, on the contrary, says *lex nationalis* is to be applied. (Weiss, *Traité théorique et pratique de Droit International Privé,* 2d ed., 1907-13, pp. 323-25.) The Hague Convention of June 12, 1902 indicates *lex nationalis,* but this treaty is now no longer law in France. Consequently, whether it is *lex fori* or *lex nationalis* that is to be applied is still uncertain. In fact, without stating what law is applied, the tendency is to apply French tests of domicile, and the courts find English and Americans to be domiciled in France under circumstances in which a British or American court would probably find that domicile of origin continued. (Pillet and Niboyet, p. 521.) Nevertheless, *lex nationalis* alone has been applied in a recent case, the *affaire* Crane.

It is not even settled in French law what the circumstances are under which an alien can validly have any domicile in France. The situation before and after the law of August 10, 1927 must be distinguished. Consider first the pre-1927 period. Article 13 of the Civil Code read: "An alien who has been authorized by decree to establish his domicile in France shall there enjoy all civil rights." Article 11, C. C., said: "An alien shall enjoy in France the same civil rights as those which are or shall be accorded to French people by the treaties of the nation to which such alien belongs." In view of these articles the question naturally arose: could an alien have a domicile in France in the absence of decree or treaty? After long hesitation, jurisprudence and doctrine finally settled upon the view that an alien could have no *de jure* domicile without decree or treaty, but could have a *de facto* domicile, for special purposes, such as jurisdiction, succession, taxation, etc. *De jure* domicile was deemed a civil right reserved to the French or those assimilated to them, *de facto* domicile a natural right open to all aliens. *De facto* domicile was considered a true domicile, not a mere residence, yet carrying with it fewer rights than *de jure* domicile. The latter domicile obtained by decree was a step towards French naturalization. The condition of an alien under a presidential decree admitting him to domicile was substantially that of a denizen at common law. Aliens *de jure* domiciled in France were on a basis of equality with French citizens as to civil rights, whereas aliens *de facto* domiciled there were under certain disabilities and entitled to those rights only which the law of nations concedes to aliens as human beings when they are in a country not their own. Such was the state of the law until lately. The law of August 10, 1927, on nationality, repealed article 13, C. C.; but without substituting anything in its place and without abrogating article 11, C. C. Consequently it is not entirely clear at this time, nor yet decided, whether the distinction between *de jure* domicile and *de facto* domicile still obtains (the former being reserved to treaty-power aliens alone) or, whether the distinction has broken down and all aliens can now have both *de jure* and *de facto* domiciles, the two being thenceforth legally the same.

From the viewpoint of divorce and separation the interest of the question is perhaps academic, because *de facto* domicile was and is sufficient for most purposes, including jurisdiction. Aliens not infrequently avail themselves of article 104, C. C., and file a declaration of domicile at the borough hall of the locality in France in which they intend to become domiciled.

It is, however, of particular interest to discuss whether or not an alien wife can today acquire a separate domicile *de facto* or *de jure* in France. Since an alien wife can become French without her husband's consent under the law of August 10, 1927, it is clear that she can obtain a separate *de jure* domicile in France. Can she become *de facto* domiciled apart from her husband in the French Republic, either with or without his consent? Unfortunately no certain answer can be given. The Tribunal of the Seine, May 14, 1926 (unreported), in the *affaire* Crane, a divorce action between Americans, conceded the right of the wife under California law to establish her own *de facto* domicile in France. The circumstances of the case were exceptional, and it is possible that the principle would not be extended or applied to other facts. In litigation between two aliens their *lex nationalis* would probably be applied, and the question answered according to this law. If the husband were French, the wife alien, article 108, C. C., forbidding separate domiciles would surely be given preference in France over a foreign law permitting it. If the husband were alien, the wife French, it is an open question whether or not the latter could claim the benefit of her husband's law or would be obliged to abide by the disability of the French. Probably the husband's law allowing separate domicile would be given preference, as article 108, C. C., does not seem to be a law of public order, which type of law article 3, C. C., makes binding upon all persons "who inhabit the territory." Unity of domicile within the family is, however, a strong *desideratum* of French law.

It is instructive to mention a few divorce and separation decisions in which conflicts of domicile have been adjudicated. A Spaniard was considered to be domiciled in France upon proof that he moved his household furniture to Paris, installed himself in his wife's apartment and in various instruments of the proceedings emanating from his *avoué* recited his French domicile. (Cassation, June 14, 1910; *Journal Clunet,* 1911, p. 209.) An American husband was held to be domiciled in Paris when it was shown that he lived the previous eighteen months in Nice, leased an apartment in Paris for a term of years and made his declaration of domicile there at the prefecture of police. (Cassation, November 10, 1920; *Journal Clunet,* 1923, p. 71.) A British husband has been held not to be domiciled in France, although he had married there, was thinking of living and entering business in Paris and his wife had leased an apartment, when it was pointed out that he had not yet personally removed from England, had not paid his wife's rental and had not leased the apartment in his own name. (Seine, June 20, 1922; *Journal Clunet,* 1923, p. 75.) A British husband was held not domiciled in France, in the absence of anything to show intent to remove from England, although the spouses had resided in Paris for a long time and the husband exercised a trade there. (Seine, January 27, 1892; *Journal Clunet,* 1892, p. 439.) It will be seen from the foregoing that *de facto* domicile of the civil law bears considerable analogy to domicile of the common law.

Chapter VII

PARTIES

Actions for divorce or separation are strictly personal and can be instituted only by a husband or wife or, strange to say, by an ex-husband or ex-wife. If a marriage has been annulled by a French court, no action for divorce or separation can be entertained thereafter. It seems, however, that an action for annulment will lie after a divorce. (Carpentier, *Traité théorique et pratique du divorce et de la séparation de corps,* 1886, vol. 1, No. 12, note.) But likewise after a valid divorce an action for separation or divorce will still lie under certain circumstances at the suit of the losing party. Since in France divorce and separation have different consequential effects for the winning party and the losing party, the former retaining, the latter surrendering certain property advantages, it is thought that if at the time of the judgment the losing party had also a cause for divorce or separation which was not invoked, he or she ought not to be prevented from instituting a later action for a judgment in his or her favor, in order to equalize effects. This is the reasoning upon which the possibility of later action is based. Such a rule could exist only in a country such as France, in which divorce or separation may be pronounced for or against either or both parties, or divorce be granted to one, separation to the other. For example, in the Salm case divorce was simultaneously awarded the wife upon her claim, separation to the husband upon his counterclaim. (Seine, April 11, 1927, unreported.) The distinct awards do not even have to be concurrent in time or embodied in the same judgment or granted in the same action.

It will seem extraordinary to common law lawyers that a validly divorced person could sue for divorce or separation, but the jurisprudence not alone in France, but in Belgium and Luxemburg, rather firmly supports this rule. (Piérard, *Divorce et séparation de corps,* 1927, vol. 1, section 221, 222, 228, p. 424, 442, *et seq.*) Accordingly, the losing party in a separation judgment can later sue the winner for separation. (Dijon, July 26, 1899 and August 8, 1899; *Dalloz,* 1899.2.452.) Similarly, a judgment of separation in favor of the wife may be converted at the end of three years into a divorce, yet the husband's counterclaim for divorce (pending in a separate action for divorce brought by the wife before the expiration of the three years) may proceed to judgment. (Angers, December 5, 1918; *Dalloz,* 1920.2.103.) The Court of Cassation, July 4, 1921 (*Dalloz,* 1923.1.240) held that a court of appeal has authority to pronounce divorce forthwith in favor of one party and to order an inquiry to take testimony upon the counterclaim of the other with a view to an eventual divorce judgment for the defendant. Piérard points out that an ex-spouse could sue "several years" after the divorce pronounced against him and no text of law says that in order to do so he must have been ignorant of the facts entitling him to judgment in his favor at the time when judgment was rendered against him. (Piérard, Vol. 1, Section 222, p. 428.) In other words, a defendant who has a cause for divorce or separation is not obliged to counterclaim, but may institute a later action.

It is not necessary that there shall be a valid or subsisting marriage between the parties in order to divorce or separate in France. Invalidity or non-subsistence is an affirmative defense in French law. So long as an ostensible marriage has taken place and the marriage has not been annulled, an action for divorce or separation will lie. Nevertheless the marriage must be *prima facie* valid, else the president of the tribunal has no power to give leave to sue and the court itself lacks authority over the subject-matter, *compétence ratione materiae.* Hence two Canadians "married" in France before a priest but without a civil ceremony, cannot litigate in relation to divorce, for such marriage is void on its face. (Paris, July 27, 1926, cited by Boyer, *Petit Formulaire. Suivi de jurisprudence. Procédure en matière de conciliation de divorce et de séparation de corps,* 1927, p. 118.)

Under article 1166 of the Civil Code, a creditor is entitled to exercise or defend his debtor's legal actions. This does not extend to divorce or separation actions, even though these have pecuniary consequences of great interest to creditors. Creditors, however, may follow the action as of right. Neither the district attorney nor any relative of the spouses can be a party so far as the principal relief is concerned, but either of these may join as co-plaintiffs or be joined as co-defendants in relation to accessory relief affecting the children of the spouses.

A person whose capacity is incomplete requires the concurrence or collaboration of those who lawfully advise or control him in order to sue or defend. A minor is emancipated by marriage; consequently he is no longer under complete guardianship (*tutelle*), but is still under limited or partial guardianship (*curatelle*). A minor should sue and be sued jointly with his limited guardian (*curateur*). The committee (*tuteur*) of an adjudged lunatic sues for separation on behalf of his ward and with leave of his family council; he cannot sue for divorce. The committee defends alone in both classes of actions. A committee (*tuteur*) sues and is sued with a convict. The committee (*conseil judiciaire*) of a feeble-minded person or a spendthrift should be joined in an action in the same manner as a limited guardian. A bankrupt or insolvent (*failli*) can himself bring and defend an action for divorce or separation, but the trustee in bankruptcy or receiver (*syndic*) should be named co-defendant in view of the property questions involved. An unadjudicated lunatic whose condition is known sues and defends by an attorney (*mandataire*) *ad litem* named by the court. A French court has no power to appoint an attorney for a feeble-minded wife interned abroad. (Douai, August 9, 1886; *Journal Clunet,* 1887, p. 175.) In the case of aliens, foreign guardians, committees, attorneys, etc., or their equivalent under different names, will usually be recognized in France without ancillary or superseding appointment. Foreign disabilities will usually be recognized in the case of aliens, but not political disabilities such as civil death or interdictions for prodigality. An accomplice is not named co-defendant (co-respondent) in French practice, but such person has a right to intervene in the action to clear his or her name. (Poitiers, July 11, 1892; *Le Droit,* July 25, 1892.) A third person wrongfully accused of adultery can intervene in the action to disprove this allegation and to recover damages for slander. (Paris, January 8, 1912; *Le Droit,* June 29, 1912.)

In French law, according to article 215, C. C., a married woman is under a general disability to sue or defend without her husband's consent, or that of a court in case of his unjustified refusal. In matrimonial actions the consent of the president (*i.e.*, the presiding justice) of the tribunal is obtained at an *ex parte* hearing before the action can be begun, no further consent being required. Alien married women, to sue or defend a matrimonial action in France, do not have to obtain their husband's or a foreign court's consent in addition to that of the president of the French court, even though they are under a disability by their *lex nationalis* similar to that applicable to French women by French law.

Concerning a possible survival of the ancient disability of alienage to sue, the situation in French law is even today not entirely clear. The Tribunal of the Seine, July 2, 1889 (*Journal Clunet*, 1890, p. 874), said: "The right of suing for divorce is comprised among the so-called 'civil rights' and their enjoyment is in principle reserved to citizens alone. The *exception* based upon the alienage of the husband, in relation to a demand for divorce or separation of the persons, does not raise, strictly speaking, a question of *compétence ratione personae* or *ratione materiae,* but raises a question whether there is a cause of action, for that which has to be determined is whether or not the plaintiff has the character and capacity necessary to bring an action of this sort." This decision does not mean that aliens entitled to civil rights by decree or treaty can always sue for divorce or separation in France while those not so entitled can never do so. Aliens not favored by treaty are frequently allowed to do this as of grace if not as of right and many treaties give court access without giving all civil rights. The treaty of April 1, 1874 with Russia entitled Russians to access to the French courts, but did not enable them to divorce; for France respected the claim of the Russian ecclesiastical courts to the exclusive right to divorce their subjects. (Seine, July 13, 1911; Paris, January 26, 1911; *Journal Clunet,* 1917, p. 602.) Notwithstanding the decision quoted, the *exception* of alienage is considered to raise a jurisdictional objection rather than an objection addressed to the old disability of alienage. Alienage as an objection to plaintiff's character is obsolete in practice, for aliens can and do sue in matrimonial actions irrespective of decree or treaty. Even an alien enemy is not denied the right to sue or defend. So a Hungarian could continue during the World War the prosecution of an action, begun in France before the War, by appealing from a judgment decided in the first instance before the hostilities. (Aix, October 6, 1916; *Journal Clunet,* 1917, p. 717.)

Chapter VIII

JUDICIAL SYSTEM

Since the Revolution, France has enjoyed legislative and judicial uniformity, save so far as Alsace-Lorraine is concerned. The courts are of the nation, not of states or provinces. Courts are either civil, penal, commercial, administrative or special, such as those for the solution of conflicts between civil and administrative tribunals, military courts, etc. Trial by jury exists only in criminal cases. Civil courts are divided into petty justice of peace courts (*tribunaux de paix*), courts of first instance (*tribunaux de première instance*), courts of appeal (*cours d'appel*) and a court of review (*Cour de Cassation*). The judges have life tenure, in the courts of record, during good behavior, but may be transferred from one judicial district to another. The territorial area of the justice of peace is the borough (*arrondissement, commune*). The *tribunal civil* serves a *département* or a special district such as the "Seine" area, which embraces Paris and suburbs. The jurisdiction of a court of appeal covers several *départements;* the Court of Cassation reviews judgments rendered in France and in the colonies and protectorates. The bench consists of three judges in the case of the tribunal, five of the court of appeal. The tribunal is divided into several terms or parts (*chambres*), each one having a presiding justice called "president." The Court of Cassation is divided into three chambers; one (*chambre des requêtes*) passes upon petitions for review and either disallows or allows them. In the latter event, the chamber refers the petition to the *chambre civile.* The *chambre penale* has no interest in divorce or separation actions. Each chamber is composed of thirteen judges called *conseillers* (councillors).

Officers of the court are besides the judges, a clerk (*greffier*), bailiffs, sheriffs, process servers (*huissiers*), attorneys-at-law (*avoués*), counsellors-at-law (*avocats*), notaries (*notaires*), etc. The number of attorneys and notaries is limited by law; their fees are fixed by authority of law, as in the case of British solicitors. This is not the case so far as counsellors-at-law (barristers) are concerned.

No distinction obtains in France between law and equity, nor are there separate courts of law and courts of equity. French law is of one sort, and this leans strongly towards equity rather than towards law in the English legal sense. The French courts are less controlled and fettered by the codes in relation to divorce and separation than are the British and American by their divorce statutes and rules of procedure. The French codes are not detailed enactments purporting to cover the whole legal field. They establish general principles, and leave many points untouched. The general judicial power in France is, therefore, very broad.

French courts have power not alone to render judgments of divorce and separation, but various accessory remedies therewith. *Accessorium sequitur principale*—hence jurisdiction for divorce and separation carries with it jurisdiction for accessory relief. They have continuing competence, jurisdiction and venue after judgment to cancel or modify the accessory relief and even sometimes to grant additional remedies. French courts have power to grant some provisional remedies even though a foreign court may already have cognizance of the divorce or separation action. Nevertheless, it seems when a foreign court is seized of an action for separation the French courts will not presume to award the provisional custody of a child, but will leave that for the foreign court to do. A *pension alimentaire* (alimony) may be awarded the winning party by judgment at any time after the divorce itself. (Nancy, April 6, 1921; *Gazette du Palais,* July 5, 1921.) The existence of a judgment of divorce or separation gives authority and jurisdiction to compel liquidation of the property regime or otherwise to enforce the effects. Provisional remedies based upon an existing judgment may even be obtained *ex parte,* but unless there is urgency they will be obtainable upon notice as in ordinary practice.

Nevertheless, notwithstanding such extensive authority, the French courts lack the power to legislate by case law. In this respect their powers fall short of those of the Anglo-American courts, and indeed are less than the powers exercised by French law courts before the Revolution of 1789. Article 5 of the Civil Code reads:

Judges are forbidden to pronounce by way of general and regulatory disposition upon the causes submitted to them.

This is the provision which ended case law (*stare decisis*) in France. Prior to the Revolution the provincial law courts, the *parlements,* had power to render so-called *arrêts de règlement,* that is to say, decisions having the force of legal precedents binding in the province. This was a partial application of *stare decisis,* namely the binding force of precedents, but in a country then lacking legislative and judicial unity, where a traveler (as Voltaire so brightly says) changed laws oftener than post horses. The French Revolution established a common judicial organization and body of law, but denied any semi-legislative power of the new courts. Consequently, it is only decisions of the three chambers united of the

Court of Cassation which are considered binding on other courts, and even then they are binding only in the same cause. Decisions in other causes have in France an argumentative value only. One decision does not make a rule, nor do even several concordant decisions.

In consequence there is an amazing diversity in the decisions of French courts. Upon nearly every debatable issue respectable authority can be found for both sides. Authors' opinions are often of equal or greater weight than a court decision. The same court has been seen to decide one way in one case and the very opposite in another closely paralleling the first and decided almost contemporaneously. Courts of first instance or of appeal will not always follow the law as laid down by the Court of Cassation. The latter not infrequently reverses its own views of the law. This flexible state of the French law must be borne in mind in considering the law of divorce and separation.

The word competence in English signifies the power of a court to award the relief prayed for; jurisdiction signifies the right to exercise that power upon particular persons or things. (Piggott, Foreign Judgments and Jurisdiction, 1903, vol. 2, p. 167.) Competence is a rarely used word; jurisdiction usually covers the relation of the court to the litigation. In fact sometimes competence embraces jurisdiction. The French word *compétence* is broader than the English; it embraces competence in the English sense and also jurisdiction and venue. *Compétence* in French law is of three sorts: *ratione materiae, ratione personae,* and *ratione loci.* Before a French court will entertain an action for divorce or separation all three must be present. The expressions *compétence ratione materiae* and *ratione personae* do not entirely coincide with the English expressions jurisdiction over the subject-matter and over the person, nor is *competénce ratione loci* always venue. Divorce and separation are civil law topics belonging to the civil courts, not the administrative or penal courts. The civil courts accordingly have *compétence ratione materiae* in relation to divorce and separation. *Compétence ratione personae* means jurisdiction by reason of the person of the litigants. French law distinguishes international conflict of jurisdictions from intra-territorial. *Compétence ratione loci* has more than one meaning. It may mean jurisdiction and venue of litigation by reason of the situation of an object within the judicial district, e.g., land. As marriage is not considered a *res* in French law, this primary meaning of *ratione loci* has no application to matrimonial actions for divorce or separation. However, *compétence ratione loci* means in a divorce action jurisdiction *a raison de la demeure* (*i.e.,* by reason of the dwelling house), namely venue or jurisdiction as to place within France where action may be brought. (Cassation, January 11, 1928, *Dalloz hebdomadaire,* 1928, p. 102.)

Before discussing the French law of *compétence* in relation to aliens, it is necessary to mention certain principles which affect that law and which differ somewhat from the common law on the same matters. Roman law has left its imprint in France not alone upon substantive but also upon adjective law. In Roman procedure *actori incumbit probatio,* which is indeed a universal rule of law, but also *reus excipiendo fit actor,* which is not of universal acceptance as applied to jurisdiction or venue. French practice has inherited both maxims from Rome and accordingly a defendant bears the burden of proof of all *exceptions* (*i.e.,* demurrers, pleas in abatement, etc.). An objection to *compétence* is one of the chief *exceptions.* In other words, the defendant must prove absence of competence, jurisdiction or venue, not the plaintiff its presence. At a time when the laws and courts of the Roman Empire were more or less uniform such a rule of burden of proof applied really to venue only and was not unreasonable. But it is hardly suited to a world divided into separate nations under diverse laws, when the choice of court by plaintiff will often decide the law applicable and may involve all the difference between winning and losing the case. For an alien defendant to have to prove a negative before a French court is no easy task, particularly when an attempt to escape the jurisdiction is considered, as it is in France, something of a reflection upon the court. The Court of Appeal of Paris in the Sickles case, June 12, 1907 (*Journal Clunet,* 1908, p. 148), remarked: "Every defendant is presumed in fact and in law to accept the jurisdiction of the judge before whom he is summoned, until he declines it."

The law of *compétence* in French matrimonial causes is not predicated upon the theory that marriage is a *res*. Jurisdiction in divorce and separation actions follows the rules of personal actions, or claims against the person, not those of real actions, or claims about or against a thing. Marriage is indeed considered a status as well as a contract, but since the Revolution the contract aspect is emphasized and the marriage status is not a *res*, as it is considered in many states of the United States. The theory of marriage as a *res* and the theory of the location of the *situs* of the marital relation where either spouse is domiciled, are quite unknown in French law. Divorce and separation actions in France are *in personam,* not *in rem* or *quasi in rem*.

Jurisdiction is independent of the possibility of pronouncing divorce and of the existence of a cause of action. For instance, there may be jurisdiction even if the defendant alleges that by his national law there can be no divorce awarded against him; "this question (*i. e.,* liability) must be decided at the time of the examination of the events and is no obstacle to the jurisdiction." (Marseilles, April 8, 1921; *Themis,* May 23, 1921; *Recueil des Sommaires,* 1921, No. 1649.) Nevertheless when the court foresees legal difficulties at trial it will on occasion dismiss the action between aliens for lack of jurisdiction.

Jurisdiction in French law is not vested or acquired over a person merely by service of process. Jurisdiction is dependent upon other factors and is independent of process. It depends upon the existence of certain facts, such as nationality or domicile, not upon whether or not a writ was served upon defendant. Personal service within the Republic does not create a jurisdiction over the person served, nor will absence of such service prevent acquisition of jurisdiction over him. This does not mean that judgment may be had without any service of process. It does mean, however, that defective service is an illegality affecting the procedure, not a defect in the vesting or taking of jurisdiction. The peculiar sanctity and efficacy which has grown up in the United States and Great Britain around personal service of process does not exist in France.

The law of jurisdiction in the private international law of France has been curiously affected by the *lex nationalis* doctrine. Status and capacity in French law are governed by the law of the nationality of the parties, not by the law of the domicile or of the forum. In consequence of a confusion between conflict of laws and conflict of jurisdictions, this doctrine is made the basis for attributing exclusive or preferential jurisdiction to the courts of the person's allegiance in matters affecting his status or capacity. Actions for divorce and separation are of this category, and in theory the national courts of the parties are presumed to be available to adjudicate and are considered to be the natural or normal judges of such matters. Divorce and separation are not considered in France either as a penalty for a misdemeanor, or as a remedy for a tort, as they act to some extent still in Anglo-American countries. Nor are they considered a statutory, as distinguished from a common law, remedy, for all remedies are based upon the codes in France and the law of 1884 is deemed a part of the Civil Code. A divorce action sounds in France more in contract than in tort.

It has been suggested that the rules of jurisdiction in France should differ between divorce and separation actions, as they do in England and America. Separation, it is argued, does not affect status, since the marriage subsists thereafter; it affects only marital rights and duties and these relate to public order. In this light *lex fori* not *lex nationalis* should be applied to determine the grant or refusal of the remedy. While there is some support in doctrine for this view, it has not found favor in jurisprudence. One may take it that the law of competence, jurisdiction and venue is the same in France in divorce and in separation actions; for separation, like divorce, does to some extent at least affect status and capacity. (Paris, June 23, 1836; Dalloz, *Répertoire de législation,* 1850, vol. 18, *Droit Civil,* no. 318.)

In relation to aliens, jurisdiction is sometimes confused in France with the question of the right of access to the courts. That is to say, when two aliens, are entitled to resort to the French courts, the latter are sometimes deemed to have potential jurisdiction over them. Where the plaintiff is under a disability and cannot sue or a defendant is not liable to be sued, there is on occasion held to be no jurisdiction. French citizens are always supposed to have access to French courts, and special jurisdictional rules have been inserted in the Civil Code to carry out this theory.

Furthermore, apart from particular treaty or statutory text and when governed by custom alone, jurisdiction in the divorce and separation actions of aliens in France is largely a matter of judicial discretion; it is of grace rather than of right. French courts may, if they see fit, decline to entertain a divorce or separation action when foreigners only are parties. The view has even been expressed that French courts are always vested with a latent jurisdiction over aliens in France, which control, according to circumstances, they may either assert or disclaim. (Paris, January 9 and 14, 1896; *Le Droit,* January 25, 1896.) The courts "decline" or "retain" what seems to be an always existing power or jurisdiction over aliens in the country, rather than "deny" or "confirm" its existence. Jurisdiction over aliens has come to be considered not so much a matter of law as of judicial policy,—jurisdiction is always present, but no relief need necessarily be granted. (Carpentier, *Divorce et séparation de corps,* 1899, vol. 2, section 5155.)

With this background, turn now to the detailed consideration of jurisdiction in private international law, then to competence, jurisdiction and venue within France.

Chapter IX

JURISDICTION IN PRIVATE INTERNATIONAL LAW

This chapter treats of the broad question whether it is a French court or a foreign court that has authority to adjudicate divorce and separation in relation to aliens.

Certain persons are in virtue of some quality or privilege entitled to sue and be sued as of right in France. Thus, article 14 of the Civil Code reads:

> An alien, even not residing in France, may be summoned before the French courts, for the fulfilment of obligations contracted by him in France toward a French person; he may be called before the courts of France, for obligations contracted by him in a foreign country toward French people.

Marriage is deemed a contract within the meaning of article 14 of the Civil Code; hence, a French citizen can always sue an alien in France for divorce or separation. Jurisdiction has been asserted in actions of a French wife against her Argentine husband (Seine, December 8, 1915; *Journal Clunet*, 1917, p. 1020); a French husband, formerly Cuban, against his Cuban wife (Seine, May 17, 1910; *Journal Clunet*, 1911, p. 1202); a French husband, formerly Italian, against his Italian wife (Tunis, December 8, 1920; *Journal Clunet*, 1923, p. 110). In these three cases the domicile of the parties happened to be in France or in a French protectorate, but the basis of the jurisdiction is not the French domicile, but article 14, C. C. Whether or not defendant is liable to be divorced in such cases is a different question, independent of jurisdiction, and one that will be studied in relation to grounds and defenses. Thus, the Court of Appeal of Montpellier, February 19, 1900 (*Journal Clunet,* 1900, p. 955) held that a Frenchman, formerly of Spanish nationality, could sue his Spanish wife for divorce in France under article 14, C. C., but they denied him the relief because the wife in Spanish law lacked the capacity to divorce, and hence as a corollary she was free of liability to be divorced.

The French courts have even gone so far as to consider an alien ex-wife, domiciled and divorced abroad, subject to the jurisdiction established by article 14, C. C., at the suit of her ex-husband, a Frenchman. Thus, the Tribunal of Chambéry, January 13, 1926 (*Recueil des Sommaires,* 1925, no. 2373) asserted authority to award the ex-husband the custody of the child contrary to the terms of the foreign divorce judgment.

The rule of article 14, C. C., applies not alone when the French nationality of the plaintiff is clear, but even when it is uncertain or in dispute. On April 9, 1914, the Tribunal of the Seine (*Journal Clunet,* 1916, p. 173) held that it had jurisdiction to grant divorce to a French woman who had married a Russian Jew in France, inasmuch as Russian law would consider her French civil marriage void because not followed by a religious solemnization. If the marriage were void she would have remained French in Russian law. In other words, the French court treated a French marriage (valid in French law) as void under Russian law, although never annulled, in order to sustain its jurisdiction to divorce the couple.

Just as a French citizen can always sue for divorce or separation in France, so too he or she may always be sued there either by an alien or by a French person. Article 15 of the Civil Code is a companion to article 14. It reads:

A Frenchman can always be called before a French court for obligations contracted by him in a foreign country, even toward an alien.

This article allows suit in France against a French citizen married abroad. The contingency of marriage in France is not expressly covered thereby. But since a Frenchman married abroad can be sued, *a fortiori* can one be there sued who married in the French Republic. By article 3 of the Civil Code the status and capacity of French citizens, wherever they may be, remain governed by French law. In consequence it is considered that the courts of France are always open to adjudicate in relation to the status of a French person. In fact, for many years French courts considered that they had exclusive jurisdiction to do so and recognized no power in a foreign court to pass upon the status of a French couple. French law still considers that French courts have paramount or preferred jurisdiction over foreign courts, even of the domicile, whenever status of a French person is to be passed upon.

The jurisdiction granted under articles 14 and 15, C. C., is mandatory upon the courts and binding upon the parties; it is of right, not of grace.

Whereas, the French law of jurisdiction is clear when one party is, or both parties are, French, it is still in an unsettled and confused condition when both parties are aliens, particularly so when they are of different foreign nationalities. No Code provision exists giving French courts jurisdiction over matrimonial actions between aliens. Consequently, by analogy with article 3, C. C., French law considers the national courts of the aliens to be the proper ones to entertain suits for their divorce or separation. Indeed, for some years French courts considered that the foreign courts had exclusive jurisdiction in such cases. Lack of French jurisdiction is still the rule, but one to which there are now so many exceptions that the rule is greatly impaired.

In harmony with the rule, French courts prior to the Russian Revolution regularly declined to divorce Russians because Russian law asserted a right to exclusive jurisdiction in the ecclesiastical courts. The rule was applied to Russian Jews in the *affaire* Levinçon by the Court of Appeal of Paris, March 17, 1902 (*Journal Clunet*, 1903, p. 342). The court also held that the French law concerning separation of Church and State is of internal public policy, not of international public policy; this internal public policy could not affect the status of aliens. Consequently a religious disability of foreign law would be observed in France in so far as it affected the status of aliens. The rule has also been applied to Russian Orthodox Christians (Paris, February 1, 1912; *Journal Clunet*, 1912, p. 857) and to Ottoman Jews (Seine, January 20, 1913; *Journal Clunet*, 1914, p. 177) and to Greeks (St. Etienne, December 27, 1911; *Journal Clunet*, 1914, p. 184). The Tribunal of the Seine, January 25, 1922 (*Journal Clunet*, 1924, p. 667) of its own motion declined to take jurisdiction to divorce Czecho-Slovak parties, for the reason that by old Hungarian law in force in Slovakia, domestic judgments alone are valid in matrimonial actions and a French judgment of divorce would there be denied *exequatur*. In relation to Russians, these decisions have become obsolete, for the Russian courts of the Soviet, unlike the old ecclesiastical courts of the empire, do not claim the exclusive right to divorce Russians. (Paris, April 30, 1926; *Journal Clunet*, 1926, p. 944.) Spanish ecclesiastical courts apparently do not claim this either; at any rate, a Spanish husband cannot avoid French jurisdiction in a separation action brought by his Spanish wife by contending that under Spanish law separations are governed by ecclesiastical law and that the

Church courts are alone competent to award this relief. (Algiers, March 7, 1898; *Le Droit,* June 10, 1898.) The practice of French courts in yielding jurisdiction over aliens whenever by the aliens' national law their national courts are considered solely entitled to adjudicate, has been seriously criticized. André-Prudhomme has aptly said: "A state cannot have its jurisdictional power limited by the legislation of another state." (*Journal Clunet,* 1924, pp. 667, 668.) The rule is none the less still firmly established.

It may be mentioned in passing that in the Zamoyska case the Tribunal of the Seine declined jurisdiction so as not to have to apply to two Austrians a religious disability which would have prevented their divorce. This view has not prevailed. It is now law that jurisdiction is not affected by religious disability, though it is affected by a claim of the foreign law to exclusive jurisdiction. The foreign religious disability, however, will be enforced by the French courts in relation to grounds and defenses.

The rule of French lack of jurisdiction over the status of aliens applies also in some cases when there is no claim to exclusive jurisdiction by the foreign national courts. The Tribunal of the Seine, January 20, 1902 (*Journal Clunet,* 1902, p. 809) dismissed for lack of jurisdiction a divorce action between Germans domiciled in France, upon proof that the German courts would entertain the suit without residence or domicile of the parties in the Fatherland, and at the same time they are awarded temporary alimony and suit-money to enable the wife to sue in Germany. Likewise, the fact that aliens were married in France is not of itself sufficient to sustain the French jurisdiction for separation or divorce. Mere matrimonial residence of the spouses in France is also insufficient. This was held in the Sickles case by the Court of Appeal of Paris, June 12, 1907 (*Journal Clunet,* 1908, p. 148).

An American husband was domiciled in New York, but had a house in Paris. He was Secretary of the American Legation in Brussels. His wife, also American, sued him for divorce in Paris. Upon objection to the jurisdiction and proof that defendant was resident in France but domiciled in the United States, the Tribunal dismissed the action so far as the principal relief was concerned, but granted alimony *pendente lite,* custody of the children, separate residence, etc. The Tirveillot case, decided by the Tribunal of the Seine, February 23, 1898 (*Journal Clunet,* 1898, p. 924), is in the same sense. A Frenchman acquired United States citizenship and later married a French woman in New York. The wife became American by marriage. The husband brought suit for divorce in America. While this was pending, the wife returned to France, recorded the marriage in the French *régistres de l'état civil* (*i.e.,* marriage records) and then sued in France for separation. The husband contested the French jurisdiction on the grounds that he was a United States citizen domiciled in New York for the last twenty years, and that an earlier action was then pending before the foreign court. The wife contended that the naturalization was fraudulent under American law and co-pendency of a foreign action was no defense. The Tribunal declined to investigate the validity of the naturalization, as no violation of French law had been alleged, dismissed the action for lack of jurisdiction, awarded three hundred francs a month temporary alimony, refused to award suit-money, and confirmed the wife's attachment of the husband's property in France made to secure her eventual rights upon the liquidation of the property regime of the spouses.

The rule of non-jurisdiction over aliens cannot be defeated by joining a French person as co-defendant, nor will the addition to the prayer for relief of a demand for other relief besides divorce or separation cause the court to retain cognizance of the latter demands. The Court of Cassation, December 26, 1917 (*Journal Clunet,* 1918, p. 714) held that if in principle French courts are without jurisdiction to separate Italian spouses, nevertheless, they could award provisional remedies such as alimony, custody of children and separate residences while dismissing the prayer for separation.

Turn now to the exceptions to the rule. The first exception is based upon treaties. (Article 11, C. C.) The Hague Convention is no longer in force in France, but some special treaties still exist. The Franco-Swiss Treaty of June 15, 1869, and the Franco-Belgian Treaty of July 8, 1899, expressly concede to French courts jurisdiction in litigation interesting Swiss and Belgians domiciled in France, but this does not necessarily mean that French courts are obliged to adjudicate upon the status of these Swiss or Belgian couples. Cases exist which hold that such litigation is within the treaty, others hold that it is not. Thus the Tribunal of the Seine, February 9, 1921 (*Journal Clunet,* 1921, p. 176) held that a Belgian wife (Marie Louise Logan) formerly American, could sue her Belgian husband (de Sinçay) in Paris, whether or not the couple were domiciled in Belgium. In another case the Court of Appeal of Douai, January 5, 1903 (*Journal Clunet,* 1903, p. 829) held that under the treaty Belgians are governed by the same rules of divorce jurisdiction as French. In this case, the defendant husband, on the day following the wife's petition to the president of the French tribunal for leave to cite the defendant to attend a conciliation hearing, unsuccessfully endeavored to evade the French jurisdiction by removing his domicile to Belgium and declaring the change at the borough hall. But the treaty jurisdiction is not mandatory upon the courts. So the Tribunal of Compiegne, February 18, 1922 (*Journal*

Clunet, 1922, p. 672) conceded that Swiss spouses were entitled to sue for divorce in France under the Franco-Swiss Treaty, but denied the relief prayed for because the "parties do not have a normal personal statute." It seems that the property regime of the couple had been changed in Switzerland during the marriage and the wife, being feeble-minded, had been placed under a committee with her consent and without judicial intervention, both occurrences contrary to French public policy. If the French court had pronounced divorce, it would have been unable to liquidate the property regime in observance of Swiss law. In consequence the court declined jurisdiction and left the parties to submit the problems to the Swiss courts.

A number of treaties have been made between France and other powers which contain merely the so-called "free access" to the courts clause, *clause de libre et facile accès auprès des tribunaux.* Such clauses are found in the Treaties of January 6, 1862, and February 6, 1882, with Spain; of March 9, 1853, with Portugal; of April 1, 1874, with Russia. These treaties are held to remove the disability of aliens to sue. Thus, Spanish subjects may litigate in France for separation, but not for the conversion of the separation into divorce, since by Spanish law they both lack capacity to divorce. (Bar-sur-Aube, December 29, 1888; *Journal Clunet,* 1896, p. 151.) But the treaty clause does not give all civil rights to treaty-power aliens, and the jurisdiction is permissive, not mandatory, so far as the courts are concerned. For example, the Treaty of Frankfort of May 10, 1871, between France and Germany, containing the most favored nation clause as applied to the "treatment of the subjects of the two nations," does not compel the French courts to retain cognizance of matrimonial causes between Germans, but gives Germans access to the French courts for such actions, which the courts may entertain or dismiss for want of jurisdiction in their discretion.

Neither the Consular Convention of 1853 between France and the United States, nor any other treaty between these countries, affects the disability of alienage or jurisdiction in relation to divorce or separation. According to Lachau: "As to treaties with the United States, jurisprudence considers them to be conventions having only commercial relations as object." (Lachau, *De la compétence des tribunaux français a l'égard des étrangers en matière civile et commerciale d'après la jurisprudence française,* 1893, p. 331.) Americans cannot claim the benefit of the jurisdictional clauses of the Franco-Swiss Treaty of June 15, 1869. (Havre, March 6, 1878; *Journal Clunet,* 1878, p. 382.) This situation does not mean that United States citizens have no access to the French courts in matrimonial actions in which only aliens and no French citizen is involved, but it does mean *inter alia* that they have no access thereto as of right, but only as of grace.

It is probably correct law to say that the "free access" clause merely removes the ancient disability of alienage, without affecting jurisdiction or capacity to divorce or liability to be divorced. It would not impose a liability upon a treaty-power alien to submit to the French jurisdiction. Neither a treaty-power alien nor a non-treaty power alien can oblige a treaty-power alien to litigate in France merely because the latter enjoys access to the courts by treaty. Hence, a Spaniard has access to the courts under the Franco-Spanish Treaty, but has no right to sue in France a non-resident British subject under article 14, C. C. (Paris, February 18. 1902; *Journal Clunet,* 1920, p. 573.)

It is probable that an alien entitled by treaty to enjoy all civil rights under article 11 of the Civil Code would be so assimulated to a Frenchman as to be able to invoke article 14, C. C., in order to sue in France a resident or non-resident alien without his consent. Such treaties are rare, but exist in relation to French protectorates.

The second exception is based upon a presidential decree. (Article 13, C. C., now repealed.) An alien *de jure* domiciled in France by presidential decree is so far assimilated to a Frenchman as to be able to invoke article 14, C. C., against another alien and to have article 15, C. C., apply against him at the suit of another alien. In other words, an alien so domiciled can always sue or be sued for divorce or separation in France. An Englishman sued in France for divorce surrendered his decree and set up alienage in an endeavor to defeat the jurisdiction. The tribunal paid no attention to the surrender, as suit had already been begun before he had relinquished *de jure* domicile. (Seine, December 11, 1889; *Journal Clunet,* 1889, p. 814.) Since admission to domicile by decree has been abolished by the law of August 10, 1927, this exception has lost practical interest.

Present *de facto* matrimonial domicile in France is the third exception. The Hague Convention expressly recognized the concurrent jurisdiction for divorce purposes of courts of the nationality and of the matrimonial domicile. Consequently, from 1904 to 1914 aliens of countries parties to the Convention could divorce or separate in France upon proof of *de facto* domicile there. Has the jurisdiction based upon domicile survived in the Republic the denunciation of the Convention? The Tribunal of the Seine, March 23, 1908 (*Journal Clunet*, 1908, p. 1128), entertained the suit of a British husband domiciled in France against his Russian wife, neither country being parties to the Convention. The Tribunal said: "It is sufficient, indeed, that domicile shall have been lawfully established in a place for it to be in such case attributive of jurisdiction for divorce." The decision was, however, inspired by the Convention. This decision is contrary to that of the same court, dated January 20, 1902, already cited, in which jurisdiction was declined over a German couple domiciled in France in view of the fact that they could litigate in Germany. The Tribunal of Papeete, May 3, 1892 (*Journal Clunet,* 1893, p. 146) asserted that aliens can divorce in whatever country they are domiciled.

In the *affaire* Prince de Looz (a case decided before the special Franco-Belgian treaty was made) a Belgian husband sued by his wife in France, was required by the French court in order to avoid the divorce jurisdiction to prove his alienage and his domicile in Belgium. He proved his alienage, but failed to prove his Belgian domicile. Until his majority, his domicile by operation of law had been with his guardian (*tuteur*) in Belgium. He claimed that nothing since then indicated a change on his part. The French courts, nevertheless, considered him domiciled in France because he had resided there since his majority. Consequently the court retained cognizance of the case. (Seine, June 6, 1890; *Journal Clunet,* 1890, p. 483: Paris, November 4, 1890; *Journal Clunet,* 1890, p. 875.)

A line of cases indicates, however, that there must be something besides mere matrimonial domicile in France before the courts will set aside the rule. Thus, a *heimatlos, apatride* (*i.e.,* countryless) ex-German *de facto* domiciled in France, who had lost German nationality by reason of ten years non-residence in the Empire, could be sued for divorce in France, particularly since he had married in France and a French judgment of separation of property had already been rendered against him. (Seine, May 12, 1892; *Journal Clunet,* 1892, p. 937.) *De facto* matrimonial domicile will suffice to sustain the jurisdiction when there is *renvoi* besides, namely, a reference back to French courts by foreign law. For example, in the *affaire* Chance, the Tribunal of the Seine, October 16, 1912 (*Journal Clunet,* 1913, p. 566), decided that it had jurisdiction to divorce Americans domiciled in France because Illinois law referred divorce to the courts of their domicile. In such case the defendant may be obliged to stand suit in France, but the court in its discretion may dismiss the action, for jurisdiction is never mandatory upon the judicial authority when both parties are aliens.

Does the third exception concede French jurisdiction when but one party is domiciled in France? Article 875 of the Code of Civil Procedure says a plaintiff must present his petition for separation to the "President of the Tribunal of his domicile." This, however, has been held to be a rule only of intra-territorial jurisdiction or venue, assuming the international jurisdiction already exists. An alien husband cannot lawfully sue in France his non-resident alien wife, whom he deserted abroad, simply because he has become *de facto* domiciled in France. A British wife cannot leave her husband in England, establish merely a separate residence in France and sue her non-domiciled husband there without his consent. (Seine, June 20, 1922; *Journal Clunet,* 1923, p. 75.) It is understood that in the Colby case decided in 1928 the husband came alone to France from America to establish residence; the action was dismissed for want of jurisdiction. But, as in the Crane case, an American wife can set up a bona fide separate domicile in France under circumstances in which American law would recognize her right thereto and then in France sue her American husband who had remained in the United States, if it be the fact that she could not sue him in America without renouncing her French domicile and residing a period of time in her own country. (Seine, May 14, 1926, unreported.)

Mere *de facto* domicile of defendant in France is also insufficient to bring the case within the third exception, in view of article 875, C. C. P. While this article cannot establish international jurisdiction, it may defeat it. Likewise matrimonial residence, but not domicile in France, would not suffice to give jurisdiction; this is also true of plaintiff's domicile in France and the defendant's simple residence there, or plaintiff's residence and defendant's domicile. The domicile must be real, not *fictif*. In fact, the matrimonial domicile must be present, not past. The Hague Convention allowed suit at the last common domicile of the spouses. French private international law seems no longer to recognize this concession.

A recent case decided by the Tribunal of the Seine, April 26, 1923 (*Journal Clunet,* 1923, p. 850) is illustrative of the necessity that France shall be the present domicile of the parties and the insufficiency for jurisdictional purposes of the fact that France was the place of the last, though not the present, matrimonial domicile. In 1914, an action for divorce was instituted in France by a German husband against his German wife, the couple being then domiciled in Paris. At the outbreak of the war, he left France for Switzerland where he established his domicile. The husband's French action remained still pending. The wife stayed on in France, where she sued the husband in 1921 in a separate action for divorce. She did not counterclaim in his action. The court in the wife's action issued a *commission rogatoire* to the Geneva court to hear the defendant for purposes of conciliation. The husband attended the hearing and orally objected to the French proceedings on the ground that he was an alien domiciled in Germany. In 1922, while the wife's French action was still in course, the husband obtained a divorce in Germany by default. He thereupon set up his judgment in further bar to the wife's action, but this was not sustained by the court, which, however, dismissed the complaint for lack of jurisdiction, the defendant having no domicile in France at the time the wife's suit was brought. The fact that the husband's action in France was still pending, never having been dismissed for laches, did not estop the defendant from objecting to the jurisdiction in 1921, domicile and residence having been really changed in the interval.

By far the most important exception to the rule of non-jurisdiction over alien couples is the fourth, namely, that founded upon denial of justice. The doctrine has been so extended that whenever the plaintiff can show a good reason for bringing suit in France the courts will in their discretion decide to assert jurisdiction notwithstanding defendant's protest. If nationality or domicile is uncertain or non-existent, it is considered the "duty" of French courts to take cognizance of the action. But when there is a remedy abroad the French courts will not take cognizance of the case. The Court of Cassation on April 30, 1927 (cited by Boyer, p. 95) declined jurisdiction in an action for divorce brought by an American husband against his American wife upon proof that an action for separation instituted previously by her in which he could counterclaim for divorce was pending in the United States. There is no lack of examples of this exception; only a few of the principal ones will be cited.

The Court of Appeal of Paris, November 16, 1892 (*Journal Clunet,* 1893, p. 370), allowed a Belgian husband to sue his Belgian wife for divorce in France upon proof that by Belgian law a subject living in France could not bring suit without removing to the Kingdom and living there for six months. It was considered a denial of justice to compel plaintiff to leave France and wait half a year before he could obtain relief. In view of the similar residence requirements of the American states, this decision is of particular importance in relation to the matrimonial actions of United States citizens in France. The principle of this case was used to decisive advantage in the Crane case, already cited.

Jurisdiction under this exception has been asserted to divorce Roumanians, upon proof that the wife could not sue her husband in Rome because he had diplomatic immunity as Secretary of the Roumanian Embassy, nor in Bucharest because he was domiciled in France, not Roumania, a local domicile being a prerequisite to suit in Roumania according to Roumanian law. (Seine, November 9, 1917; *Journal Clunet,* 1918, p. 656.) In this case jurisdiction was not founded upon the French domicile, but upon the fact that defendant could not be sued anywhere else, French domicile being mentioned only as constituting an obstacle to Roumanian jurisdiction in defendant's national law. In another case, the Roumanian wife of a Russian Jew was allowed to sue for divorce in France, where the parties had been civilly married, upon proof that by Russian law the marriage would be deemed void, and upon failure by defendant to prove he had a domicile outside France or to point out any foreign court before which an action would lie. (Seine, January 19, 1920; *Journal Clunet,* 1920, p. 198.) During the civil war in Russia after 1918, Russian Orthodox Christians were allowed to divorce in France in view of the dissolution of the ecclesiastical courts and Holy Synod in Russia. (Seine, June 11, 1921; *Journal Clunet,* 1921, p. 525.) Russian Jews could do so in France in view of the chaotic conditions in the Soviet dominions. (Seine, December 24, 1921; *Journal Clunet,* 1922, p. 117.)

There is a fifth exception to the rule; an exception predicated upon the general principle of French law that the territorial courts have jurisdiction over aliens whenever public order is concerned. Persons injured by a crime, a *délit* (felony) or a *contravention* (misdemeanor) have a civil action for damages which may be conducted either with the penal prosecution, yet subordinate thereto, or independently thereof and subsequently thereto. In the case of adultery, which is sometimes a *délit* under the Penal Code, an action for divorce is not a civil action for damages, but is a separate action relating to the felony. It seems, nevertheless, that there is jurisdiction over aliens resident but not domiciled in France when the adultery complained of took place there. Such was the decision in the Gould case. (Cassation, December 8, 1920; *Journal Clunet,* 1921, p. 518.) It is still an open question whether or not the commission of *excès* (violence) or *sévices* (cruelty) constituting crimes, felonies or misdemeanors would come within the exception. It is probable that mere torts would not do so.

Voluntary submission in the French jurisdiction is a sixth exception. In French law jurisdiction for purposes of divorce or separation may be given by consent of the parties. This is not the case in the United States or in Great Britain. The anonymous case "S—S" is in point, in which it was held that Americans married and permanently established in France might submit their marital differences to the French courts. The Tribunal of the Seine, March 4, 1895 (*Journal Clunet,* 1896, p. 602) saw no reason for dismissing this action of its own motion, the defendant not objecting to the jurisdiction, particularly as the acts complained of took place in France.

What amounts to consent? The Tribunal of the Seine, August 6, 1888 (*Journal Clunet,* 1890, p. 883) decided that French courts have jurisdiction to divorce aliens only when the parties expressly consent; if defendant defaults this indicates lack of consent and the court should decline jurisdiction of its own motion. The same court,

December 20, 1886 (*Journal Clunet,* 1886, p. 710) held just the opposite. The Tribunal, upon defendant's default, asserted jurisdiction to divorce two Russians, the couple having married in France and the wife having been formerly French. The decision was based upon the view that alienage is a purely personal defense, that a defendant must expressly raise the jurisdictional question if he objects to the court and if he defaults the court will not raise the issue for him. The election of a *domicile fictif* in advance of suit to receive the writ would be express consent to the jurisdiction, but such election in the power to the attorney to enter an appearance for defendant after service would not be consent; such domicile is always elected at the attorney's office in the instrument and nevertheless the jurisdiction may be contested.

An estoppel or waiver is an implied consent. If a defendant sues for divorce in France and the action is still pending, he cannot object to the jurisdiction in a suit by the other spouse. This was the rule laid down by the Tribunal of Versailles and Court of Appeal of Paris in the Gould case. But it seems a defendant may nevertheless successfully object if he has really changed domicile and residence between the two actions. (Seine, April 26, 1923; *Journal Clunet,* 1923, p. 850.)

Apart from these six exceptions, there are some cases in which for special reasons the French courts have arbitrarily taken jurisdiction over aliens. These cases depend upon their special facts. They are *sui generis* and cannot be classified properly under one of the six exceptions.

In relation to all these exceptions to the rule of non-jurisdiction over aliens it is a grave and still unsettled question whether or not there is an underlying condition or prerequisite that both parties shall be domiciled in France. The fact is that in most of the cases both the parties have been so domiciled. The Tribunal of the Seine,

November 19, 1920 (*Journal Clunet,* 1921, p. 184) remarked that French jurisdiction over aliens is subject to "one essential condition," namely "that the parties shall have in France a domicile in fact for many years and that they shall have lost all right to sue in their country of origin which they shall have left without intent to return and where they no longer have a domicile." Furthermore, the Ministry of Justice is supposed some time ago, in a confidential circular to the district attorneys, to have instructed them in performing their duties, which are similar to those of the King's proctor in England, to oppose the grant of divorce to aliens unless these shall have actually been in France continuously for at least six months before suit. The district attorneys are far too surcharged with other work to control effectively the divorce litigation of aliens and in practice they do not do so. It is rumored also that since 1927 the president of the 4th chamber of the Tribunal of the Seine charged with the conciliation of alien litigants, has been advised to apply the six-months' test before granting a plaintiff leave to sue.

The president does at present scrutinize rather carefully the evidence on domicile and requires aliens to present a copy of long lease taken out several months earlier and an invoice showing importation of household goods and furniture from abroad, and even lately a French income tax receipt. If the tribunal becomes aware that the aliens have been but a short time in France, it is liable to dismiss the action of its own motion. Nevertheless, there is no statutory domicile or residence requirement. Speaking of the various exceptions to the rule of nonjurisdiction over aliens, Carpentier says: "In all these hypotheses the possession of a true domicile is not even necessary. It is sufficient that the spouses shall be established in France in a permanent manner and act without fraudulent intent, particularly when the offense was committed in France, and the wife was French before marriage." (Carpentier, *Divorce et séparation de corps*, 1899, vol. 2, sec. 5139.) He adds that the residence shall nevertheless "be of a nature to exclude an early return to a foreign country and shall imply renunciation of the domicile which they have had there" (Section 5140). It may, therefore, be concluded that jurisdiction over aliens will be taken in France only when both the aliens are bona fide domiciled or at least have been resident in France for a substantial period of time and when, in addition, there is some good reason for asking the aid of a French court.

It will be noted from the foregoing, that the question of domicile is not the sole one involved in the French jurisdictional issue. It is frequently an incidental aspect. A defendant usually has to prove his own foreign domicile and alienage and his subordination to suit abroad in order to avoid the French jurisdiction. It is not incumbent upon nor does it suffice for a plaintiff to prove French domicile of himself or of defendant in order to sustain it. This conception of jurisdiction over the person is different from that of Anglo-American law.

The French law concerning international jurisdiction over aliens is in an unsatisfactory and unsettled state. This is largely responsible for the recent American divorce scandal. Had there been in French law a clear-cut statutory six-months domicile requirement, instead of the question of jurisdiction being left to the six exceptions and judicial discretion, there would have been far less opportunity to impose upon the courts.

Chapter X

COMPETENCE

When it is decided that some French court has international jurisdiction over the parties, then the question arises, what category of French court has authority to divorce or separate them? Article 326 of the Civil Code says, in relation to paternity of children: "The civil courts only shall be competent to decide claims relating to status." The same principle applies to other matters of status, such as divorce and separation.

Article 234 of the Civil Code provides that matrimonial causes shall be brought before the civil tribunal of first instance. This court consists of a bench of three judges, without a jury. No special chamber or division of the court is reserved for divorce or separation actions, save in Paris, where since 1927 these actions between aliens are placed upon the calendar of the 4th chamber. The justice of peace, an inferior civil tribunal, has no power to entertain a divorce or separation action, but may grant certain provisional remedies which bear upon the principal action.

Only the civil courts in France have any competence over divorce and separation; there is no such power in a commercial or administrative court. Family tribunals no longer exist since the promulgation of the Civil Code. Can it be said that the ecclesiastical authorities have no longer any voice in matrimonial affairs? The courts of the Catholic Church still function in France. Rabbis still purport to divorce Hebrews. Have their "judgments" no civil value? So far as French couples are concerned, the answer is clear: they have no executory force nor are they *res judicata.* The situation is the same when one party only is French, the other alien. But is this the case where both parties are aliens? Probably the answer is still the same. The state has exclusive authority in France to adjudicate with civil effect. The Tribunal of the Seine, December 24, 1921 (*Journal Clunet,* 1922, p. 117) declined to recognize any power in a French rabbi to divorce Russian Jews, saying: "Just as the principle of the secularization of marriage in France is opposed to giving any civil effect in France to a religious marriage, so likewise the purely religious dissolution of marriage by the intervention of the religious authority cannot in any fashion take place in France, even if made in conformity with the personal statute of the aliens."

Nevertheless, French courts have recognized a divorce pronounced by a French rabbi between Ottoman Jews. (Nancy, June 17, 1922; *Journal Clunet,* 1922, p. 985.) In another case the recording upon the ecclesiastical register in Russia of a French rabbinical divorce between Russian Jews, was deemed to entitle the divorce to recognition in France. (Seine, December 27, 1912; *Journal Clunet,* 1914, p. 172.) The divorce instrument granted by the rabbi was considered not as a French ecclesiastical divorce but as a step in the procedure, the Russian authorities converting the instrument into a Russian divorce. This attitude of recognition of some power in a rabbi over members of his faith is based upon the idea that as Russia and Turkey recognize such a divorce of their subjects, why not France? These cases are anomalous and the jurisprudence has not been extended to recognition of Catholic Church separations or annulments of marriage rendered in France or in relation to French citizens.

It has been held that the French courts lack *compétence ratione materiae* when the plaintiff fails to show that he was *prima facie* validly married to the defendant. (Paris, July 27, 1926, cited by Boyer, p. 118.) In the case mentioned a mere religious marriage in France was insufficient subject matter for dissolution by divorce. A religious marriage valid under foreign *lex loci celebrationis* would be sufficient to satisfy the competence requirement of French law even though the marriage be invalid in substance. The invalidity would be a defense on the merits, not an objection to the competence.

Chapter XI

JURISDICTION AND VENUE

When the civil courts of France have international jurisdiction and are competent, then the question must be answered: which civil court has cognizance of a divorce and separation action?

Article 234 of the Civil Code, as reënacted by the law of 1884, provided that suit for divorce could be brought only before the civil tribunal of the borough (*arrondissement*) in which the married couple were domiciled. The law of 1886 on procedure abrogated this provision, without enacting anything in its place. Only two texts of law now relate to territorial jurisdiction or venue. Article 875 of the Code of Civil Procedure says:

> The spouse who wishes to sue for separation of the persons shall present to the President of the Tribunal of his domicile a petition stating the facts summarily; he shall annex thereto the supporting documents if there are any.

This article is found in title nine of book one, part two of the Code. The title is headed, "Of Separation of the Persons and of Divorce," but the article speaks only of separations.

Article 59 of the Code of Civil Procedure reads:

> In personal actions, the defendant shall be sued before the court of his domicile; if he has no domicile before the court of his residence.

This article is but the application of the maxim: *actor sequitur forum rei,* divorce and separations being actions *in personam* and not *in rem* according to the civil law. It would seem that this article (as well as article 875, C.C.P.) might have a bearing upon international as well as intra-territorial, jurisdiction. This is indeed the view of some authors. It is the weight of authority, however, that article 59, C.C.P. relates only to the selection of the particular court among the courts of France, not to the selection of courts of France or of some other country as the proper jurisdiction.

Article 875, C.C.P., speaking of plaintiff's domicile and article 59, C.C.P., speaking of defendant's, usually relate to the same court, as by operation of law husband and wife are during marriage considered to be domiciled together, but after judicial separation this is no longer the case. It seems therefore that for divorce purposes after a separation and in some other cases there might be a conflict between the two articles. In such case article 59, C.C. P. would probably prevail.

The rule of article 59, C.C.P. is not absolute and territorial jurisdiction is subordinate to international. Thus, a French citizen can sue an alien in France under article 14 C.C. although the defendant have neither domicile nor residence in the country. (Paris, December 11, 1855; *Sirey,* 1885.2.302.) If an alien or French defendant has no domicile or residence in France, but is nevertheless within the international jurisdiction, then article 59 C.C.P. does not apply. In such contingency the maxim *actor sequitur forum rei* is reversed, and the court of the domicile or residence in France of the plaintiff has cognizance of the litigation. (Cassation, February 16, 1916; *Gazette du Palais,* May 22, 1919.) So, a husband who conceals the place of his domicile in order to prevent his wife from obtaining divorce, may nevertheless be sued at the last matrimonial domicile (Nancy, July 4, 1888; *Recueil des arrêts de Nancy,* 1889, p. 66); or at the wife's residence (Paris, November 25, 1895; *Gazette du Palais*, 1895. 2.776). If it is known that defendant has a domicile or residence in France but its location is not known, the last known domicile or residence in France is the one meant by article 59 C.C.P. This domicile, to determine the jurisdiction in actions of divorce and of separation of the persons, is not required to satisfy any condition of subsequent duration. A change of domicile after presentation of the petition does not divest jurisdiction. (Cassation, July 27, 1825, *Sirey chronologique*, 1825-1828, vol. 8, p. 161.) Nor need domicile have been established for a given period before suit. The place of the commission of the tortious offense giving rise to the action for divorce or separation has no bearing in French law upon the question of *compétence* within France.

The proper court in which to convert a separation into a divorce is not necessarily the court which awarded the separation, but the court indicated by article 59, C.C.P. These courts may not be the same, as the separated wife has in the interval taken up a separate domicile.

The court that grants divorce or separation has a continuing jurisdiction in relation to it, as to enforce, explain, correct, change accessory relief, etc. This is the case even when both parties have removed their domicile and gone abroad since the judgment was rendered. (Cassation, August 22, 1884; *Dalloz*, 1885.1.206.) Similarly the mere existence of a judgment of divorce in France gives jurisdiction in a later action to compel liquidation of the property regime of the ex-spouses or to prevent the use by the ex-wife of the ex-husband's name. This rule applies even to rabbinical divorces in France. Hence, in the case of Turkish Jews divorced by a Paris rabbi, an action lies before the tribunal to compel the ex-husband to repay the wife's dowry in the money stipulated in the marriage articles without taking exchange fluctuation into account. (Nancy, June 17, 1922; *Journal Clunet,* 1922, p. 985.) Article 1476 C.C., which refers to article 770, C.C., gives jurisdiction to liquidate the regime to the tribunal of first instance of the place where the marital community was dissolved. Hence the Court of Cassation quashed a judgment of a court of appeal granting a divorce and naming one of its own judges to report upon the accounts of the liquidation. (Cassation, October 23, 1911; *La Loi,* October 30, 1911.) A judge of the tribunal, not of the court of appeal, should have been named for this purpose. If the husband has changed domicile since the divorce judgment was rendered, the proper court before which to sue him for the liquidation of the regime is nevertheless the one which rendered the judgment. (Cassation, August 14, 1811; *Sirey,* 1811, p. 353.)

Under articles 472 and 554 of the Code of Civil Procedure the proper court to enforce a judgment is the one that rendered it. A suit to revoke alimony awarded with a separation under article 301, C.C. is not a new action but an incident of the old action; hence suit should be brought in the same court that rendered the separation judgment, not in the new court of the domicile of the defendant. (Rodez, June 6, 1912; *Recueil de Procédure civile,* 1912, p. 369; *Recueil des Sommaires,* 1913, no. 1865.)

To what extent the granting of provisional remedies concerning property in a divorce or separation action will be influenced by the situation of the *res* is uncertain in French law. A French spouse would be entitled to, or would be subject to, provisional relief whether the property affected were in France or abroad. An alien spouse would be situated similarly in relation to real estate in France, in view of article 3 of the Civil Code; probably also in relation to items of his personal property considered *ut singuli*, and perhaps to personalty considered *ut universalis* if he were domiciled in France.

Aliens do not often raise in issue the question of French territorial *compétence ratione personae vel loci;* usually the international jurisdiction only is contested by reason of alienage. Nevertheless, the Tribunal of Nice, December 6, 1920 (*Journal Clunet,* 1923, p. 71) was called upon to pass upon both objections. Defendant contested the legality of his being sued for divorce in Nice. He asserted that before suit was brought he had sold his business in that city and had removed to Paris. The Tribunal held that the action was properly brought in Nice because in defendant's power of attorney to his *avoué* he had used the expression *"demeurant à Nice"* (living in Nice), also because the sale of his business had been unknown to the plaintiff wife, the alleged domicile in Paris was not sufficiently proved, the change of residence was recent, and it was "probably temporary."

Chapter XII

GROUNDS IN THE CIVIL CODE

In this chapter will be treated the various grounds for which divorce or separation may be obtained according to French internal law. Questions concerning the applicability of these grounds to aliens will be considered later.

Articles 229-232 and 310 of the Civil Code, as re-enacted by the law of 1884, enumerate all the possible reasons for divorce. These articles read:

Article 229: A husband may sue for divorce on account of the adultery of the wife.

Article 230: A wife may sue for divorce on account of the adultery of the husband.

Article 231: The spouses may reciprocally sue for divorce for violence, cruelty or gross insults of the one toward the other.

Article 232: The condemnation of one of the spouses to a corporal and degrading punishment shall be for the other a cause of divorce.

By article 306, C. C., whenever there is a ground for divorce the plaintiff may instead sue for separation.

French authors unanimously refer to the existence of three, not five or six, causes or grounds for divorce: (1) adultery; (2) penal condemnation; (3) violence, cruelty and gross insults. It would seem more logical to divide (3) into its component parts, for divorce may be obtained for violence, cruelty or gross insults. Gross insults is a general ground; the others are specific. Article 310, C. C., provides for the conversion of separation into divorce. It is not considered a ground for divorce, but a matter of procedure, there being no new trial on the merits. The French viewpoint will be followed and accordingly the law of conversion of separation into divorce will be reserved for a later chapter.

It will be of interest to note that several of the grounds set forth in the law of 1792 have been omitted from the Code; namely, incompatibility, insanity, desertion for two years, absence for five years, emigration (*i.e.*, for political reasons), and mutual consent. Several of these causes have nevertheless found their way back into the law in the guise of gross insults.

The grounds of French law are limitatively enumerated, but the limitation is more theoretical than substantial because "gross insults" is so broad and so elastic a term that practically any state of facts warranting divorce can be brought under it. It is considered in France that society has an interest in seeing that marriages which occasion scandal shall be dissolved, equal to its interest in seeing that marriages which do not occasion scandal shall be preserved. The courts have a wide latitude in appraising and weighing the facts and in deciding whether or not divorce in the particular case is justified. In the case of adultery and penal condemnation there is no occasion to test the gravity of the facts, but in cases of violence, cruelty and gross insults, gravity is a vital element.

In practice, however, not infrequently trivial offenses are successfully magnified into grounds and an award of divorce has become largely a matter of judicial discretion. The Court of Appeal of Caen, April 20, 1855, remarked that the legislators of 1884 considered divorce preferable to separation, hence "an award of divorce should be the general rule, and the refusal of the prayer an exception which must be justified by grave and particular reasons." The Court of Cassation, January 12, 1887, stated that this extraordinary view was inexact. (*Recueil des arrêts des Cours d'Appel de Rouen et de Caen*, 1887, p. 252.) Nevertheless, the idea is still prevalent and nearly nine out of ten applications for divorce are allowed.

Prior to 1908, it was the prevailing view that less serious reasons need be shown to obtain separation than divorce, notwithstanding article 306 C. C. which drew no such distinction. The distinction was based upon the fact that conversion of separation into divorce under article 310 C. C. as it then read was permissive and not mandatory. Hence separation could be granted under circumstances for which the court would not grant divorce. The law of June 6, 1908, made article 310, C. C., mandatory, so the basis for the distinction no longer exists. It seems, however, that the courts now lean in the opposite direction, for proportionately fewer cases of separation eventuate than of divorce.

It is the weight of authority in France that there is a distinction between "peremptory" (*péremptoire*) and "permissive" (*faculative*) causes for divorce, but as to which causes are of the one sort, which of the other, there is no unanimity of opinion. The principal interest in the distinction lies in this: peremptory causes "when proved, dispense with all debate, all appreciation by the judge and render a negative decision impossible." (Labiche, Senate report on the proposed law of 1884, *Journal Officiel*, June 21, 1884, p. 1130.) Some authors maintain nevertheless that it is sounder law to reject such a distinction. (Piérard, vol. 1, sections 94, 95, p. 205, *et seq.*) It is the view of most authors, such as Baudry-Lacatinerie, Coulon,

Demolombe, that adultery and penal condemnation are "peremptory" causes. There is some support for the view that violence and cruelty are also of this class. All authorities that accept the distinction agree that gross insults are a "permissive" cause only. It has been held that once adultery is proved as a fact it is so peremptory a ground that it is not necessary for the court to inquire into or take into consideration the circumstances under which it occurred. (Orthez, June 11, 1890; *La Loi*, November 21, 1890.)

In relation to gross insults, jurisprudence concedes that a court may decline to grant relief no matter how fully the facts may have been established, but in relation to the other grounds, it is still unsettled whether or not the award is in the court's discretion, notwithstanding complete proof. It seems that when proof of gross insults fails, the court may nevertheless grant divorce if, owing to the notoriety of the case, reconciliation is impossible. (Toulouse, January 30, 1896; *La Loi*, March 21, 1896.) It is probably correct to conclude that if an allegation of adultery or penal condemnation should go to trial and were not proved, the court would decline to award divorce to plaintiff in view of this failure of proof. All grounds are not in practice of equal weight and judicial discretion plays an important part in the decision.

It is also a subject of difference of opinion in France whether or not the offense to constitute a ground for divorce or separation must be the violation of a marital duty established by the Code. Gillet, speaking for the *Tribunat* during the debate upon the Code, remarked: "Furthermore, all these causes are based upon the very reciprocity of their obligations. . . . The Code restricts thereto all the causes for which the conjugal society can be ended at the request of one only of the parties." Nevertheless, according to Carpentier, facts which will warrant divorce may be entirely foreign to the marital duties. (Carpentier, *Divorce et séparation de corps,* 1899, vol. 1, section 233.) In practice the question is of academic interest, for nearly every offense justifying divorce may be viewed as a violation of some one of the many enumerated duties.

A spouse must in most cases at least have felt the offense constituting the ground. *Volenti et consentienti non fit injuria.* Hence, only the injured party can invoke the ground. No accord to divorce or separate without cause is tolerated by the law, as this would amount indirectly to divorce or separation by mutual consent, which is forbidden expressly by article 307, C. C., in the case of separation and forbidden impliedly in the case of divorce. Grounds are not mutually exclusive; that is to say, relief may be asked under the head of several grounds and for the same acts considered in different aspects. For example, adultery may be set up *per se* under articles 229 or 230, or as a gross insult under 231. Actions may be brought simultaneously for adultery, cruelty, etc. No legal distinction exists between the sexes as to the causes for divorce. Yet Carpentier remarks: "In practice, however, as we shall see, the courts seem always to look with more indulgence upon adultery by the husband than by the wife, or show themselves less strict in their requirement of proof to establish the latter than the former." (Carpentier, *Divorce et séparation de corps,* 1899, vol. 1, Sec. 162.) In other matters than adultery, the courts seem on the contrary more generous to women than to men, and it is easier for a wife to get a divorce than for a husband. The courts do hold women to a higher standard of morality and conduct than men, but treat them in litigation with greater consideration.

To constitute grounds, the acts complained of must be wrongful. *Qui jure suo utitur neminem laedit.* Acts constituting merely the exercise of a right for a legitimate purpose and without ulterior motive cannot be a ground for divorce. Consequently an accusation of adultery made before the police magistrate will not be deemed insulting if the accusation was warranted by appearances even though unfounded in fact. (Paris, July 13, 1870; *Sirey,* 1870.2.268.) The bringing of a suit for divorce is not *per se* so insulting that when it fails the defendant is himself entitled to obtain a divorce. (Angers, April 13, 1896; *Dalloz,* 1896.2.439.)

In principle, acts to be a reason for divorce or separation must have been performed by one spouse against the other. Nevertheless, cruelty to a child by the mother is considered sufficiently insulting to the father for a divorce in his favor. (Seine, March 31, 1890; *Le Droit,* April 19, 1890.) Offensive conduct towards a relative by marriage may also constitute an exception to the principle. For instance, a husband so grossly insults his wife as to warrant her in divorcing him when he refers to her grandmother as having been a public prostitute and her father a convict. (Paris, March 27, 1896; *Dalloz,* 1896.2.222.) If one party instigates a third person to commit the offensive acts, appearances will be disregarded for the reality, and the instigator will be deemed liable to divorce, for instigation is itself a gross insult. Libelous and unwarranted allegations in a pleading emanating from the party's *avoué* will not constitute grounds for separation unless made at the party's personal suggestion. (Paris, January 10, 1852; *Dalloz,* 1852.5.499.) A party is not liable to have separation pronounced against him by reason of improbable and offensive remarks made by his witness. (Lyon, February 5, 1891; *La Loi,* March 18, 1891.)

To be actionable for divorce or separation, acts must adversely affect the spouse in his or her person, not in his or her property alone. This rule is not absolute. It is a gross insult for a husband to pawn his wife's jewels without her knowledge or consent. (Gien, December 29, 1896; *La Loi,* December 30, 1896.) It will also warrant separation in favor of a wife, that her husband made away with money which was her separate (*paraphernal*) property. (Nimes, July 16, 1849; *Sirey,* 1852.2.45.) Yet the acts against property need not amount to larceny to constitute grounds, for this crime does not exist in French law between husband and wife.

Mere occurrence of the offensive acts, save in the case of penal condemnation, will not be sufficient to sustain the action. Just as the innocent spouse must have felt the offense, so too the guilty spouse must have intended offense, must have had *animus injuriandi.* Knowledge of the nature of the act and wrongful intention must coexist. For example, if a person marries a second time in good faith, thinking the first spouse dead, the first spouse being nevertheless still alive, the sexual relations in consequence of the invalid marriage will not amount to adultery under the Civil Code, since volition to do wrong is not present. But if bigamy were intentional, the felony of adultery would be coupled with the crime of bigamy, and divorce would be warranted *a fortiori.* (Seine, November 4, 1897; *Gazette des Tribunaux,* December 3, 1897.) Since the mind must go with the act, an insane person cannot lawfully be divorced for acts done while insane; nor can a kleptomanic be divorced for theft. Habitual drunkenness does not excuse acts done under the influence of liquor, but if the intoxication were an isolated instance of rare occurrence even violence or cruelty committed thereunder might be excused. Lack of mental maturity may attenuate the gravity of offensive acts. So a very young wife would not always be considered responsible for slanderous utterances against her husband.

The law is not yet in a settled state regarding the significance of time of occurrence of the wrongful acts. The question whether or not acts which occurred before the marriage can be used as a basis for divorce or separation cannot be answered precisely. Acts of adultery, violence and cruelty, to be actionable for divorce or separation, must necessarily have occurred after marriage. But in the case of gross insults this is not always so. Prenuptial acts which project their effects into the period after marriage may constitute grounds. The offensive effect, not the cause, would be the occasion for relief. For example, separation would be pronounced in favor of a husband on account of the pregnancy of the wife by another man if the fact had not been discovered by the husband until after marriage. This would be emphatically the decision if the situation had been concealed from him. That this would be the decision if there had been no concealment or if the woman did not know her condition is not so certain. The fact that the wife had a lover before marriage is not a reason for divorce when after marriage the husband discovers this unpleasant surprise. (Seine, April 17, 1891; *Le Droit,* May 10, 1891.) Nor can a wife divorce a husband because he had a mistress before she married him. (Seine, June 4, 1897; *Gazette des Tribunaux,* October 6, 1897.) It would be different if the guilty relations continued thereafter. Divorce will be granted a wife for misconduct committed by the husband during the engagement. (Paris, March 19, 1887; *Gazette du Palais,* March 22, 1887.) The *fiancé* owes, it seems a duty of loyalty to the *fiancée.* A husband who commits larceny before marriage and is convicted after it, may be divorced for the conviction if a corporal and degrading punishment is inflicted upon him, but probably not if the sentence is lighter, for all convictions are not grossly insulting to the guilty person's spouse.

GROUNDS IN THE CIVIL CODE

The time during marriage when the offensive acts were committed is not of decisive importance in French law. Condonation, laches and prescription will be considered in relation to defenses. It is possible to invoke acts long since pardoned, if the offending spouse gives new grounds for relief. This is expressly stated to be the case by article 244, C. C. The old acts serve to support the new ones, and together they may constitute a course of conduct warranting divorce, even though the old acts and the new ones taken separately might not. Offensive acts occurring during the course of the action, if they are of a nature similar to those already alleged, may be brought to the attention of the court and may complete a set of facts previously insufficient as proof. An act which does not amount to a ground when it occurred may nevertheless be invoked as a ground upon change in the law making it this. Thus acts performed before the enactment of the divorce laws of 1792 and 1884 could be successfully invoked in actions instituted under these laws. It seems, however, that this would not be true of a prior conviction to a degrading and corporal punishment. Acts which take place after a valid divorce or annulment cannot serve as grounds for divorce or separation.

The fact that the offensive acts were performed outside of France or were innocent so far as relates to divorce or separation by the law of the place where they occurred is immaterial so far as the Civil Code is concerned, but may have a bearing upon the matter in the case of aliens whose litigation is governed by their national law. The fact that the marriage was solemnized in France before 1884, when there was no divorce law, is not a reason for denying divorce in an action instituted after the enactment, and does not operate to make later offensive acts free of the divorce consequence provided by the Code.

A brief consideration of each ground separately will be helpful as a further explanation of the French law on grounds.

Under the law of 1794 and the Civil Code as it existed until 1816, a wife could always be divorced for her adultery, whereas a husband could be divorced only for adultery aggravated by keeping his paramour in the home. When divorce was reëstablished in 1884, the difference between the sexes was abolished so far as civil matters were concerned. The old rule remains in force in relation to adultery as a felony under the Penal Code, article 339. Acts of sexual intercourse do not amount to adultery unless they are consummated, that is (*semble*) there must be penetration and ejection. Marriage must also exist and a wrongful intent. Unnatural offenses with a person of the same sex do not constitute adultery. An attempt at adultery is actionable for divorce as a gross insult. (Cassation, December 18, 1894; *Dalloz* 1895.1.260.)

According to article 7 of the Penal Code the punishments which are *afflictive* and *infamante,* namely, corporal and degrading, are, besides the death penalty, life imprisonment at hard labor, imprisonment for a term of years at hard labor, imprisonment for from five to twenty years in a fortress (*détention*), imprisonment for from five to ten years in prison (*réclusion*) and exile. Under article 232, C. C., it is the grade of the penalty, not the nature or gravity of the crime punished, that determines whether or not there is ground for divorce or separation. The commission of a *délit* (felony) or *contravention* (misdemeanor), as, for example, vagrancy or disorderly conduct, not punished in the manner indicated by article 7, P. C., would not be a ground under this heading, though it might under the subhead of "gross insults." Naturally, it is only a final penal judgment that can be invoked under article 232, C. C. *Réhabilitation* (quashing), as stated in article 634 of the Code of Criminal Procedure, effaces the conviction itself and will consequently prevent divorce or separation based upon condemnation. Pardon, commutation of sentence or completion of sentence will not prevent divorce or separation, as the fact of condemnation remains.

Violence and cruelty are usually treated together by French writers because the line of demarcation between them is rather vague and the words are somewhat redundant. By violence (*excès*) is usually meant any act of a nature to put in jeopardy the life or health of the victim. Cruelty (*sévices*) embraces acts which, without imperiling life or health, render life odious or unbearable. Both operate physically, whereas gross insults operate mentally or morally. Violence requires an overt act, whereas cruelty or gross insults may be either positive or negative in character; that is, may be acts or omissions. Hence, mental cruelty and assault without battery would be classified as gross insults and not as violence or cruelty. Furthermore, not every assault with battery constitutes violence or cruelty within the meaning of article 231, C. C. A French husband has a right to chastise his wife moderately. False imprisonment may amount to violence, cruelty or gross insults, according to circumstances. The acts or omissions to be actionable must usually be, not isolated instances, but habitual or repeated. However, one attempt at murder will suffice; a single slap may or may not. A wife acquitted in a criminal court of attempted homicide upon her husband, may nevertheless be divorced in the civil court on account of the violence committed upon him. (Seine, August 13, 1885; Paris, October 20, 1886; *Dalloz,* 1888.2.101.) Acts provoked by the scandalous conduct of the victim will not justify pronouncement of divorce or separation against the perpetrator.

GROUNDS IN THE CIVIL CODE

By far the most important cause of divorce in France is *injures graves*. It is by no means easy to give a satisfactory English equivalent of this term. It is customary to translate the term by the words "gross insults," but this is not entirely exact. It is not *diffamation* (slander or libel) that is meant, but rather the *injuria* of the Roman law; *omne quod non jure fit*. (Piérard, vol. 1, section 125, p. 247.) Possibly the words "grievous wrong" or "grave tort," or "gross offense" would convey more clearly the French sense. Kelly uses the words "dishonorable treatment." (Kelly, The French Law of Marriage, Marriage Contracts, Divorce and the Conflict of Laws Arising Therefrom, 2d ed. 1895, p. 177.) The expression "gross insults" will, nevertheless, be used. This is Cachard's translation. (Cachard, The French Civil Code, 1895, article 231, C. C.)

The sub-ground "gross insults" comprises any words or writings, acts or omissions, of one spouse adversely affecting the other in his or her reputation or honor. Publicity or communication to a third person is not essential to constitute the offense, but may aggravate this. Although the word "insults" is in the plural, this does not mean that there must be a plurality of acts or omissions constituting a course of conduct. A single insult if sufficiently gross and precise will suffice for divorce or separation. More than a dozen different subdivisions exist of this sub-ground, and many cases, besides, which defy classification. Such subdivisions as concealment of childbirth, communication of venereal disease, unwarranted jealousy, non-protection by a husband, etc., do not require detailed discussion herein. Others merit this,—particularly desertion, the favorite cause with French and aliens.

Article 214 of the Civil Code reads:

GROUNDS IN THE CIVIL CODE

A wife is bound to live with her husband, and to follow him wherever he deems it proper to live; the husband is bound to receive her and to supply her whatever is necessary for the wants of life according to his means and condition.

The divorce law of 1792 provided that desertion for two years should be a distinct cause for divorce. This cause was omitted from the Code of 1804. Consequently, it is held that mere violation of article 214, C. C., is not a reason for divorce unless it is grossly insulting. An action for the restitution of conjugal rights is the proper remedy for most commonplace breaches of the duty of cohabitation.

When is desertion considered grossly insulting? If the acts or omissions contrary to article 214, C. C., are unjustified and an evasion of marital responsibility, they are deemed offensive. It is largely a question of intent and reason for the breach of duty. It would not be insulting for a husband to leave his wife and remove to a foreign country to recoup his fortune if he hoped to return and kept in touch with her by letters. A mere business trip, even though prolonged, would not be desertion. The prayer of a wife for divorce will be rejected when the desertion by the husband and his refusal to return are found to have been arranged beforehand by the spouses. (Seine, May 8, 1896; *La Loi,* June 21 and 22, 1896.) But desertion accompanied or followed by offensive circumstances will be a reason for divorce or separation. Excessive prolongation of absence without excuse or reason will be insulting, though there is no time fixed by law or custom beyond which non-presence becomes desertion or abandonment. The insult of desertion may be inflicted in any number of ways; for example, by the abrupt or discourteous manner of departure, by the conduct while away, by the terms used in declining to come back, or by the financial want in which the other spouse was left. A wife who leaves her husband and secretly removes the children is guilty of a gross insult for which her husband may divorce her. (Algiers, February 5, 1894; *Le Droit*, April 15, 1894.) If a wife refuses to live with her husband for puerile reasons, she grossly insults him. (Paris, April 17, 1888; *Le Droit*, April 19, 1888.) A wife who deserts her husband to live abroad and refuses to return may be divorced on that account. (Seine, April 14, 1891; *Le Droit*, May 10, 1891.) A husband is entitled to divorce when his wife refuses to live with him and petitions the Vatican for an annulment of the marriage. (Seine, July 27, 1888; *Pandectes françaises*, 1889.2.27.)

The offensive character may be given to a desertion by letters stating a firm intention never to resume life in common. (Bordeaux, March 31, 1897; *Gazette des Tribunaux*, September 24, 1897.) In order to obtain clear evidence of such refusal to resume marital relations it is customary for the deserted party to send a bailiff (*huissier*) to the deserting party to summon him or her to return. The deserting party states orally to the bailiff his unwillingness to do so, in language whose terms are purposely derogatory to the deserted one. The bailiff draws up a report (*procès verbal*) of what was said and delivers it to the *avoué* who sent him. Such report is conclusive evidence, unless and until special proceedings are taken to falsify it. In nearly all the American divorces in France which are not seriously contested this is the method used to establish grounds for divorce.

Non-support may next be considered. Article 212 of the Civil Code says: "The spouses owe each other fidelity, support and assistance." This article is deemed to make the duty of support mutual, although the primary duty is upon the husband under article 214, C.C. Non-support is not *per se* insulting, for there may be good reason for it. For example, the husband may have no resources or the wife may have deserted him. If the one party has financial resources, while the other has not, the fortunate one is in duty bound to contribute towards the other's support and an action lies for alimony or for compulsory support to be supplied in the home in lieu of divorce or separation. In order to obtain termination of the marriage or relaxation of the conjugal bond for non-support, this must be grossly insulting. As in the case of desertion, this character may be given in a variety of ways, similar to those already suggested. If the wife has an income of her own, sufficient for her support, she is not in a particularly good position to suggest that the failure of the husband to support her is insulting.

By article 213 of the Civil Code, a wife owes her husband obedience. When the wife goes upon the stage against her husband's wishes, this involves a sufficiently grave disobedience and insult to warrant him in divorcing her.

Vulgar abuse among people of low social condition will not be deemed insulting within the meaning of article 231, C.C., but it will be so regarded if indulged in by persons supposedly well brought up. Malice or intent to libel or slander is essential, else there is no insult. Truth would probably not excuse the language or writing, but provocation might do so. The so-called "debt notices" in which a husband advertises in the press that his wife has left him and that he will not be responsible for her debts, are frequently, but not always, deemed insulting. For example, it would be insulting to publish such notice if the wife had been granted a separate residence by order of the president during the pendency of her divorce action and had a substantial fortune of her own. Malicious prosecution or the bringing of an unfounded action to disavow paternity of a child will usually give rise incidentally to grossly insulting statements or acts. But divorce cannot be pronounced for a passing display of ill-humor or for mutual recriminations and quarrels. (Paris, November 24, 1894; *La Loi,* January 3, 1895.)

Some acts of one spouse contrary to the religion of the other may be so grossly insulting as to warrant a court in awarding divorce or separation to the victim. Nevertheless, the disestablishment of the Catholic Church and the emphasis now laid in France upon religious freedom render the state of the law on this sub-division quite unsettled. A change of religion by one spouse during marriage will not warrant divorce against him or her, but if the wife should secretly educate the children in a faith disapproved by the husband, this might give warrant. It has been held that a refusal by the husband to take part in a religious marriage solemnization after the civil one has already taken place, is a sufficient cause for separation, even if action is brought many years after the civil marriage and after a protracted *de facto* separation in the interval. (Angers, January 29, 1859; *Sirey,* 1859. 2.77.) It is probable that this case would not be followed today, unless the husband had before the civil marriage promised to participate in a religious solemnization. Civil marriage being the only one valid in France, it is not proper to compel submission to a religious rite which has no legal effect, under penalty of divorce for refusal. It is only the breach of a promise to go before a priest that would give the refusal an insulting character. It has been held that if a Catholic priest conceals his calling and marries, his Catholic wife may divorce him on that account. (Seine, May 18, 1888; *Le Droit,* May 24, 1888.) This is a very unusual case, because by civil law a priest has capacity to marry, his disability existing only in Canon law, which latter law has in France no civil standing. The Catholic Church also forbids divorce. In other words, the husband's violation of the religious scruples of the wife warranted her in seeking a remedy equally reproved by her Church.

Intemperance of one spouse is not *per se* grossly insulting to the other, but habitual drunkenness will be a reason for divorce if accompanied by degrading manifestations or if it leads to arrest for disorderly conduct.

Refusal of sexual intercourse is not a gross insult, unless it is voluntary, confirmed and unwarranted. It has been held that deliberate refusal of intercourse by a husband is not only sufficient cause for divorce, but for damages as well. His obduracy amounted to a quasi-delict or tort which imposed a duty of compensating the "material" and "moral" injury suffered by the wife, to the amount of fifty thousand francs. (Montpellier, November 27, 1897; *La Loi*, June 11, 1898.) The mere fact that the marriage was once consummated would not excuse the couple from intercourse forever afterwards, but the courts have not ventured to indicate the length of the permissible interval between acts of intercourse. If the complaining wife long after marriage still remains a virgin, it is incumbent upon the defendant husband to explain and justify his inactivity. (Douai, April 29, 1884; *Sirey*, 1884. 2.92.) A husband is entitled to a divorce if he is unable to hold intercourse owing to absence of the "encouraging disposition" which a husband "is entitled to expect of his young wife." (Toulouse, January 30, 1896; *La Loi*, March 21, 1896.)

Embezzlement, receiving stolen goods and attempted rape by one spouse reflect sufficiently upon the other to warrant the latter in obtaining a divorce or separation. It is in these cases the criminality and disgraceful character of the acts, not the degree of punishment or penalty, which constitutes the insult. It is not even necessary in such cases that the guilty party shall have been prosecuted to conviction. Gambling by the husband is not necessarily insulting to the wife, but would become so if it should lead to the dissipation of the family fortune. Questionable conduct, even short of bad conduct or misconduct, may sustain an action for divorce. For instance, divorce has been granted to a wife because her husband evinced undue affection toward a young girl received by them into the home, and took her to the theater and dinner in the wife's absence. (Seine, November 28, 1890; *Pandectes françaises,* 1891.2.148.) If a wife displays excessive independence in conduct, lack of reserve and disregard of conventions, occasioning public criticism and gossip, her husband is so grossly insulted as to be justified in separating from her. (Riom, December 22, 1886; *Dalloz,* 1887.2.230.)

It will be observed from this review that mere absence, sickness, insanity, impotence, sterility, loss of fortune and incompatability are not of themselves sufficient grounds for divorce. Under some special circumstances, it is possible for them to become insulting, and then they could be invoked in a divorce or separation action. Usually, however, reliance must be placed upon other classes of acts or omissions. This is true notwithstanding the fact that the effects upon domestic relations of acts or omissions not considered *per se* grossly insulting may be as grave as or graver than those considered of this nature. It will seem rather forced and far-fetched to speak of desertion as a gross insult, yet it is only by such indirection that it has come within the divorce grounds, and the same is the case in relation to most of the subdivisions of gross insults above described.

Chapter XIII

GROUNDS IN PRIVATE INTERNATIONAL LAW

In the United States and Great Britain a divorce court can grant relief for grounds stated in its own law only, no foreign law being considered. This is because the action is one sounding in tort for a particular remedy granted by statute, not by the common law, and because remedies, as matters of procedure, are governed by *lex fori* in these countries. No inquiry is made there into the capacity of a plaintiff to obtain a divorce under his *lex domicilii*; apparently because *lex fori* and *lex domicilii* will nearly always be the same since jurisdiction depends upon domicile. In France, the legal theory is quite different. Divorce and separation are remedies for breach of contract. No distinction is made between statutory and other remedies, for all are statutory. Since domicile is not the sole or even the dominant test of jurisdiction, *lex fori* and *lex domicilii* in many cases do not coincide. Furthermore in most cases *lex nationalis* not *lex domicilii* or *fori* governs capacity. In the civil law divorce and separations are considered matters of status and capacity in substantive law, rather than matters of remedy in adjective law. The outcome of this is that French courts make a study of capacity in relation to the divorce and separation of aliens. This in turn leads to a requirement not alone that the acts complained of shall come within the grounds of the French Civil Code, but also within those of the national law of the aliens.

Before the Revolution, when Frenchmen were Parisians, Normans, Orleanists, Burgundians, etc., status and capacity were considered to accompany the person wherever he went and were fixed by the custom of the province in which he was domiciled. When France became unified and adopted the Civil Code in place of the provincial customs, such as the *coutume de Paris, coutume d'Orleans, lex domicilii* gave way to *lex nationalis.* Article 3 of the Civil Code expressly provides that a Frenchman is governed as to his status and capacity by French law wherever he may be; that is, in or out of France. While the Code says nothing about the status and capacity of aliens, a rule corresponding to that of article 3 is applied to them by analogy. Aliens in France are as a general principle governed in relation to status and capacity by their own national law.

The reason for the reference by French law to a foreign law is not international courtesy or comity. The Dutch school of thought in private international law does not prevail in France, as it does in England and America. The rule of *lex nationalis* as to status and capacity of aliens is a matter of law in France, not of comity, although it is of unwritten law or practice since the Code does not specifically mention it. The rule is based upon a desire that French law shall be applied to Frenchmen abroad, and in order that foreign nations shall so act, France applies a similar principle to aliens. France is not alone in doing this. Practically all the continental countries now follow *lex nationalis.* The Institute of International Law in 1887 voted that before a country should permit its courts to divorce aliens the latter should have capacity to divorce in *lex nationalis* and grounds in *lex fori.* Capacity was to be deemed existent if divorce were a known institution in the alien's country. The Hague Conference of 1894 resolved that there must be not alone capacity to divorce in general but in particular, that is to say, there must be grounds both in *lex nationalis* and in *lex fori.*

The Hague Conference of 1900 followed this latter view with a slight attenuation, and this was the solution adopted by the Hague Convention. The rule *lex nationalis* was therefore statutory in France for ten years, but its adoption long preceded the Treaty and survives its denunciation.

The Tribunal of Vesoul, December 15, 1896 (*Journal Clunet,* 1897, p. 335) held that a Belgian admitted to domicile in France by presidential decree was still governed by Belgian law as to status and capacity, and in particular as to the grounds for which he could divorce or be divorced in France. It is only when a person has no nationality or no known nationality or when his national law is contrary to French public policy or for some other sufficient reason that a different law than *lex nationalis* will be applied to him in relation to status and capacity. In such unusual cases the old rule *lex domicilii* or *lex fori* is applied, or if it be the wife whose nationality is uncertain or whose law is distasteful to the courts, then the husband's national law may be applied to her or the law of the place where the marriage was solemnized. For example, a *heimatlos, apatride* (*i.e.,* countryless) person, formerly Austrian, of the Catholic faith, living in France, can divorce, since French law applies to aliens domiciled in France who by reason of loss of nationality cannot invoke in relation to capacity the law of their country of origin. (Nantes, November 28, 1901; *Journal Clunet,* 1902, p. 590.) The Court of Appeal of Algiers, June 7, 1902 (*Journal Clunet,* 1907, p. 409), remarked: "The status and capacity of an individual whose nationality is indeterminate can only be governed by the law of his domicile. Indeed public policy is interested in it that every inhabitant shall be governed by laws fixed and determined in advance."

GROUNDS IN INTERNATIONAL LAW

Does the foregoing explanation mean that aliens can divorce in France for grounds set forth in their own national law without the application to them of the grounds of the Civil Code? Aliens having divorce capacity in national law may indeed so divorce in Italy, although there is no divorce available to Italians. Some French courts have inclined to an equally broad view. For instance, the Tribunal of Dieppe, April 2, 1896 (*Journal Clunet,* 1899, p. 360), said: "The provisions of their national law concerning divorce are applied to aliens in France, to the exclusion of those of French law." The Court of Appeal of Paris, December 17, 1920 (*Journal Clunet,* 1921, p. 521), granted Dutch subjects each a divorce against the other, the one for cruelty, the other for adultery, upon proof that those were grounds in Dutch law and without saying a word about the grounds of the Civil Code of France. The Tribunal of the Seine, November 5, 1920 (*Journal Clunet,* 1921, p. 185), divorced Greek subjects upon proof that adultery was a ground in Byzantine law, and without reference to the French ground.

The view of the exclusive applicability of national law is however not the prevailing one. Between 1816 and 1884, when there was no divorce law in France, aliens could not divorce in France though authorized to do so by their own national law. Belgians cannot today divorce in France by mutual consent as they can in Belgium; nor can a Swiss citizen divorce in France for insanity as permitted by Helvetian law. (Weiss, *Manuel de Droit International Privé,* 1914, p. 511.) French courts grant a divorce or separation to aliens on Civil Code grounds or not at all. (Laurent-Bailly, p. 30.) Nevertheless, *lex nationalis* is considered with *lex fori,* which latter indeed enjoys a certain preëminence. The two laws are applied more or less concurrently. To obtain divorce or separation in France today the facts must amount to grounds in both French and national laws. If the particular ground is not present in the two legislations, or if either legislation forbids divorce or separation on the facts or in general, the remedy prayed will not be awarded by a French court unless perhaps there are very exceptional circumstances.

It is not necessary that there be absolute coincidence between the French and the foreign grounds. General analogy is sufficient. It must be demonstrated that plaintiff would be entitled in both countries to a divorce for the same reasons. From 1904 to 1914 under the Hague Convention, this requirement was still further attenuated. According to this treaty, nationals of the ratifying or adhering powers could divorce or separate in the territory of another treaty-power provided they proved a ground under *lex nationalis* and under *lex fori*, though the two grounds might be different. For example, aliens might invoke French penal condemnation as a French ground and sterility as a national ground, the former being no cause in national law, the latter no cause *per se* in French law. Since the Convention is no longer law in France, it is uncertain whether or not this attenuation could now be invoked. The French law is in an unsettled state on the question of how exact must be the coincidence between the grounds of French and foreign law before the French courts will pronounce divorce or separation. It is not alone necessary to show what the foreign law is, so that it may be compared with the French, but to show that the facts fall within the foreign as well as within the French grounds. This task is simple in the case of a clear-cut ground such as adultery. It is no easy matter in cases of violence, cruelty, etc.; that which may be violence in foreign law may not amount to this in French law.

In this relation a conflict of qualifications of the offensive acts may very easily arise. The private international law of France on this point is very complicated. Not only is foreign law to be applied to qualify acts in relation to foreign grounds, but also in relation to French grounds. In other words, *lex nationalis* solves conflicts of qualifications and foreign law decides in the case of aliens the question whether or not the acts complained of fall within one or another of the grounds of the Civil Code. This is a surprising manner of solution, for one would expect that French law would decide whether or not the facts fall within a French ground, and foreign law would decide whether or not they fall within a foreign ground. For example, it is not adultery within the Civil Code for an Algerian Mohammedan to hold intercourse with several wives, but it is so for him to hold intercourse with a person to whose sexual possession he is not entitled. (Algiers, June 27, 1921; *Journal Clunet*, 1922, p. 650.) In other words, the French view of what is adultery in relation to wrongdoing does not apply to an Algerian in view of the polygamy permitted by Algerian domestic law. In the *affaire* Levinçon, the Court of Cassation, May 29, 1905 (*Journal Clunet*, 1905, p. 1006) applied Russian qualifications, not French, to decide whether performance of religious rites in relation to the divorce of Jews was a matter of substance governed by *lex nationalis* or of form governed by *lex fori*. In Russian law, unlike French law, such rites relate to status and capacity, not to judicial procedure. Russian qualification was accepted; consequently, as French courts had no power to perform the necessary rites, but only Russian ecclesiastical courts could do so, the action was dismissed.

The practice of referring to national law in relation to grounds for divorce and separation is reasonably satisfactory when the foreign country to whose law reference is made enjoys unity of civil legislation and has rules for the solution of conflict of laws similar to those of the French. But the practice is by no means of easy application where the reference is to the legislation of a nation whose civil law is not uniform, for example, the United States, the British Empire, Argentine, Brazil, Poland. Until lately there was no national Civil Code in Germany or Switzerland and unity of civil legislation there is still incomplete. Even Spain, though it now has a Civil Code, has also its *fueros,* or local civil laws, in Catalonia and in some other provinces. Even in France, the civil laws of Alsace-Lorraine are not quite the same as those in the other *départments* (provinces, states). In the United States there is no federal divorce or separation legislation, but separate territorial laws in the District of Columbia, Alaska, Porto Rico, the Philippines, the Canal Zone and Hawaii. The civil laws differ in the forty-eight sovereign states, four only of which have enacted the Uniform Annulment of Marriage and Divorce Law. Separate civil laws obtain in England, Scotland, Ireland, Canada, Australia and the British Colonies.

How is *lex nationalis* to be applied to aliens who are citizens or subjects of such states? *Lex nationalis* ought not to be applied to them at all. *Lex domicilii* would fit their situation far better. This was the rule applied to inter-provincial conflicts in France under the old regime. In the case of persons from Alsace-Lorraine, *lex nationalis* (French law) is indeed applied to them, but *lex domicilii* (Alsatian law) is used subordinately thereto. According to Weiss, *lex domicilii* decides what law within a given country shall be considered. (Weiss, *Manuel de Droit International Privé,* 1914, p. 372.) For instance, in an action concerning the distribution of the estate of an Ottoman subject, national law was held to govern, but the Hatti Humayoum of February 18, 1856 was considered by the court in order to decide whether distribution should be made under Turkish or Byzantine law applicable within the Turkish Empire respectively to Ottoman Turks and Ottoman Greeks. (Seine, July 3, 1914; Paris, July 5, 1921; *Journal Clunet,* 1921, p. 958.) The concurrent application of *lex domicilii* and *lex nationalis* fits cases in which the aliens are still domiciled in their own country, but not cases in which they are domiciled in France or some other country not their own. In such cases either *lex nationalis* or *lex domicilii,* but not both, ought logically to be applied.

A further complication exists when the reference of French law is to a country whose rules for the solution of conflicts of laws differ from those of France. Is the reference to the so-called "internal" law of the foreign country, which solves the point at issue, or to the whole body of the foreign law, including the foreign private international law? If the reference is of the latter sort, the solution of the reference may be referred back to French law or to the law of still another country. This is the well-known *renvoi* problem. It is now the weight of authority in France, that the reference is to the whole foreign law and that a reference back to French law is to be accepted. But unless the parties suggest and prove a *renvoi* the courts require evidence of the grounds in internal law. By reason of the foregoing, in various cases involving American and British litigants the grounds of the internal foreign law have been applied, e.g., the Gould and Knibloe cases. In others the grounds of the Civil Code alone have been applied.

The Tribunal of the Seine, May 7, 1908 (*Journal Clunet*, 1909, p. 474) in the case of two British subjects, remarked: "Whereas, according to English law the status of persons and especially the grounds for divorce are determined, not by the national law of the spouses but by the law of their domicile at the time of the institution of suit, and this is so without distinguishing between marriages contracted abroad and in marriages contracted in England; hence, French law alone is applicable to the case at bar, Mr. de Grandcourt inhabiting Paris." Although opposed by nearly all legal writers, the doctrine of *renvoi* had been definitely accepted by jurisprudence. The Court of Cassation in the Soulié will case, all chambers united, adopted *renvoi* simply as a matter of convenience. (Cassation, March 1, 1910; *Le Droit,* March 30, 1910.) *Renvoi* has since then been applied to various sorts of conflicts of law. It is, nevertheless, still opposed on occasion by a few recalcitrant lower courts, such as that of Boulogne-sur-Mer. It is not yet settled, however, that French law allows *Weiterverweisung,* namely, *renvoi* to another foreign law instead of back to French. (Pillet and Niboyet, *Manuel de Droit International Privé,* 1925, section 310, p. 385.)

The view has been expressed that *lex domicilii* not *lex nationalis* governs Americans in France. The Tribunal of the Seine, March 12, 1921 (*Gazette des Tribunaux,* February 23, 1922) in the Coxe case, said: "The law which governs the status and capacity of American citizens in France in so far as concerns the causes for divorce, is determined not by their national law but by their domicile. This law is, therefore, French law if the spouses were domiciled in France at the time of the solemnization of their marriage and if they have continued to live there in an uninterrupted manner since this event." It cannot, however, be said that this is the weight of authority. French courts still refer to *lex nationalis* and require proof either of grounds in the internal law or proof of a *renvoi* to French law under the American rules of private international law. Renvoi has come to be the favorite method of making French grounds alone applicable. The decision in the Coxe case should be interpreted in this sense.

Could the difficulty of applying *lex nationalis* to the divorce actions of Americans be solved in some such way as the following? The French courts would regard the country or sovereignty as a whole, not considering the specific law of local subdivisions (states) of the Union; accordingly, a citizen of one of the United States could obtain a divorce in France even upon a ground not recognized in his own state if the ground were recognized in any other state, because as a citizen of the United States he is free to change his domicile to any state which recognizes the ground for divorce which he possesses, and the French courts would, therefore, entertain his action if the ground be recognized anywhere in the United States. An American lawyer practicing in Paris has suggested this, but no reported case has been found which supports the view, nor the opinion of any French text-writer. During the rush years of 1923 to 1927, some divorces of Americans may perhaps have been secured on some such theory as this, but the theory does not recommend itself. In public international law, France does regard the sovereignty as a whole, but not in private international law. In the Valentino case the French courts referred to Indiana law, in the Gould and Knibloe cases to New York law, in the Chance case to Illinois law. A French court if it understood American law would not deliberately apply Nevada grounds to New Yorkers, on the theory that they could remove to Reno if they wished. The French courts intend the reference to foreign law seriously. A New York or Massachusetts citizen is not at liberty to migrate for divorce; this is a fraud on his state law. The status of a citizen is governed by some law at a given time, not by any law in or beyond the Union, to which he may choose to go. It would not properly satisfy the French reference to *lex nationalis* in the case of Americans simply to prove that somewhere "in the United States" the facts of the case constitute a ground. It would be like proving Australian grounds for Londoners.

Nevertheless, there is a very serious problem indeed in deciding to which American state law the French private international law intends to refer, particularly when the Americans are no longer domiciled in the United States and may have lost state citizenship. Usually there is no controversy before the French court as to whether New York, New Jersey or another state law is to be applied. If the question were controversial, there is no telling on what theory the court would decide. The law of the state of the present matrimonial domicile is, of course, the first choice. If the couple are domiciled outside the Union when action is brought, then the law of the state of last common domicile would seem logically applicable. In the Valentino case, the couple claimed domicile in France and were the one Italian, the other American. They were married in Indiana, so the grounds for divorce set forth in the law of that state were referred to. In the Chance case Illinois grounds were applied for the same reason to two Americans domiciled in Paris. In the Gould case, New York grounds were applied, the couple being domiciled in that state, resident in France and married in Scotland.

If the law of the American state or states to which the spouses are or were in some way attached does not contain a ground which coincides with a French ground, the usual practical way to solve the difficulty and still secure divorce is by *renvoi,* namely, a reference back to French internal law by American private international law. For whereas there is extreme diversity in grounds for divorce between the several American states, there is still among them substantial uniformity in the basic rules of private international law. A *renvoi* to French internal law on the grounds for divorce usually may be shown to exist by the laws of every state with which the parties have been connected by birth, marriage, domicile or otherwise. The usual theories upon which a *renvoi* is predicated are these: by American law, status and capacity are governed by the law of the domicile, the courts of the domicile of the parties have jurisdiction, divorce and separation are remedies governed by *lex fori* alone. These same general principles apply in the British Empire. Even Latin-America favors *lex domicilii* rather than *lex nationalis*. Consequently, upon *renvoi* to French law, either as *lex domicilii* or *lex fori,* the grounds of the Civil Code have been exclusively applied in several divorce and separation actions between or concerning such aliens as Americans, British and Argentinos. In the case of New Yorkers, when adultery is not in issue, *renvoi* to French law on grounds is practically the only proper way to get a divorce in France, in view of the strictness of the divorce law in their own state.

Consider now the application of the foregoing principles to litigation between two aliens of the same nationality, then between two aliens of different nationalities, and then between an alien and a French citizen.

When there is no such thing as divorce in the law of a foreign country, this is considered to mean that marriage is there regarded as indissoluble. Consequently, the nationals of such country are deemed to lack divorce capacity, that is, they both lack ability to divorce and are free from liability to be divorced. Several countries of Catholic faith are in this class, e. g., Spain, Italy, etc. Indissolubility is there the rule, even though the marriage may have been solemnized in France or another country wherein divorce is known. France respects the implied as well as the express divorce prohibition of foreign law. For instance, it has been held that two Italians can separate but cannot divorce in France. (Colmar, April 7, 1925; *Journal Clunet,* 1926, p. 74.) Also, this is the case of two Spaniards (Pau, January 16, 1897; *Journal Clunet,* 1897, p. 535); Portugese (Seine, June 12, 1889; *Journal Clunet,* 1890, p. 107); and Austrian Catholics (Nice, January 17, 1921; *Revue Lapradelle,* 1921, p. 508.) A British judgment of separation between British subjects cannot be converted into a French divorce under article 310, C. C., since conversion without another trial and without further cause is unknown in English law. (Dieppe, May 5, 1904; *Journal Clunet,* 1908, p. 465.)

The law is unsettled on the point whether Irish and certain Canadians can divorce at all in France or can only separate. In the McBride case, an Irish wife sued her Irish husband in France for divorce. The parties were found to be still domiciled in Ireland, the children having been baptized there and the couple having been married in France at the British consulate instead of at the borough hall. The tribunal awarded separation, but not divorce, on the theory that there is no divorce in Irish law and such law applies to status and capacity of Irish parties domiciled in Ireland. On appeal it was argued that divorce is possible between Irish subjects judicially separated inasmuch as the plaintiff could petition Parliament for an Act of Divorce. The Court of Appeal of Paris considered this fact insufficient to warrant a French court in divorcing them, notwithstanding the fact that a judicial inquiry is held in England before a bill of divorcement is enacted into law. (Seine, August 8, 1906; *Journal Clunet,* 1907, p. 373; Paris, January 30, 1908; *Gazette des Tribunaux,* April 22, 1908.) In the case of Canadians just the reverse has been indicated. The Court of Appeal of

Douai, January 29, 1924, (*Journal Clunet,* 1924, p. 398) declared that it had power to divorce Canadians, although in Canada an act of parliament may be the only available remedy. The court regarded a Canadian legislative divorce as if it were judicial in character, and discussed the grounds usually sufficient to obtain the act. These grounds were considered similar to the gross insults of French law. It was found, however, that plaintiff was not entitled to a divorce on the merits.

Aliens within the French jurisdiction and praying a French court for relief known to their national law and to French law and for reasons considered suitable in both countries will receive such relief. Thus, two Spaniards *de facto* domiciled in Algiers and entitled to access to the courts under the France-Spanish Treaty of January 7, 1862 will be granted separation for gross insults. (Cassation, June 14, 1910; *Journal Clunet,* 1912, p. 209.) It is unnecessary to cite further authority for this proposition, as practically all the divorces and separations granted to aliens in France are based upon concurrent application as to grounds of *lex nationalis* and *lex fori.* Nevertheless, there are cases in which *lex nationalis* will be excluded for one or another reason.

A rather anomalous decision has lately been rendered which should be considered at this stage. The Tribunal of the Seine, February 15, 1922 (*Journal Clunet,* 1922, p. 396) pronounced divorce between Polish citizens domiciled in Paris and married in Belgium, notwithstanding the marriage would be deemed void in Polish law for lack of a religious solemnization and the Polish law forbids divorce when one party is Catholic and the other Jewish. The tribunal held that the French principle of the secularization of marriage implies the validity in France of a purely civil marriage solemnized abroad and the purely civil dissolution of that marriage when the facts constitute a ground either under the law of the place of solemnization of the marriage or under the law of the domicile of the spouses. In such case no attention is to be paid to the religious disability of the spouses. In other words, national law is to be disregarded so far as it imposes a religious disability. This is contrary to the decision of the Court of Cassation in the Levinçon case, in which a Russian religious disability was respected. Furthermore, it is novel even in France to suggest that the law of the place where the marriage was solemnized has such relation to the grounds for divorce. Also, it is quite unprecedented to hold that the grounds of *lex domicilii* or of *lex loci celebrationis* in the alternative will be applied, instead of the grounds of *lex nationalis* and *lex fori* currently, or instead of those of *lex fori* alone if *lex nationalis* in the particular case is contrary to the public policy of the forum. It is probable that this decision will not be considered authoritative.

It is, nevertheless, correct to say that a *lex nationalis* contrary to French policy will be disregarded by French courts. It is by no means easy to decide what French public policy is in relation to divorce. Before 1884, divorce itself was contrary to French public policy. A foreign prohibition of divorce is not now contrary to French public policy, and such prohibition will usually be respected. French policy is not opposed to mere differences of details in grounds. This is true at any rate if the foreign grounds are more limited than the French. For example, adultery is of itself a ground in French law, but British law for many years required with adultery such aggravating circumstance as bigamy, incest, rape or desertion for two years. A British wife has been awarded divorce against her British husband for adultery aggravated by desertion for upward of two years. (Boulogne-sur-Mer, December 14, 1925; *Journal Clunet,* 1927, p. 70; Seine,

June 24, 1910; *Journal Clunet,* 1914, p. 922.) But divorce has been refused a British wife when her husband's adultery was aggravated by desertion for less than one year. (Boulogne-sur-Mer, February 5, 1926; *Journal Clunet,* 1926, p. 977.) It was suggested to the tribunal that French grounds alone should be applied upon *renvoi* to the *lex domicilii,* but the court declined to follow the *renvoi* doctrine, notwithstanding it is now well established in France under the eminent authority of the Court of Cassation.

Can it be said that foreign grounds which are broader than French grounds will be disregarded as being contrary to French public policy? Divorce by mutual consent or for insanity will not be granted in France to aliens even if their national law concedes this right. The reason for refusal is not so much the fact that the foreign law is disregarded as the fact that French grounds are to be concurrently applied and these circumstances, *i. e.,* consent, insanity, happen not to be grounds in French law. One may conclude that a more liberal foreign law on grounds will be inoperative to the extent that it goes beyond the French, but a more restricted foreign law will be observed.

The French private international law in relation to divorce and separation presents many other complications. Thus, the rights and duties of husband and wife are defined in articles 203 to 226 of the Civil Code. These articles apply to French couples, not always to aliens. The rights and duties under foreign law differ sometimes substantially from those of the Code. Suppose a foreign husband violates the rights of his wife under foreign law but not under French. Could she divorce him on this account in France? No precise answer can be given. The courts and authors have not developed the law to so fine a point. Article 205, C. C., concerning the duty of filial support, applies to aliens in France; hence, a non-resident alien son can be required to support his parent in France. (Cassation, July 22, 1903; *Journal Clunet,* 1904, p. 355.) An American son-in-law will be required to support his French mother-in-law. (Article 206, C. C.) (Justice of the Peace, Paris, 16th *Arrondissement,* July 10, 1903; *Journal Clunet,* 1904, p. 356.) Support, therefore, is a matter of public order in France. Hence it is posible that an alien husband guilty of non-support of his wife's parent in France could be divorced there for gross insults to the wife, even if he owed no support in his national law. Yet it can be argued that a judgment for restitution of conjugal rights or for alimony, without divorce, would be the proper remedy in such cases.

Change of nationality of both spouses will perforce exclude one of two foreign laws, the old or the new. If both spouses bona fide change nationality to the same country, French law will consider their status and capacity governed by the law of the country of their new allegiance. This will be the case even though they may have changed from a country which has no divorce to one which has, or the reverse.

Consider next the situation of aliens of diverse nationalities. In principle the status and capacity of each alien ought to be applied to him in French litigation. So, if the plaintiff husband were German, the defendant wife Danish, there should be applied French grounds in general, German grounds to test the ability of the husband to divorce, and Danish grounds to test the liability of the wife to be divorced. It can be argued, however, that the husband's law should predominate over the wife's. But the practice has not consistently followed any particular theory. The Tribunal of the Seine, November 29, 1904 (*Journal Clunet,* 1905, p. 187) applied French grounds alone in an action brought by an American wife against her Turkish husband, upon the theory that when there is diversity of nationality within the family *lex domicilii* applies. In the Salm case an American wife from New York was granted a divorce from her Austrian husband for gross insults and he was given a separation from her for these also; although gross insults are not a ground in New York, and there is no divorce in Austria for Catholics, and the parties asserted their domicile to be in Paris. In the Valentino case, desertion, a ground in Indiana law, was applied to the suit of an American wife against her Italian husband; there being no divorce law in Italy and the parties being found to be domiciled in Paris. French grounds were not even mentioned in this case. (Seine, January 19, 1926, *Journal Clunet,* 1926, p. 663.) In other words, capacity of the wife to divorce in her own national law outweighs non-liability of the husband to be divorced in his! It is still apparently undecided how the French courts would solve the conflict, if both aliens had capacity under their national laws, but the grounds differed. It might not be easy to apply the grounds concurrently.

If the diversity in foreign nationality is occasioned by the naturalization of one spouse to evade a restriction of his former national law, it seems the French courts will inquire into motive and will apply the old and not the new national law (Laurent-Bailly, p. 43). If naturalization were to the French, this would not always be true.

According to the French rules for the solution of conflicts of laws, when one litigant is alien, the other French, the capacity of the alien should be tested by foreign law, that of the French party by French law. Such would be the case when from the outset of the marriage relation the diversity existed. But if the parties once had a common nationality, and one of them became French, it is not yet settled whether it is the different national laws of each that is to be applied or their last common national law. Strong authority exists for both views on this question. The Hague Convention indicated the application of the last common national law, but this is no longer in force in France. So the question is not governed by written text. There are two opposite lines of cases in this relation.

Consider the first line. The Tribunal of the Seine, February 24, 1903 (cited by Laurent-Bailly, p. 47) declined to divorce a Portuguese wife restored to French nationality by decree for the following reason: "Whereas F. is still Portuguese and both spouses have today a different personal statute, the wife French law which allows divorce, the husband Portuguese which does not; it is reasonable in order to solve the conflict between the two legislations to decide in favor of the law under which the couple were placed by their marriage, namely, Portuguese law." The same view has been applied to a French husband formerly Spanish in an action for divorce brought by him against his Spanish wife. (Algiers, January 27, 1892; *Journal Clunet,* 1892, p. 662.) In the Knibloe case, a wife formerly American, but restored to French citizenship by decree, could not divorce her American husband domiciled in New York for habitual drunkenness, as this was found not to be a ground in New York. (Havre, November 17, 1923; *Journal Clunet,* 1924, p. 1000.) The theory of the case was that acts "innocent" when committed cannot be made "guilty" by the subsequent change of nationality of one spouse. A case decided by the Tribunal of Dieppe, June 19, 1905 (*Journal Clunet,* 1905, p. 1009) is also instructive. A British subject married a Frenchwoman, who thereby became English. She sued for divorce, but was awarded separation only, because by British law the husband's offenses did not justify divorce. The wife was then restored to French citizenship by decree. At the end of three years, she applied to convert the separation into divorce under article 310, C. C. This was refused on the ground that the law under which the marriage was "placed" at its inception continued to govern it. The Hague Convention was cited as authority for this proposition, although legally inapplicable to a British subject since Great Britain was not a treaty-power. It is to be noted that these cases are not in fact dependent upon the Hague Convention. In them it is the French law of the wife that has not overcome the foreign law of the alien husband.

Consider now the opposite line of cases. The Court of Appeal of Lyon, December 17, 1925 (*Journal Clunet,* 1926, p. 384) in the *affaire* Ferrari, stated that the principle of unity of legislation applicable to marriage has a theoretical and argumentative value only since the denunciation by France of the Hague Convention. In consequence, an Italian husband cannot prevent his wife from divorcing him upon her recovery of French nationality. Thereafter, her status and capacity were governed by French law as provided by article 3 of the Civil Code. "The agreement of the spouses at the time of the marriage does not control the latter's future characteristics, such as may result from changes in legislation or personal statute." This is now the weight of authority, since the Court of Appeal of Lyon decided as it did in view of the quashing of a contrary judgment by the Court of Cassation, July 6, 1922 (*Journal Clunet*, 1922, p. 714). It has accordingly been held that a French husband formerly Italian can divorce his Italian wife, but she cannot counterclaim for divorce against him. (Tunis, December 8, 1920; *Journal Clunet,* 1923, p. 110.) A French husband, formerly Cuban, can divorce his Cuban wife, although Cuba has no divorce law. (Seine, May 17, 1910; *Journal Clunet,* 1911, p. 1202.) The French law of the husband prevailed in these cases over the foreign law of the alien wife, save in the Ferrari case in which the French law of the wife was supreme over the foreign law of the husband.

The difficulty of deciding which law, French or foreign, is to prevail was rather neatly avoided by the Tribunal of the Seine, December 8, 1915. (*Journal Clunet,* 1917, p. 1020.) The court found a *renvoi* from Argentine law to French law as *lex domicilii;* consequently, a French wife was allowed to divorce her Argentine husband on French grounds, although there is no divorce law in the Argentine.

It is to be borne in mind, however, in the case of diversity of nationality, that while the grounds of an alien wife's law may be applied in relation to her capacity, nevertheless, if her husband is French, the standard of her conduct will be governed by French law. The reverse is also true; the standard of conduct of the French wife of an alien husband will ordinarily be governed by the husband's national law, not by French law. In the case of two aliens of diverse nationality, the national law of the husband will be applied to the standard of conduct. This is due to the fact that there must be unity of legislation within the family concerning the marital rights and duties, even though there be no unity of nationality. (Pillet and Niboyet, section 452, p. 547.) The national law of the husband would, therefore, generally predominate in France over that of the wife, save in cases in which for reasons of public policy French law will apply to the litigation. In the case of Americans and British, under whose law the marital rights and duties are governed by the *lex domicilii,* there may be a *renvoi* to French law not alone as to the grounds for divorce or separation but also as to the standard of conduct between the spouses. Such *renvoi* would make French internal law qualify the alleged acts as guilty or innocent.

Chapter XIV

DEFENSES IN THE FRENCH CODES

The Civil Code contains an enumeration of grounds but not of defenses in divorce and separation actions. The latter are found scattered in the various provisions of the Civil Code and in the Code of Civil Procedure among defenses applicable to actions in general. Traverses will be considered in Chapter XVII, on Preliminary Procedure. Lack of jurisdiction and of capacity to sue, freedom from liability to suffer divorce, etc. have already been discussed. The other principal defenses will now be studied, leaving however the manner and time of pleading them and their effect as a permanent or temporary bar to the action for presentation in a later chapter.

Article 244 of the Civil Code, as amended by law of June 26, 1919, reads:

> An action for divorce abates by the reconciliation of the spouses which has taken place either after the occurrence of the facts alleged in the complaint or after the complaint itself. In either case the plaintiff's action is dismissed; he may nevertheless bring a new action for a cause arising or discovered since the reconciliation, and invoke the former causes in support of the new complaint. The action is also extinguished by the death of one of the spouses which has taken place before the *jugement* or *arrêt* pronouncing divorce has become final.

This article is the basis for the defenses of reconciliation and abatement. The French word *réconciliation* is broader than the English condonation, for the latter does not always imply resumption of relations as does the former. *Pardon* is the French equivalent for condonation. Reconciliation may be express or implied, by words or deeds. To be effective it must be carefully considered, serious and susceptible of endurance. (Evreux, December 2, 1924; *Gazette du Palais,* February 5, 1925.) A reconciliation apparently effected before the president of the tribunal at the conciliation hearing may be in fact merely a sham into which the judge has led the unwilling parties. Such ostensible but unreal reconciliation is not a defense; it may be repudiated, if this is done promptly after leaving the presence of the judge. Reconciliation to be effective must be voluntary and not constrained; it must be free from error or fraud. Reconciliation is always impliedly conditional upon the reformation of the offending spouse. "If this condition is not realized the pardon disappears and the grievances are reborn." (Pierard, vol. II, Sec. 489, p. 63.) But reconciliation must be otherwise unconditional. A period of time for further life together accorded by a wife to her erring husband as a trial reconciliation is deemed conditional and inoperative unless followed by an unconditional pardon. Continuance of life together after knowledge of the offensive acts is not necessarily reconciliation. (Bordeaux, Fructidor 9, Year XII; *Sirey,* XII.2.219.) This is particularly true when life together was continued in the interest of young children. (Cassation, December 11, 1893; *Dalloz,* 1894.1.341.) It is not reconciliation for a wife to return home to nurse her husband during an illness. (Lyon, July 30, 1891; *Gazette des Tribunaux,* September 26, 1891.) Sexual intercourse held under duress would not be a reconciliation.

Pardon is also a defense in French law. It seems to be the law in France that a guilty party may invoke a pardon even if he did not accept it at the time it was given, for a pardon may be unilateral and still bar the action. A pardon is a renunciation of the cause of action. It differs from reconciliation, which latter is necessarily bilateral and takes two persons and a meeting of the minds to be effectuated. Renunciation of action is not the same as reconciliation or pardon. It is not pardon for a wife to dine with her husband or to be seen in his company after suit was brought. Even sexual intercourse is not necessarily a pardon, but would probably be considered such if a child were conceived. A demand made by a bailiff acting for the innocent party, that the guilty one shall resume marital relations is not reconciliation, condonation or renunciation, even when the latter offers to comply therewith. Hence, the demand of a husband made through a bailiff that the wife return home to him is not a bar to his later action for her adultery, and though his letters for the same purpose are couched in affectionate language.

If either spouse dies before the action has reached the stage at which the judgment has become "final," the action and judgment abate. A judgment is not "final" until the time to appeal and to *opposer* (*i. e.*, open a default) has expired. Hence a judgment of separation becomes *ipso facto* void if a party dies before the time to appeal has elapsed. (Bordeaux, January 27, 1873; *Sirey,* 1873.3.267.) This is true also of divorce. It is immaterial that the death be that of appellant or respondent, of the winner or loser. Nevertheless, death after the judgment has become final but before it is recorded in the "register of civil status" (*registres de l'état civil*) does not prevent recording, nor does it render the judgment void. The abatement ends the judgment in its pecuniary effects upon the property of the spouses as well as in its personal effects upon the parties themselves. An action once abated cannot be revived or continued by the heirs even if abatement occurs on appeal and if the revival is sought only in relation to the property aspects and in order to bring about a revocation of the pecuniary advantages made in the marriage articles in favor of the losing side. (Cassation, July 27, 1871; *Sirey,* 1871.1.109.)

Considerable difference of views exists in doctrine and jurisprudence as to whether or not there is any statute of limitations applicable to divorce or separation actions. Some authorities consider that no relief can be granted if thirty years elapse between the offensive acts and the beginning of suit, others set the limitation at three years, others at one. It seems to be the weight of authority that there is no time prescription against the action. (Carpentier, *Divorce et séparation de corps,* 1899, vol. 1. section 1899.) It has been held that the thirty year limitation of article 2262 of the Civil Code does not apply to matrimonial actions. Hence acts over thirty years old can be made the basis of a divorce action. (Abbeville, May 20, 1884; *Sirey,* 1885.2.168.) The lapse of time may, however, amount to laches under particular circumstances or be evidence of reconciliation or pardon. If over three years intervene between steps in procedure the proceedings may be dismissed. (Article 394, C. C. P.) This is called *péremption d'instance,* (abandonment of action). The cause of action is not lost on that account.

By article 171 of the Code of Civil Procedure the codependency of another earlier action between the same parties and for the same relief will be a defense to the later action. *Litispendence* (copendency) can be set up only when the first action is pending in France. Hence the Tribunal of the Seine, April 8, 1910, and the Court of Appeal of Paris, January 10, 1911, (*Journal Clunet,* 1911, p. 893) retained jurisdiction of a divorce action between Dutch subjects domiciled in Paris, notwithstanding the pendency of an action in Holland. The wife in this case started suit in Paris a few days before the husband did so in Holland. The offensive acts took place in France. Article 266 of the Dutch Civil Code conceded jurisdiction to courts of the domicile in cases of malicious desertion. Under the Hague Convention, which then applied both in France and Holland, concurrent jurisdiction is recognized in the national and domiciliary courts, without any pre-eminence being given the one over the other. Under those circumstances the French courts considered that they, as courts of the domicile, being seized first by one spouse, need not yield to a court of the nationality, seized second by the other. Now that the Hague Convention is no longer law in France, the rule of article 171, C.C.P. is quite unaffected by treaty. Hence today the French courts are at liberty entirely to disregard the proceedings pending before other courts. Codependency of a foreign action, however, will usually lead a French court to decline jurisdiction over aliens.

The French law presents unusual features in regard to what actions can be copending without rendering the copendency defense available under article 171, C. C. P. A plaintiff may sue for divorce on one ground in one action and on another ground in a separate action. There may be as many actions as the plaintiff has grounds. The plaintiff may sue on one set of facts on one ground in one action and another set of facts based on the same ground in another action. The plaintiff may sue for divorce in one action and conversion of separation into divorce in another. No rule exists in France which requires a plaintiff to set forth all his known causes of action in one action or to introduce all known facts in support of his grounds in one suit. Of course, a defendant may obtain consolidation of these various actions for *connexité* (*i. e.*, closeness of relationship), but the defense of *litispendence* does not bar them. In consequence, copendency of action is not frequently available as a defense in French law. In the *affaire* de Beauffremont, the Princess was successful in securing separation in a third action setting up different facts and causes after two failures, "and nothing would have prevented beginning over again indefinitely." (Piérard, Vol I, section 275, p. 535.)

The copendency with a divorce or separation action of an action for annulment will bar proceeding on the separation or divorce action until the question of annulment shall have been decided. A stay can be obtained as of right in a divorce or separation action, if an action for annulment is brought at any time before the judgment has been transcribed into the register of civil status. (Carpentier et Frejoneu du Saint, *Répertoire alphabétique du droit français,* 1899, vol. 17, Divorce, p. 596, no. 49.) Apparently also an action for divorce or separation cannot be pursued if a penal prosecution for the offensive acts is in progress. This was expressly stated to be the law by article 235 of the Civil Code, but the law of 1886 abrogated the provision. Nevertheless, according to several authorities the old adage *le criminel tient le civil en état* (*i. e.,* criminal proceedings stay civil), still applies, and a stay of the action could doubtless be obtained if this reason were invoked.

The French law concerning *res judicata* has been materially affected by the copendency rule. Article 1351 of the Civil Code reads:

> The authority of prior adjudication only extends to that which has been the object of a judgment. The remedy asked must be the same; the complaint must be founded upon the same cause; the controversy must be between the same parties and between them in the same character.

Whereas, copendency of a foreign action is not a bar to an action in France, the existence of a foreign judgment may be such bar. This matter will be treated in a separate chapter. Domestic judgments only will be considered now as a defense. Mention has already been made that a French judgment of annulment will bar a later divorce action, but that the existence of a judgment of divorce or separation will not prevent the bringing of a later action by the losing party. A judgment of separation will prevent the winning party from obtaining later a divorce on the same facts and for like grounds, except, however, divorce upon conversion under article 310, C. C. A spouse who has obtained a divorce, but who has abstained from seasonably executing it, whereby it has become void, can obtain a second judgment and can execute the latter and *res judicata* will be no defense to the second action. (Arras, April 2, 1924, *Recueil Douai,* October, 1924.)

Furthermore, the facts adjudicated in one action may be invoked in a later action coupled with new facts, for the use of old facts with new ones is expressly permitted by article 244 of the Civil Code. A judgment makes *res judicata* only the facts in issue in the action. Other facts brought out in evidence establishing the same or a different ground are not made *res judicata* by the judgment. If a divorce is denied on a given state of facts, the same facts cannot later be alleged in a separation action. (Seine, May 31, 1892; *Le Droit,* June 30, 1892.) Nevertheless the contrary has also been held, for the reason that the relief prayed for is different in the two actions. (Douai, December 27, 1886; *Jurisprudence de la Cour de Douai,* 1886, p. 376.) It seems a denial by a court of jurisdiction to separate aliens does not prevent a later assertion of jurisdiction to divorce them, although the circumstances may not have changed in the interval. This is quite consistent with the French theory that jurisdiction over two aliens is a matter of discretion rather than of law. It has been held that a contested judgment rendered by a court which lacked *compétence ratione materiae* is nevertheless *res judicata.* (Cassation, June 12, 1907;

Dalloz, 1909.1.461.) This is also in harmony with the French rule that a judgment can be contested by the parties only by appeal, opening default, review or new trial and until it is quashed or superseded it is binding, notwithstanding the court which rendered it had no statutory power to do so.

If the marriage is void, the invalidity is a complete defense to an action for divorce or separation, without annulment being asked. If it is merely voidable the defense of illegality can be raised only by counterclaim asking annulment. It is not necessary that the marriage shall have previously been declared void by a court in order for the defense of illegality to be available in a divorce or separation action. For example, the Court of Appeal of Dijon, March 20, 1922 (*Journal Clunet,* 1922, p. 409) granted divorce to a wife against her second husband, holding that her second marriage was valid because her first marriage was void in England as bigamous on the part of the first husband. The court investigated the validity of the first British marriage, although it had never been annuled. In this case the second husband had set up invalidity of the second marriage and the wife in an attempt to sustain it had set up invalidity of the first. In a recent case, a religious marriage solemnized in France between Canadians was treated as void and the action for divorce between such parties was dismissed for lack of *compétence ratione materiae.* (Paris, July 27, 1926, cited by Boyer, p. 118.)

It is a defense in an action for divorce or separation that the grounds are tainted by collusion or connivance. If one party conspires with a third person to produce a state of facts constituting a ground, this can be interposed as a defense to defeat the action. Yet it has been held that a husband who agreed to the wife's adultery might still be granted a divorce, the agreement being void. (Seine, May 28, 1891; *Le Droit,* June 15 and 16, 1891.)

There is no peremptory rule in the French law of divorce or separation that a plaintiff must come into court with clean hands to obtain relief. A wife who arranged with a woman to commit adultery with her husband and then posted neighbors to catch them, will not be granted a divorce, as she is not supposed to have felt the insult. (Seine, May 14, 1889; *Le Droit,* April 19, 1889.) A wife is not entitled to divorce when she not only tolerated but even favored the adulterous relations of her husband with a concubine, stipulating indeed at the time of the marriage that he should continue to live with his mistress, and in the same case it was held that the husband cannot obtain a divorce from the wife even for adultery since he married her solely to participate in the fortune and to give his name to her child and had no illusions concerning the likelihood of her conjugal fidelity. (Paris, July 18, 1893; *Sirey,* 1893.2.267.) It seems, nevertheless, that when a wife conspired with another woman for the latter to become the husband's mistress, divorce should be pronounced both against the scheming wife and the husband who fell into the trap.

Provocation of the offensive acts by plaintiff is a defense when there is the relation of cause and effect and coincidence in time and place between the acts provoking and those provoked. But the provocation need not be direct or immediate, or a part of the *res gestae.*

It is generally considered that recrimination is not a defense in actions for divorce and separation. For example, gross insults of plaintiff will not be a defense in an action instituted by reason of gross insults committed by the defendant, even though the insults of the plaintiff produced those of defendant. Nevertheless, there is some authority that *compensation des torts* (*i. e.,* set off of offenses) in the case of the non-peremptory grounds, more particularly gross insults, will prevent divorce or separation. In such cases recrimination is sometimes confused with provocation. It has been held that a husband and wife can each obtain separation against the other for their respective infidelity. (Paris, June 9, 1860; *Sirey,* 1860.2.449.) The adultery of the wife will not prevent her from obtaining a separation if the husband was not only unfaithful, but also brought his mistress into the home. (Cassation, May 9, 1821; *Sirey,* 1821.1.431.)

Anything which savors of agreement to divorce or separate when there are no grounds is void, as contrary to the principle of article 307, C. C., which forbids separation by mutual consent. It seems that an agreement to procure a divorce is not necessarily invalid if there are grounds for such relief and the action is not fraudulent. Thus, it would perhaps be lawful for a spouse guilty of adultery to admit the offense in writing and to agree to allow the innocent party to divorce him and to settle upon the basis of support during the litigation.

No agreement to live apart during marriage has any legal value in French law, consequently such an agreement is not a defense even to a complaint for desertion or refusal of cohabitation. No estoppel exists to deny the validity of such an accord. This legal situation is an outgrowth of article 307, C. C. which forbids separation by mutual consent. If judicial separation by consent is forbidden, *a fortiori,* contractual separation must be. Furthermore, article 48 of the Code of Civil Procedure forbids compromise of an action concerning status. By analogy it is illegal to contract without judicial proceedings concerning a change in status. The Court of Cassation, June 14, 1882 (*Sirey,* 1882.1.421) held that every agreement which has for its object a voluntary separation of persons and property has an unlawful motive and is absolutely void. Even a notarial instrument of this sort will be deemed non-existent. A contract is void which has the effect of a voluntary separation even without its expressly so providing. In fact, a financial agreement whose consequence is to maintain a state of separation will be void, as tending to promote a voluntary separation. A separation agreed to by way of compromise of litigation is intrinsically illegal and may be repudiated by either party against the other's wishes. Accordingly a husband may resume the administration of community property notwithstanding the terms of an authentic (*i. e.,* notarial) instrument depriving him thereof. An agreement which allocates to each spouse a portion of the common property and determines for the future their life incomes, is of a character reproved by the law. An agreement to obtain judicial separation without cause is void and the illegality would carry with it a clause which stipulates a penalty to be paid by whichever spouse fails to observe the covenants. It has been held that the payment of alimony cannot be ordered by the court when the parties are only *de facto* and not *de jure* separated. (Bordeaux, February 11, 1887; *La Loi*, December 18, 1887.) Parties cannot renounce by separation agreement the right to demand a judicial separation. (Caen, April 11, 1818; *Sirey,* 1818.2.372.)

It has been held, however, that the illegality of a voluntary separation agreement applies only to those clauses which maintain and regulate the voluntary separation and not to clauses which simply carry out the terms of a judgment of separation of property. (Pau, June 20, 1894; *Dalloz,* 1895.2.11.) Also the parties can agree *pendente lite* upon separate residences and payment of alimony, etc. In other words, they can arrange a provisional *modus vivendi,* but such agreement is subject to the control of the court and can be modified by court order at any time upon application of one party or both. Furthermore, even a void separation agreement will operate as a discontinuance of a pending action; that is, application may be made to dismiss the action (without prejudice to its renewal) by reason of such agreement. A separation agreement made during the pendency of an action which contains a clause whereby the parties agree that the case shall be struck from the calendar is void, and the actual removal from the calendar in pursuance of the agreement does not extinguish the action. (Seine, March 15, 1887; *Journal des Avoués*, 1887, p. 227.)

The legal position in France of foreign separation agreements between aliens will be considered in a later chapter.

According to article 236 of the Civil Code the president of the tribunal at the outset of the litigation fixes by order the separate residence *pendente lite* of the wife, whether she be plaintiff or defendant. Article 241 C.C. states that if she is at any time unable to show that she is living at such residence, the husband may discontinue paying her alimony and her suit cannot proceed. It is not clear whether this provision is merely a reason for an indefinite stay or whether it is a defense which will lead to dismissal of the action. If the non-observance should endure three years, the action being meanwhile stayed, the husband would be entitled to a dismissal of the suit for laches under article 397, C.C.P. Possibly he could obtain dismissal before three years under article 241, C.C., but this is undecided. Usually the wife returns to the residence or the court excuses her absence or fixes her another residence. If she has good reasons for her departure, the mere lack of judicial consent will not prevent the action from continuing. Thus, a wife ordered to live with her parents can follow them to their new home without further leave of the court. Article 241, C.C. would not be applied if the wife left the place indicated in order to support herself and her children more easily elsewhere. The article is not mandatory upon the court, but is permissive. The court may even allow a wife to proceed though she be persistently in default thereunder. If the husband is in arrears of alimony before the wife changes residence, he cannot set up article 241, C.C. as a defense in the action or as a justification for his continued failure to pay the alimony. (Seine, January 16, 1890; *Le Droit*, January 17, 1890.) After suit has been instituted, the parties are at liberty to agree upon the location of a separate residence for the wife, and her departure therefrom will not be a reason for stopping her suit. Article 241, C.C., in other words, applies to the departure of a wife without good reason from a separate residence fixed *pendente lite* by the judicial authority.

Article 403 of the Code of Civil Procedure reads:

> Discontinuance, when it shall have been accepted, involves by operation of law consent that matters shall be restored on both sides to the same condition as they were in before the complaint.

A plaintiff usually cannot discontinue after defendant has appeared if the latter objects. Defendant in such case can counterclaim and proceed in spite of the discontinuance. (Lille, January 18, 1924; *Dalloz hebdomadaire*, 1924, p. 180.) Sometimes it appears that consent is not required until after joinder of issue by answer or by conclusions. Nevertheless the "judicial contract" (*contrat judiciaire*) logically should be deemed formed upon appearance, even when jurisdiction is contested. The bringing of an action for separation of property while a divorce action is in course will not amount to a discontinuance of the divorce proceedings, although divorce if granted would produce separation of property. (Paris, Messidor 1, Year XII; *Sirey*, XII.2.201.) But the bringing of a divorce action while a separation action is pending will be deemed a discontinuance of the separation action if the facts alleged in both actions are the same. (Riom, June 13, 1893; *Dalloz*, 1894.2.481.)

A discontinuance usually operates without prejudice to renewal of the action, but this is not always the case. Sometimes a discontinuance will bar the action. A discontinuance based upon a voluntary separation agreement would not prevent renewal, since such agreement is void. It is really an anomaly to give it even so much recognition as to found a discontinuance upon it. If suit is first brought for separation and this action is discontinued, an action for divorce cannot later be brought on the same grounds, for the first action is considered a final election of remedy and the discontinuance ends the right of action. It seems, therefore, that divorce and separation are parallel remedies. Plaintiff's election of separation as remedy creates a vested right in the defendant not to be divorced for the same cause. Plaintiff cannot deprive defendant of this right by bringing a later action for divorce. (Aix, November 27, 1809; *Sirey,* 1809.2.149.) This is one case in which discontinuance ended the cause of action, as well as the action.

It is to be noted that it is no defense in French law that the marriage was for convenience only, that the litigation has been induced by another person, or that defendant has reformed. These facts may nevertheless be considered in attenuation of the gravity of the offense in the case of non-peremptory grounds; for an award of divorce or separation is largely discretional. No legal term in French law corresponds precisely to the English term estoppel, nor is estoppel a separate defense, but acts or omissions which would amount to an estoppel by deed or conduct in Anglo-American law may constitute a defense in French law, under other defense headings.

Chapter XV

DEFENSES IN PRIVATE INTERNATIONAL LAW

It is by no means an easy matter to say when the defenses of internal French law may be interposed in an action between two aliens or between an alien defendant and a French plaintiff or between a French defendant and an alien plaintiff. It is quite true that defenses are intimately related to procedure, hence *lex fori* applies, but defenses relate also to the merits, to status and capacity, therefore *lex nationalis*, according to the French theory, should receive some consideration. In general the same rules of conflict of laws apply to defenses as to grounds. To be available to an alien defendant the defense ought to be present simultaneously in both foreign and French law.

When treating of private international law in relation to grounds, cases were cited showing that in an action between two aliens of the same nationality the absence of a divorce law in *lex nationalis* prevents the grant of divorce in France. This absence affects not alone the capacity of the plaintiff, but the liability of the defendant, and both points of law may be raised by the defendant. A defendant may set up plaintiff's want of capacity to divorce and defendant's freedom from liability to be divorced. Mention has also been made that in an action between two aliens of different nationalities, capacity of the plaintiff outweighs incapacity of the defendant, but that in an action of a French plaintiff the cases are still divided on this matter. The defense of lack of jurisdiction, under the rules of French private international law, has also been treated.

A foreign defense, that is a defense based on foreign law, will not be allowed by a French court when it is against French public policy and when there is no similar defense in French law. Thus, the Court of Cassation, July 6, 1922 (*Journal Clunet*, 1922, p. 714) in the *affaire* Ferrari, held that a separation agreement made in Italy between Italians and confirmed by the Italian court is void in France for reasons of public policy. Hence a wife restored to French nationality by decree may set up, in a divorce action brought by her against her Italian husband, grounds which occurred in Italy before the separation agreement was made. In other words, the existence of a separation agreement valid in Italian law could not be used as a defense by an Italian defendant sued by a French plaintiff. The Court of Appeal of Lyon, December 17, 1925 (*Journal Clunet*, 1926, p. 384), to which the Ferrari case was sent for retrial by the Court of Cassation in pursuance of the above decision, followed this view to its logical conclusion and held that since the Italian separation agreement could not be converted into a French divorce under article 310, C. C. neither could it be a defense in the divorce action. The wife was accordingly deemed to have preserved and not lost her grounds for divorce, "in view of an agreement whose validity is not recognized by French law."

The principle that a foreign defense will not be recognized in France when it is opposed to the public policy of the forum applies in an action between two aliens. This is also illustrated by the Gould case. The American wife was unsuccessful in her attempt to set up her husband's adultery, by way of recrimination, in defense to his action instituted for her own adultery. Recrimination is a defense in New York, but not in French, adultery cases.

Consequently it is the law in France that to be available to an alien, a defense must exist by his national law as well as by French law, unless *lex nationalis* is excluded for reasons of policy. If the defense is known to both laws, but differs as to details in the two countries, a serious question arises as to how they are to be concurrently applied, and this is a question which has not yet been satisfactorily answered by courts or authors.

Chapter XVI

FOREIGN AGREEMENTS AND JUDGMENTS

It often happens that aliens seek divorce or separation in France after making separation agreements in their own country or after foreign matrimonial litigation. Foreign agreements and judgments affect the marital rights and duties in France to some extent. What is the attitude of French law toward such foreign judgments and agreements?

Article 546 of the Code of Civil Procedure says:

> Judgments rendered by foreign courts, and instruments received by foreign officers, shall be susceptible of execution in France only in the manner and cases contemplated by Articles 2123 and 2128 of the Civil Code.

Concerning foreign agreements texts of law are few. Article 2128 of the Civil Code says simply:

> Contracts made in foreign countries cannot establish a mortgage upon property in France, unless there are provisions contrary to this principle in political laws or in treaties.

This article has but a remote bearing upon divorce or separation, though it has a bearing upon foreign marriage contracts.

Article 6 of the Civil Code says:

> It is not possible by private agreement to derogate from the laws which interest public order or morality.

Agreements between French citizens made abroad and relating to their status or domestic relations would be governed by French law as to substance in view of article 3, C. C., but by foreign law as to form, by reason of the maxim *locus regit actum.* Such contracts between aliens would be governed in France by *lex nationalis* as to substance, save when French public policy is concerned, and by *lex loci actus* as to form.

Mention has been made already that by French law no agreement which maintains or facilitates a voluntary separation is lawful. Foreign agreements between two aliens, even though valid by *lex nationalis* are void in France as contrary to public policy. This was held by the Court of Cassation, July 6, 1922, (*Journal Clunet,* 1922, p. 704) in the Ferrari case in relation to an Italian separation agreement. In view of this decision a British or American party could (*semble*) repudiate in France a valid English or American separation agreement. Perhaps the decision of the Court of Cassation will be later qualified, since the principle of respect for vested rights validly acquired abroad under local law ought to be applied in France. One may conclude, however, at the present time that foreign agreements of a nature condemned by French law in relation to French parties would probably be void in France so far as aliens are concerned; *a fortori* this would be so if one party were French.

Consider now the position of foreign judgments of divorce and separation. Foreign judgments of annulment will not be considered in this book. It will here suffice to say that rules apply to them in all essential points similar to those which relate to foreign divorce and separation judgments. A paucity of texts of law exists in France on the subject of recognition in France of foreign judgments. Article 2123 of the Civil Code provides:

Likewise a mortgage cannot result from judgments rendered in a foreign country unless they shall have been declared to be executory by a French court; without prejudice to provisions to the contrary which may exist in political laws and in treaties.

This text is not particularly illuminating, but tradition has left its influence upon the French custom in relation to foreign judgments. Article 121 of the ordinance of 1629, called the Code Michaud, provided that foreign judgments in so far as they related to French subjects should have no effect in France, but so far as aliens only were concerned, they should be recognized by a domestic judgment giving them executory force without reopening the controversy on the merits. Some authorities hold that this ordinance is still in force, but the prevailing opinion is that since the French Revolution the ordinance is no longer law. No distinction now exists as to the conditions required for securing *exequatur* between foreign judgments affecting French and aliens and foreign judgments affecting aliens alone. (Seine, July 5, 1881; *Journal Clunet,* 1882, p. 530.) The combination of article 546 of the Code of Civil Procedure with article 2123 of the Civil Code leads one to conclude that foreign judgments cannot receive compulsory enforcement in France without the aid of a judgment of *exequatur* of a French court, but that is about all the law that is expressed by the Codes. The rest of the law in France is based upon custom and treaties. *Exequatur* proceedings may be combined with other actions and *exequatur* may be given at the same time as other relief or may precede it.

The Hague Convention of June 12, 1902 obligated the ratifying and adhering powers to recognize and give effect to foreign judgments of divorce and separation rendered by courts of other treaty-powers in relation to treaty-power citizens or subjects, provided the judgments were rendered in conformity with the Treaty. France withdrew from the Hague Convention and is not today a party to any convention or union of several powers on matters of foreign judgments. Nevertheless, a few separate treaties have been made by France, with various neighboring countries, which should be mentioned. Thus, matters decided by judgments of the courts of the contracting parties are declared to be *res judicata* by the Franco-Sardinian Treaty of 1760, extended later to all Italy; by the Franco-Swiss Treaty of June 15, 1869 and by the Franco-Belgian Treaty of July 8, 1899. France has no such treaty with the United States or Great Britain or with any others than those named. The World War treaties need not be mentioned, since the provisions therein about judgments concern only those regarding war claims.

In France, in relation to foreign judgments, a distinction is drawn between respect for vested rights and the acquisition of rights. Executory force is considered to be acquisition of a new quality, not a mere consequence of respect for vested rights. No domestic judgment can be executed in France until it possesses the executory formula added by the clerk of the court in the name of people calling upon all public authorities to enforce; *a fortiori* a foreign judgment requires such formula before it can be enforced. The formula can be added only by virtue of a French judgment called *exequatur*.

To obtain *exequatur* four conditions, perhaps five, are requisite. *First:* The foreign judgment must be valid in the foreign country under its laws. But a foreign provisional judgment is nevertheless susceptible of *exequatur*. (Seine, July 5, 1881; *Journal Clunet,* 1882, p. 530.) The fact that a British judgment for alimony may be modified in England is not an obstacle to collection of arrears in France and such judgment may be given *exequatur*. (Paris December 19, 1924; *Journal Clunet,* 1926, p. 76.) An Italian separation judgment, awarding custody of a child to the husband, may also be given *exequatur* (Paris, July

6, 1892; *Journal Clunet,* 1892, p. 1022); though an award of custody is always revocable in Italy.

Second: The foreign judgment must have been rendered by a court having international jurisdiction according to the French rules of private international law. This is said to mean that when a French court would have jurisdiction, no foreign court also has it. It has been asserted that this rule "is absolutely fundamental and our jurisprudence has always consecrated it with the most extreme rigor." (Pillet and Niboyet, section 613, p. 686.) Thus a British default judgment of divorce for adultery and cruelty against a French husband will not be given *exequatur,* because the French wife should have sued in France where the husband was domiciled. (Seine, June 4, 1885; *Journal Clunet,* 1885, p. 548.) Nevertheless, the condition does not appear to be quite so drastic as Professors Pillet and Niboyet consider it. For instance, a California divorce against a French citizen was given *exequatur* by the Tribunal of the Seine, April 6, 1922 (*Journal Clunet,* 1922, p. 674), yet by articles 14 and 15, C.C. the French courts would have jurisdiction. In this case Viscount M. married an American woman in Paris, but the parties went to live in California. The wife won a divorce there for non-support. The ex-husband applied to the French court for *exequatur* to permit the recording of the judgment in France and the rectification of the French marriage records, without which he could not remarry in France. For some reason, which does not appear in the report, the ex-wife contested the action and set up that the grant of *exequatur* to the California judgment would be contrary to French public policy. The tribunal nevertheless granted *exequatur* for the reasons that the judgment was valid and final in the state where rendered and pronounced divorce for a reason susceptible of acceptance by French courts. The second condition of

French law would seem therefore to be satisfied when the foreign court is one either of the nationality or of the domicile of the parties, but the matter is by no means free from uncertainty. In view of the extreme breadth of French jurisdiction, the second condition, if applied as suggested by Pillet and Niboyet, would prevent practically all foreign judgments affecting a French citizen, and also many judgments affecting aliens, from ever receiving French *exequatur.* If the condition were reduced to the limits of French statutory jurisdiction under articles 14 and 15, C.C., the second condition would still be too drastic and would operate to deny the right of *exequatur* to a foreign judgment whenever French courts could have had even concurrent jurisdiction with the foreign courts.

Third: The foreign judgment must have applied to the controversy rules of private international law similar to those prevailing in France. (Pillet and Niboyet, sec. 613, p. 691.) This means that French law must have been applied to the status of French citizens, and *lex nationalis* to that of other aliens or at least law similar to these. Viscount M.'s case just cited is in point as to a French citizen, the ground of divorce (*i. e.,* non-support) of California law being deemed equivalent to the ground (*i. e.,* gross insults) of the French. A San Salvador judgment of *divorcio* (*i. e.,* separation) between French citizens based upon mutual consent will not be recognized in France. (Seine, May 2, 1918; *Journal Clunet,* 1918, p. 1182.) The Tribunal of the Seine, February 6, 1901 (*Journal Clunet,* 1901, p. 967) declined to recognize a German divorce granted to Italians, because by Italian law they could not divorce. But the same court on November 18, 1901 (*Journal Clunet,* 1902, p. 103) decided just the reverse, for the reason that it is no concern of the French courts to inquire what effect the German judgment would receive in Italy, it sufficing that its execution in France involves no consequences contrary to French legislation. A Swiss divorce judgment between Swiss parties, in which the husband was awarded the property acquired by the spouses during marriage, was denied the Swiss effects as to the liquidation of community property, because the regime was that of French legal community, the marriage having taken place in France without written contract and the couple being domiciled there at the time. (Seine, January 25, 1882; *Journal Clunet,* 1882, p. 74.) In other words the Swiss judgment was denied recognition in this relation because the Swiss courts had failed to apply French law.

Fourth: The foreign judgment must not be contrary to French public policy. A German divorce judgment has been denied *exequatur* because it contained ironic and libelous remarks concerning France. (Seine, November 23, 1922; *Journal Clunet*, 1923, p. 295.) A Serbian ecclesiastical divorce between Serbians married in France was denied *exequatur* by the Tribunal of Marseilles, November 25, 1925 (*Journal Clunet,* 1926, p. 388) because the judgment forbade the parties ever to remarry without the consent of the bishop. Such a restriction is contrary to French public policy. The court would not sever the award of divorce from the restriction upon remarriage, giving as reason that French courts must either accept or reject a foreign judgment *in toto,* since they cannot modify it or enforce part only.

When a foreign court is seized of a divorce or separation action between its own nationals, the French law admits that the foreign government may award different accessory relief from that provisionally awarded by a French court. Indeed, the French judgment may provide that its own provisional relief shall end when the foreign court has taken cognizance of the action and not when it has finally adjudicated. If, however, the French provisional judgment has set a time limit for its own duration, the foreign court (according to the French view) cannot modify the provisional relief in the interval. A foreign judgment purporting to do so would not be recognized in France. France recognizes no power in a foreign court to substitute other provisional remedies on the same matters for those awarded by a French judgment. (Seine, July 18, 1889; *Pandectes françaises,* 1890.2.29.)

Fifth: The foreign judgment must be a proper adjudication on the merits. The existence of this fifth condition is open to serious question, but in many cases French courts will allow the merits to be reopened, on the theory that the facts are not *res judicata.* A foreign judgment entitled to *exequatur* is *prima facie* evidence, but it may be more than this. Four principal views exist on this issue: (1) That article 121 of the ordinance of 1629 is still in force. By it a foreign judgment affecting aliens only is *res judicata,* whereas affecting the French it is not; (2) that a foreign judgment is always *res judicata* on the merits; (3) that a foreign judgment is subject to "unlimited control," that is to say, a French court can permit or refuse to allow reinquiry on the merits; and (4) that a foreign judgment is never *res judicata.* When a foreign judgment is rendered against a French citizen it is said to be the "duty" of the court to try the matter over again. (Seine, June 12, 1906; *Gazette du Palais,* December 4, 1906.) In practice, when foreign judgments are denied *exequatur* it is usually for the reason that the foreign court lacked jurisdiction according to French rules or applied some other law than that indicated by French private international law, rather than for incorrect adjudication on the merits. (Pillet and Niboyet, sec. 623, p. 704.)

Besides the California divorce already mentioned, other foreign divorces and separations have been given *exequatur* in France without inquiry on the merits. Usually this has been done to enable the parties to bring the French marriage record up to date. For example, *exequatur* has been given for such purpose to a Belgian divorce between French parties (Seine, August 2, 1887; *Journal Clunet,* 1888, p. 86); a Mauritius divorce between French parties (Seine, May 29, 1897; *Journal Clunet,* 1898, p. 129); a Tahiti divorce between natives of Huahine (Papeete, May 3, 1892; *Journal Clunet,* 1893, p. 146); an Argentine judgment of *divorcio* between French parties (Pau, November 2, 1907; *Journal Clunet,* 1908, p. 473). An Italian separation between Italians has been given *exequatur* so that third persons should know the wife's status. (Pau, December 16, 1909; *Journal Clunet,* 1910, p. 558.) A Chilean *divorcio* rendered between French spouses was given *exequatur* to enable the wife to sue for restitution of her separate property. (Dax, January 16, 1908; *Journal Clunet,* 1909, p. 154.) *Exequatur* has been given to an Italian separation awarding custody of the child to the husband. (Paris, July 6, 1892; *Journal Clunet,* 1892, p. 1022.) Finally *exequatur* was given a British divorce judgment between British subjects awarding alimony, to permit execution and attachment. (Paris, December 19, 1824; *Journal Clunet,* 1926, p. 76.) While the merits were not reëxamined in the foregoing cases, nevertheless the existence of the first four conditions was verified by the court.

Of course, there are numerous cases in which *exequatur* to foreign divorce and separation judgments has been denied. A foreign penal judgment will not be given *exequatur* so that it can be used as a basis for divorce under article 232, C. C. (Gex, February 3, 1897; *Gazette des Tribunaux,* May 6, 1897.)

A foreign judgment between aliens will produce in France the effects indicated by their national law. (Seine,

December 10, 1896; *Journal Clunet,* 1897, p. 543.) This will be the case not only of effects expressed in the judgment but also the consequential effects indicated by the foreign law. (Seine, January 30, 1903; *Journal Clunet,* 1906, p. 1130.) Thus, the contractual capacity of a German ex-wife divorced in Germany is determined by German law. (Nogent-le-Retrou, June 7, 1878; *Journal Clunet,* 1879, p. 277.) But public policy may restrict this rule of private international law. Since French judgments operate only *in personam* under article 1351 C. C., a foreign judgment *in rem* will be given effect only *in personam* in France. (Moreau, *Effets internationaux des jugements en matière civile,* 1884, p. 54.) It is likely furthermore that a foreign judgment would not be allowed to produce greater or substantially different effects in France than those of a similar domestic judgment. (Pillet and Niboyet, sec. 627, p. 706.)

The remedies available to enforce a foreign judgment are those indicated by *lex fori* both as to form and substance. For instance, if a domestic judgment is enforceable by arrest of the person, this will be allowed a foreign judgment given *exequatur* even if by foreign law it is not so enforceable where rendered. (Paris, December 2, 1848; *Sirey,* 1849.2.32.) Garnishment of salary has been allowed in France under a British judgment, notwithstanding the fact that this remedy is not available for such purpose in England. (Seine, December 10, 1896; *Journal Clunet,* 1897, p. 543.) The Court of Appeal of Paris, December 19, 1924 (*Journal Clunet,* 1926, p. 76) allowed a British wife to collect arrears of alimony by execution and attachment of royalties payable to her ex-husband by a French company. The defendant, a British subject, argued that a British judgment of divorce could not be enforced in this way in England; that by English law the award was subject to reduction and that execution could not be levied without a second British judgment. The French court held that the manner of enforcement of a foreign judgment given *exequatur* in France is governed by French law and that execution and attachment are proper remedies in France even if unavailable in England.

It would seem, however, that a French court would have power if it so wished to grant enforcement of a foreign monetary judgment for part only of the relief. A foreign award of alimony might be reduced. For instance, the amount of damages awarded by a British money judgment between aliens was cut in half in a French judgment of *exequatur.* (Paris, January 19, 1905; *Gazette des Tribunaux,* February 17, 1905.) But the power to reduce the amount of a foreign money judgment has been denied. (Douai, March 17, 1900; *Journal Clunet,* 1902, p. 593.) Whether or not a French court can modify a foreign judgment when granting *exequatur* is therefore still unsettled and cases are conflicting. Apparently foreign judgments other than money judgments cannot be varied.

It must not be supposed that *exequatur* is essential before a foreign judgment can receive any recognition. Foreign judgments even without the executive formula do have a very considerable recognition in France as of grace and based upon respect for vested rights. One may indeed say that a foreign judgment will produce in France without *exequatur* all effects which do not involve levy of execution upon property or coercion of the person. For example, the Tribunal of the Seine, February 10, 1893 (*Journal Clunet,* 1893, p. 365) held that a Dutch divorce judgment between Hollanders *ipso facto* produces effect so far as status and capacity are concerned without *exequatur,* but none other and that in order to compel surrender of the custody of children under the accessory relief provisions thereof *exequatur* is necessary and will be refused when a defendant enjoys diplomatic immunity. Divorced aliens can remarry in France without necessity of obtaining *exequatur* of their judgment. Thus the Tribunal of the Seine, April 12, 1923 (*Journal Clunet,* 1924, p. 107) declared *exequatur* to be unnecessary for such purpose in the case of Germans married in France and divorced by German judgment, which "is valid *ipso facto* in France without any necessity for the French courts to enforce it by *exequatur.*" A Canadian judgment of separation between French citizens granted for gross insults may be converted without *exequatur* into a French divorce. (Seine, July 20, 1920; *Gazette des Tribunaux,* August 24, 1920.) Two Polish Jews divorced by mutual consent in Warsaw can obtain the supervision of the French court over the liquidation of their community regime without *exequatur* of the Polish divorce judgment and this even in the absence of the notarial instrument setting forth the terms of the liquidation required by Polish law. (Paris, April 30, 1924; *Journal Clunet,* 1925, p. 121.) A Swiss divorce judgment between Swiss citizens will operate in France without *exequatur* to supercede the effects of a French separation. (Bordeaux, June 19, 1883; *Journal Clunet,* 1883, p. 629.)

A foreign judgment may also be used without *exequatur* as *prima facie* evidence or even set up by way of defense as *res judicata* of the matters decided. It can also be so used as the basis for some kinds of relief, e. g., annulment of marriage. While *exequatur* is unnecessary to enable a foreign judgment to be set up as *res judicata* it is nevertheless subject to the four or five conditions already mentioned before it will be recognized to this extent.

In an annulment action of a French citizen against a Brazilian, a *divorcio* pronounced in Brazil between Brazilians was considered in evidence and given full faith and credit as a separation without inquiry on the merits. (Seine, June 28, 1913; *Journal Clunet,* 1916, p. 170.) The

Tribunal of the Seine, January 25, 1882 (*Journal Clunet,* 1882, p. 74) recognized without *exequatur* or inquiry into the merits a Swiss divorce judgment between Swiss parties domiciled in France as to the change in their status, but declined to give effect at all to the accessory terms of the judgment relating to the liquidation of the property, as the regime was general community which had arisen by reason of marriage in France without notarial contract and should be liquidated in accordance with French, not with Swiss, law.

Numerous examples are found of the application of these principles to divorces pronounced in the United States. The leading case in France is the *affaire* Le Goaster. An American married a French woman in France. Shortly thereafter he brought suit there for divorce, but lost it as the insults on the part of the wife had been provoked by him. He then went to Florida, without giving his wife an opportunity to accompany him or to go to him there. He obtained a default decree of divorce in Florida and custody of the children on the false assertion that he did not know his wife's address and that she had deserted him. He then married another woman in England and returned with her to France. Thereupon the first wife sued him for divorce. Defendant set up the Florida judgment in bar to the action. It was held void by the Tribunal of Yvetot and Court of Appeal of Rouen because based upon false findings of fact. Furthermore, for some reason not stated in the report, the judgment was not considered to be an authentic instrument. Possibly it had not been authenticated by the state authorities and the French Consul. Consequently, the first wife was awarded divorce, custody of the children and three hundred francs a month alimony, namely, one hundred and fifty francs for herself and seventy-five francs for each child. The Court of Cassation affirmed the French judgment; the Florida divorce being deemed a fraud upon the wife, since she had never been served with process. (Yvetot, June 22, 1907; Rouen, December 11, 1907; *Journal Clunet,* 1909, p. 137: Cassation, November 11, 1908; *Revue Lapradelle,* 1909, p. 227.) The Le Goaster case indicates that a foreign judgment is admissible in evidence without *exequatur,* and even without proper authentication, that it is not *res judicata* between aliens but may be reviewed on the merits, that fraud vitiates it, that foreign service of process by publication is insufficient service upon a person deserted in France.

Other American divorces have also been disregarded by French courts. Thus, the Tribunal of the Seine, February 4, 1882 (*Journal Clunet,* 1882, p. 544) so treated a Utah decree. French citizens were married and lived together in New York. They returned to France, where the husband sued to annul the marriage. He was unsuccessful, so he went back to America and obtained a Utah divorce by default on constructive service. He followed this by naturalization in America and remarried. He returned to France with his second wife and was promptly prosecuted there for bigamy and adultery and sued for separation by his first wife, as in 1882 no divorce law existed. The Tribunal held in the civil action that the defendant could not set up alienage to defeat the jurisdiction because he had become naturalized in fraud of French law and in order to validate his divorce and that he must stand trial on the merits of the separation action. The court indicated also that at trial the Utah divorce would be no defense as it had been obtained in fraud of the wife.

A Louisiana divorce decree, on somewhat similar facts, was considered void in France, although not obtained by default. In this case the American court had failed to apply French law to the status of the parties and French citizens before 1884 lacked capacity in French law to divorce and were correspondingly free from liability to be divorced. (Seine, April 24, 1883; *Journal Clunet,* 1883, p. 160.) A New York divorce between Baron and Baroness Blanc was considered insufficient without *exequatur* to sustain a French judgment forbidding the ex-wife to use the ex-husband's name on the stage in France, but this relief was given on the theory that even if plaintiff were still defendant's husband he could prevent so disgraceful a use of his name. (Seine, December 15, 1897; *Journal Clunet,* 1898, p. 130.)

Another important American case was decided by the Tribunal of the Seine, January 28, 1891, and Court of Appeal of Paris, April 5, 1891. (*Journal Clunet,* 1891, p. 227.) French citizens were married and lived in Chicago. The husband deserted the wife and returned to France, whereupon the wife divorced him in Illinois by default on constructive service. The husband learned of the suit a few days only before judgment was entered. The ex-wife thereupon remarried another Frenchman in Wisconsin. The second husband later sued in France to annul the marriage. The French courts granted him this relief, but awarded the wife six thousand francs a year alimony from the second husband because she had married him in good faith, thinking her Illinois divorce valid. The Illinois divorce was considered void and not a defense as *res judicata* because the Illinois court lacked jurisdiction over the husband, he being then domiciled in France where the wife could have sued him, and because no suitable opportunity had been given him to defend, and because the ground of wilful desertion of Illinois law is not the same as the gross insults of the French law. The decision states that a foreign court can divorce a French couple only when the jurisdiction is voluntarily accepted or when the defendant cannot show a domicile where he can be sued, and when the grounds of French law are applied.

From this review it will be noted that only one American divorce (that of California) has successfully run the gauntlet of the French courts; that four, namely of Utah, Florida, Illinois and Louisiana, have been refused recognition for one reason or another; and that one, of New York, has been considered in evidence without acceptance or rejection. Can it be said that the French courts give full faith and credit to American divorces? Can it be said that such American divorces as those of Utah and Florida deserved faith?

Foreign judgments to be used in France, either with or without *exequatur,* must be previously registered at the *enregistrement* (stamp office) for stamp duty. The Tribunal of the Seine, July 24, 1897 (*Journal Clunet,* 1899, p. 555) held that a certified copy of a British divorce judgment annexed to the French marriage record of two British subjects without registration, ought to have been registered. Hence the parties were sued for one hundred eighty-seven francs fifty centimes, by the treasury (*fisc*) after the marriage solemnization and were compelled to pay. It seems that a certified copy of a Belgian divorce, to be annexed to the French marriage instrument, is exempt from registration and stamp duty. (*Usage en France de l'expédition d'un acte de divorce passé en Belgique, Journal Clunet,* 1924, p. 93.)

Chapter XVII

PRELIMINARY PROCEDURE

When an alien is considering divorce or separation in France, the first thing he usually does is to confer with an attorney or solicitor of his own country. If he finds himself outside of France, he should by all means consult his home counsel before removing to France, in order to ascertain the possibilities of the litigation and its probable effects upon his person and property in his own country. If the alien is already established in France at the time when his marital troubles become acute, he usually seeks the advice of a member of the legal profession of his country practicing in Paris or Nice. These foreign advisers, registered at their consulates upon production of evidence of their professional character, have a recognized standing in France to advise and certify upon foreign law. Their eventual intervention in the suit is essential in order to supply the *certificat de coutume* (*i. e.,* expert evidence) on *lex nationalis* required by the court. The foreign legal adviser retains for the client a French *avoué* (solicitor, attorney) and *avocat* (barrister, counsellor). Unfortunately a number of unofficial French divorce intermediaries exist, called *agents d'affaires,* who interest themselves in divorce business, but without having any recognized standing in the civil courts. Sometimes they are *agréés* (*i. e.,* admitted) to practice before the commercial courts, a permission which any person even without special legal training may receive. In any event in divorce or separation litigation a French *avoué* and *avocat* have to be retained, and, of course, an alien client may go directly to them. If he does so, the French *avoué* will retain a foreign legal adviser before trial is reached to supply the requisite expert evidence.

The initial work on the case is usually done in France by the foreign legal adviser. If the client or clients are not at the time bona fide domiciled in France, he sees to it that they lease an apartment, make their declaration at the prefecture, etc. He assembles the necessary evidence, engages the bailiff to make formally the usual demands upon defendant, signs the *certificat de coutume* (*i. e.*, certificate of foreign law) and performs other services. It is necessary for the client to give a power of attorney to the French attorney-at-law, as a power is essential to justify recording the judgment, etc. It is of course possible for some of the preliminary arrangements to be made from New York or London, by a member of the legal profession in these countries acting through his correspondent in France. At the present time the foreign law offices in Paris usually require that both the parties shall come to France in person, in order to establish the necessary domicile, supply evidence of grounds, receive citation and writ of summons, attend conciliation and receive service of the judgment. The foregoing is the preliminary routine ordinarily followed in France in the case of divorce and separation actions between aliens or interesting an alien.

How is the litigation actually started and conducted? In France, the procedure in matrimonial actions differs in important respects from that of other actions, but between the procedure in divorce and in separation minor differences only exist. Procedure in divorce actions is covered mostly by the Civil Code, but any deficiencies are supplemented by the Code of Civil Procedure. The procedure indicated in the Civil Code is paramount over that indicated in the Code of Civil Procedure in case of discrepancy. Article 307 of the Civil Code says that articles

236 to 244 of the Civil Code which cover divorce procedure apply to separation also. Most of the other articles apply likewise by analogy. Consequently procedure in both classes of actions is substantially the same.

Articles 875 C. C. P. and 234 C. C. treat of the manner of beginning suit; the former relating to separation, the latter divorce. Article 234 of the Civil Code reads:

> The spouse who wishes to bring an action for divorce presents in person a petition to the president of the tribunal or to the judge acting as such.

This article of the Civil Code was not mentioned in article 307, C. C. In separation actions the initial procedure under article 875, C. C. P., is nevertheless the same, except that presentation of the petition in person is not essential. (Bayonne, August 7, 1894; *La Loi,* November 16, 1834.) This initial procedure in matrimonial actions differs from the initial procedure of other civil actions. French legal actions are ordinarily started without petition, simply by serving a citation calling upon defendant to attend before the justice of the peace for an attempt at conciliation, and upon the failure of the attempt a writ of summons for trial is served without leave of any judge.

The petition for divorce or separation is prepared by the plaintiff's attorney. It is not sworn to or verified by the party, nor is it necessarily signed by him. The petition sets forth in a summary way who the parties are, the facts of the case and the suggested grounds. (Article 875, C. C. P.) It indicates the intention of plaintiff to sue for divorce or separation. It prays the president of the tribunal to give leave to plaintiff to cite the defendant to appear before the judge for an attempt at conciliation. The petition does not usually contain a prayer for accessory relief, but this may be requested orally when attending before the president.

PRELIMINARY PROCEDURE

According to article 875 of the Code of Civil Procedure the petition should be accompanied by any available written evidence, but the omission thereof does not invalidate the proceedings. In practice the only evidence usually submitted at this time is that relating to jurisdiction, nationality and domicile in France. For example, in the case of aliens there ought to be submitted if possible all or some of the following: a stamped and registered copy of the lease of an apartment executed over six months before action began, a bill of lading showing importation of household goods, a *certificat de domicile* of the *concierge,* a French income tax receipt, a *carte d'identité* (identity card) issued by the prefecture of police, a foreign passport, and a copy of a declaration of domicile filed at the borough hall. Evidence on the grounds, such as letters, police reports, etc., are generally reserved for presentation to the court at trial.

The plaintiff appears in person before the president in chambers or at the judge's home, without placing the petition upon any calendar and without giving notice to the president or clerk or to the defendant. In the case of aliens in Paris, since 1927, the petition is presented to the president of the 4th chamber of the Tribunal of the Seine. In other districts, the plaintiff goes before whichever president is on duty for such purpose on the day of presentation. If the plaintiff is unable by reason of illness or infirmity to appear in person, the president and clerk of the court are required by law to go to the party to receive the petition. If the plaintiff lives in France but outside of the judicial district and is unable to attend in person, the president may issue letters rogatory (*commission rogatoire*) to another president to receive the party in person or to go to the latter. (Algiers, March 30, 1909; *Rev. Alg.,* 1911, p. 377; *Recueil des Sommaires,* 1912, no. 4646.) For example, the court of the husband's domicile in France would invite the court of the wife's residence in France to receive her petition when she is sick, poor and unable to travel by reason of young children. But if the plaintiff lived abroad, in Brazil for example, her petition would be refused if not presented in person and no commission would be issued to a French consul or Brazilian court to receive it. The Court of Appeal of Algiers, February 2, 1885 (*Sirey,* 1886.2.181) reversed an order of the president of the Tribunal of Tizi-Ouzan (Algeria) for the issuance of a *commission rogatoire* addressed to the president of the Tribunal of Nautua or Annecy (France) to receive the petition of a French wife resident in Switzerland.

The plaintiff alone attends upon the president, without *avoué* or *avocat* or other adviser, except perhaps an interpreter. The president listens to the plaintiff at this *ex parte* hearing and endorses on the petition an order prepared by the clerk authorizing the plaintiff to cite the defendant to come before the president on a given day for an attempt at reconciliation. It is possible for the president to issue a *commission rogatoire* to another court to hear the defendant, but not to hear the plaintiff in regard to the petition. (Douai, April 27, 1921, *Recueil Douai,* 1921, p. 241.) The president of the first court would conduct the conciliation hearing himself in the light of the report of the second court as to the defendant's attitude, the plaintiff only being present at *conciliation.* The president of the French tribunal can even commission a Swiss court to hear a German defendant. (Seine, April 26, 1923; *Journal Clunet,* 1923, p. 850.) Laurent-Bailly mentions a case in which the tribunal of the Seine commissioned the French consul in St. Petersburg (Russia) to endeavor to conciliate the parties (Laurent-Bailly, p. 139). The precedent is of doubtful authority as the duty of conciliation cannot be delegated; the most that can be done is to delegate a preliminary hearing of one party before the *conciliation* hearing itself takes place. Article 238, C. C., does not permit the president to delegate to another judge the conciliation hearing. (Riom, October 19, 1910; *Gazette du Palais,* 1911.1.741.)

The president cannot lawfully decline to give a plaintiff leave to cite the defendant. (Agen. December 8, 1885; *Receuil des arrêts d'Agen,* 1885, p. 234.) Sometimes nevertheless if the president sees that the case is hopeless for lack of jurisdiction or other reason he will decline to sign the order. The order giving leave to cite defendant always appoints by name a bailiff to serve the citation upon defendant in divorce actions, but in separation actions plaintiff selects the bailiff.

It is possible for a plaintiff to obtain various provisional remedies at this *ex parte* hearing. For example, the order grants plaintiff leave to have a separate residence during the proceedings and in the case of the wife indicates where it shall be. (Article 236, C.C.) The order may also treat of the surrender of personal effects and of provisional custody of the children. (Article 238 C.C.) Apart from the order endorsed on the petition there is no official record of what was said or done at the hearing, the original petition being returned to plaintiff's attorney with the order endorsed thereon.

An appeal to the court of appeal by plaintiff lies from an order refusing leave to cite or declining to order a separate residence. It seems that an appeal by defendant lies from an order issuing a *commission rogatoire* for another court to receive plaintiff's petition (Algiers, February 2, 1885; *Sirey,* 1886.2.181.) It has been held, however, that no appeal can be taken by a defendant from the *ex parte* order even as to accessory relief, since the order is of *jurisdiction gracieuse,* that is it is non-controversial in character. (Paris, May 1, 1894; *Dalloz,* 1895.2.222.) It ought to be lawful to appeal from any award of provisional relief therein made, but the point is of academic interest since on short notice the defendant can bring the matter again before the president and ask him to vacate or change the terms of the order, or the defendant can wait until the conciliation hearing takes place and then without notice ask a change, or finally he can wait until the *assignation* (*i.e.,* summons and complaint) is served upon him and then on notice apply for this to the tribunal. All such contested orders or judgments are appealable.

The citation for conciliation is returnable not less than three days after service. To these three days must sometimes be added according to article 237, C.C. certain periods of time called *délais de distance* (*i. e.,* distance periods) which vary in duration according to the distance of the court from the domicile or residence of the defendant. The manner of computing the distance periods is indicated in article 73 of the Code of Civil Procedure. One month is the extra time given to a defendant who is in England. The additional time in the case of a defendant in America is two months. No distance period whatever is given a defendant when the citation is personally served upon him in France. This is the case notwithstanding the fact that he may be served while casually present in France, his domicile or residence being abroad. (Article 74, C.C.P.) It is still unsettled in law whether or not the distance periods apply when a defendant has elected in advance of suit a "fictitious domicile" (*i.e.,* address for service) in France for the special purpose of the proposed litigation. (H. Fort Dumanoir. *Questions et solutions pratiques,* no. 184, III, *Journal Clunet,* 1910, p. 841.)

A copy of plaintiff's petition, bearing at its foot the endorsed order of the president and a citation, is placed by the bailiff in a closed and sealed envelope, and is so served upon defendant. (Article 237, C.C.) No fixed time is indicated within which the citation must be served.

The bailiff's report that he has served the citation is evidence thereof; in fact its veracity can be contested only by special falsification proceedings. It is not possible for a defendant to waive service of process or to render service unnecessary by an admission thereof. The bailiff's report of service is essential. The service by a bailiff of the copy order, etc., is required to avoid *nullité* (nullity) of the procedure. (Article 237, C.C.) In fact all processes and most notices have to be served by a bailiff. For example, a notice of opposition to a marriage executed before a foreign notary and authenticated (*légalisé*) by the French consul, sent by mail to the "officer of civil status" in France is not a regular opposition, for such character is attached in France only to an instrument served by a bailiff. (Nice, March 25, 1890; *Journal Clunet,* 1890, p. 488, and *Journal Clunet,* 1903, p. 172.) It should be remembered, however, that various unsubstantial illegalities will be covered or cured if no appeal or petition for review is taken on the point.

In what manner does the bailiff serve the citation? Since the methods of service are the same for the citation as for the writ of summons for trial and other instruments, service will be considered in a separate chapter.

Few questions of private international law normally arise in relation to this preliminary court procedure. The president does not usually pass upon the question of jurisdiction or decide matters even provisionally in which foreign law is of moment. An alien wife is not required to produce an order of a foreign court giving her leave to sue for divorce or separation, even though she could sue in her own country only with such leave. *Lex fori* is deemed solely applicable to this initial procedure, which is considered rightly or wrongly to be purely of form and not affecting the merits of the action. Nevertheless, if the president treats of the custody of children or other accessory remedies, questions of the conflict of laws are involved and matters are dealt with *ex parte* which do in fact seriously affect the defendant.

Chapter XVIII

SERVICE OF PROCESS

The Civil Code does not prescribe particular methods for the service of process in divorce and separation actions, although it does indicate by whom the service shall be made and the contents of the papers to be served. Articles 68 and 69 of the Code of Civil Procedure give the methods of service of process.

Article 68 reads in part:

All service shall be made upon the person or at the domicile; but if the bailiff finds at the domicile neither the party nor any of his relatives or servants he shall forthwith deliver the copy to a neighbor, who shall sign the original; if this neighbor cannot or will not sign, the bailiff shall deliver the copy to the Mayor or Deputy of the Commune, who shall sign the original without cost.

Article 69, subdivisions 7, 8, and 9 are as follows:

Service shall be made upon:

7. Persons who have no known domicile in France, at the place of their present residence; if that place is not known, the writ shall be posted on the principal door of the court room of the court where the complaint is brought; a second copy shall be given to the District Attorney, who shall sign the original.

8. Those who live in French territory outside Europe and Algeria, and those who are established in countries placed under the French protectorate other than Tunisia, at the office of the District Attorney of the court where the complaint is brought, who shall sign the original and

shall send the copy directly to the Chief of the (judicial) Bureau of the colony or protectorate.

9. Persons who live abroad, at the same District Attorney's Office, which under the same conditions, shall send a copy to the Ministry of Foreign Affairs, or whatever other authority shall be indicated by diplomatic conventions.

It is clear from article 68 C. C. P. and article 237 C. C. that a defendant may be personally served by the bailiff wherever he is found in France, either at his domicile, residence or elsewhere. Thus, personal service in France upon an alien domiciled abroad but sojourning in France is valid, and in such case the service need not be made in the manner indicated by article 69 (9), C. C. P. (Paris, January 9, 1902; *Journal Clunet,* 1902, p. 321.)

Consider next the situation when the defendant is not personally served but has a known domicile in France. In such case he should be served as indicated in article 68, C. C. P., namely by delivery of the process to a relative, servant, neighbor, or, if no neighbor will accept it then, to the mayor of *commune* (borough) in which the domicile is situated. A Frenchman who lives abroad but who has retained a domicile in France must be served at such domicile under article 68 C. C. P. and not at the district attorney's office under article 69 (9), C. C. P. (Cassation, January 24, 1908; *Dalloz,* 1910.1.484.) When a defendant has a domicile in France and also a residence separate therefrom, service at the latter is inoperative. (Cassation, April 14, 1891; *Dalloz,* 1891.1.329.) It has been held in the case of a defendant domiciled in France that service at the office of the district attorney under article 69 (9), C. C. P. is void, defendant's removal to the principality of Monaco not being proved by the plaintiff. (Cassation, November 9, 1903; *Journal Clunet,* 1904, p. 712.) An alien who resides alternately in France and abroad for business reasons but who has his commercial headquarters in France can be served at such headquarters under article 68, C. C. P.; for his headquarters amount to a domicile within the meaning of this article. (Lyon, March 28, 1879; *Journal Clunet,* 1880, p. 102.) Service upon a Frenchman at his "former" domicile in France is valid when his removal to America is "fictitious" and the defendant sold his house and made a declaration of intention to change domicile at the borough hall merely to obstruct his wife's divorce action. (Cassation, November 20, 1889; *Journal Clunet,* 1890, p. 278.)

Suppose a defendant is known to have a domicile in France though its location is unknown, but he has a residence in France and that is known, where is he to be served? He should be served at such residence. (Article 69 (7), C. C. P.) But if the residence is not known then the process should be posted at the court house and a copy delivered to the district attorney in compliance with subdivision (7) of article 69, C. C. P.

The situation is more complicated when husband and wife are *de facto* or *de jure* separated during the course of the marriage. The domicile of a French wife is always that of her husband unless she is judicially separated from him. Consequently, one might suppose that a husband could serve the wife at his own domicile even if she were in fact absent therefrom. But this would be unfair, particularly if she had left him for cause or if he had established a new domicile without her. Therefore it has been held that when the couple are *de facto* separated, a husband must serve process at the wife's residence if he knows or could find out where she is. (Alais, February 4, 1920; *Gazette du Palais,* May 7, 1920.) In the case of a wife entitled to a separate residence *pendente lite,* process must be served upon her at such residence. So, service at the husband's domicile of a judgment of separation upon a wife authorized to reside separately in France during the action is void. (Nancy, August 11, 1865; *Sirey,* 1865.2. 324.) Some conflict in jurisprudence exists, however, in case a wife is given leave to live abroad during the suit. For example, service upon a wife permitted to live in Belgium should be made through consular channels under article 69 (9) C. C. P. and not upon her by leaving the writ at the husband's domicile in France. Yet a husband has been allowed by leave of the president to serve his wife residing abroad by substitution under article 68, C. C. P. the process being delivered to an employee of the husband at his house and never having reached the wife. (Nancy, May 21, 1887; *Le Droit,* August 22 and 23, 1887.) The separate residence of the wife based upon the president's order applies only *inter partes. Vis-à-vis* third persons she is still *pendente lite* domiciled with her husband and may be served by them at his domicile. After judgment of separation the wife has a separate domicile under article 108, C. C. as amended by law of February 6, 1893. If in the matrimonial action it is the husband that leaves the home and establishes his temporary residence elsewhere during the suit, his legal domicile remains where it was so far as the wife and third persons are concerned. Process is served, it seems, upon the husband at his domicile, not at his temporary residence, even when he has been expelled from home by court order.

Turn now to the case of persons who have a known domicile, but this is outside of France. Service upon such a defendant is made in the manner indicated by article 69 (9), C. C. P. unless he has a residence in France, in which case he is served at his French residence under article 69 (7), C. C. P. For example, an alien domiciled abroad but sojourning in France, where he has rented a place of business, may be served in the town where this place of business is located by delivery of the process to the hotelkeeper or head waiter or servant of the hostelry where he has a *pied-à-terre* (*i.e.*, living room). (Court of Appeal of Lyon, date not stated, *Journal Clunet*, 1878, p. 375.) If the defendant has a known foreign domicile but no residence in France, service is made upon him under article 69 (9), C. C. P. by delivery of the writ to the district attorney, who is expected to transmit it to defendant through "diplomatic" (*i.e.*, consular) channels.

When process is served by delivery to the district attorney for transmission through the Ministry of Foreign Affairs, the latter sends the copy to the French consulate nearest the address given in the process as being that of defendant's foreign domicile or residence. The plaintiff is the one who supplies such address. If the foreign address is inexactly given the service is nevertheless good unless plaintiff acted fraudulently. The consulate does not seek out the party, but writes him a letter asking him to call and receive some legal papers. The consulate does not state what the papers are, nor does it know what they are, as the envelope is sealed. So far as plaintiff is concerned he has done his full legal duty when the bailiff delivers the process to the district attorney. A legal duty probably exists upon the Ministry or consulate toward defendant to see that the process is forwarded to him, but the plaintiff is not responsible for an irregular transmission of the process through the consular channels and service by delivery at the *parquet* is complete and valid notwithstanding subsequent irregularity in transmission. (Cassation, June 28, 1905; *Journal Clunet*, 1906, p. 174.) Consequently the defendant is deemed validly served even though the process may never reach him and time to appear, etc., will run against him as if the process had been received. This is indeed the rule of the Hague Convention of November 14, 1896. Nevertheless, the French courts have recoiled from pressing the rule to its logical result in all cases. For instance, it has been held that when the transmission through the consulate was absolutely prevented by a ministerial circular, ordering French consulates not to deliver process to Frenchmen in Alsace-Lorraine (Germany), a defendant domiciled in Alsace-Lorraine is not to be considered as regularly served simply by the delivery of the process to the district attorney under article 69 (9), C. C. P. (Nancy, November 25, 1893; *Journal Clunet*, 1894, p. 805.)

Consider now the topic of service upon a defendant whose domicile and residence are unknown; that is a defendant concerning whom it is not known whether he is domiciled or resident in France or abroad. In such case article 69 (7), C. C. P. applies; service is made by delivery of the process to the district attorney's office and there is no transmission to any foreign country. In the case of a defendant who at one time lived in France, but who is domiciled somewhere abroad at the time suit is brought, although he is sojourning at some place in France whose location is unknown, it seems a demand made through a bailiff and in good faith at the party's last known domicile in France is valid to interrupt prescription. (Seine, December 5, 1891; *Journal Clunet*, 1895, p. 1076.) In such case personal or substituted service under article 68, C. C. P. would be proper, not substituted service at the *parquet* under article 69 (9). When a plaintiff knows of no residence of the defendant other than a hotel at which he stopped at a comparatively remote date, the process may be served by posting (*i.e.*, placarding) and delivery to the district attorney as provided by article 69 (7), C. C. P. (Seine, November 21, 1884; *Sirey*, 1885.2.21.)

Any illegality of service is cured or covered if the defendant actually received the process in due season. (Piérard, vol. II, Sec. 460, p. 11.) A defendant waives the illegality of service founded upon the fact that the writ was not seasonably served upon him either personally or at his domicile or residence, if having actually received the process he attends the conciliation hearing without objecting to the service. A defendant can waive an error in the date set for attendance, the writ giving him a shorter time for the return than that fixed by law. These formalities of service are for defendant's benefit and can be waived. Service itself (it seems) cannot be waived, but a defect in the manner of service need not be invoked and will be cured or covered if no objection thereto is seasonably made.

It is to be noted that there is no provision in French law for service by publication. Nevertheless there is a permissive provision (article 247, C. C.) for publication of a notice of the pendency of action when a defendant was not personally served and defaulted by non-appearance. Furthermore, there is no provision in French law for personal or substituted service outside France. The delivery of the writ by the consulate is not personal service within the meaning of French law, as service in such case by substitution was already complete upon delivery to the district attorney. Substituted service upon a relative, servant, neighbor or mayor takes place without court order upon failure of bailiff to find the defendant. The bailiff may if he desires make several efforts to find the defendant to deliver the process to him in person but he is under no duty to do so. If defendant does not happen to be at his domicile or residence when the bailiff calls, the bailiff simply leaves the envelope for him. It is only in case the bailiff has to make a demand upon a party and take note of his verbal reply that a serious attempt is made actually to find him. The comedies of personal service which characterize American proceedings are entirely unknown in France, and personal service has in French law no greater efficiency than substituted service. Jurisdiction *in personam* is not created in French law over transients by the magic of personal service. Jurisdiction is quite independent of service and cannot be defeated by evading service. The manner of service is not a factor in determining whether in a given case there is or is not jurisdiction over the person of defendant. In the case of British and American defendants the foreign legal advisers usually insist that personal service in France be secured, so that the French judgment shall stand a better chance of recognition abroad than it would if the writ had been served by substitution or through the consulate. The value of the French judgment is thereby psychologically enhanced; it is also increased in foreign, though not in French, law.

In relation to aliens domiciled or resident in France, no particular hardship is usually experienced by reason of these rules. But when delivery of process is made to the mayor or district attorney for an alien defendant, the latter runs great risk of never learning of the suit until time to appear has run against him. Neither official is under a duty to search out defendant nor do they do so. The papers are simply filed away and can be unearthed only with difficulty, if at all. No proper filing system exists at the borough halls and no index which can be readily searched. The situation is equally defective at the district attorney's offices, the Ministry of Foreign Affairs and the consulates. How defective a system of service the foregoing may prove to be in the case of aliens may readily be conceived, particularly when it is applied in connection with the French rules on jurisdiction.

In the case of a married woman, process is served upon her as if she were under no disability of coverture. Minors under limited guardianship are served by delivering copies both to them and to their guardians (*curateurs*). Persons supplied by judicial authority with a committee (*conseil judiciaire*), because feeble-minded or spendthrifts, and persons applied *ad hoc* with an attorney *ad litem* (*mandataire ad litem*) are likewise so served. A convict is not served himself, but the process is served upon his guardian (*tuteur*).

The private international law of France is happily quite clear in relation to service of process. *Lex fori* of the court in which the action is pending governs. For example, in an action against a French citizen before a Belgian court service of process may be made by a letter sent to defendant in France, although the French law does not provide for service by mail. (Nantes, November 25, 1895; *Journal Clunet,* 1896, p. 625.) Similarly in an action before the British High Court it is lawful for a defendant resident of France to be served by a solicitor's clerk in the French Republic instead of by a bailiff. (Seine, July 5, 1881; *Journal Clunet,* 1882, p. 530.) The Court of Appeal of Toulouse, January 29, 1872, (*Journal Clunet,* 1874, p. 78) sustained personal service in the English manner in France, the action being before the British court. The Court remarked indeed: "The English procedure which requires that the French defendant shall have been reached by the writ presents more complete guaranties than the procedure organized by Article 69 of the Code of Civil Procedure under which one cannot always be sure that the alien will receive the writ of summons within the period fixed for appearance by Article 73 of the Code of Civil Procedure."

From the foregoing it is manifest that in the view of French law the provisions of articles 68 and 69, C. C. P. apply to both aliens and French defendants in actions instituted in France. Hence, service upon an American husband domiciled and resident in the United States, defendant in an action brought by his French wife, could be made by mere delivery of the process to the district attorney in France.

Aliens do not often contest the validity of service upon them, even when they do strenuously contest the jurisdiction. The Sickles case, however, did pass upon the applicability of article 68, C. C. P. to a United States citizen domiciled in New York, but who had a house in Paris. Process was served while he was away by leaving the instrument at his residence. The service was held to be perfectly proper. (Paris, June 12, 1907; *Journal Clunet,* 1908, p. 148.) Jurisdiction was, however, denied for the principal relief of divorce because defendant was domiciled in New York and merely resident in Paris, there being no additional circumstances which taken with residence would have led the court to assert jurisdiction.

Chapter XIX

CONCILIATION

On the return day indicated in the citation the plaintiff and defendant are required to appear together before a president of the tribunal in his judge's chambers. It is not usually the same judge that heard the plaintiff alone, for the duty of conducting conciliations rotates among the presidents of the several chambers (*i. e.,* terms, parts). Article 877 of the Code of Civil Procedure requires the parties to appear in person, unaccompanied by anyone save an interpreter if this is necessary. The presence of a mother who attended with her married minor daughter was held to invalidate the divorce procedure. (Blidah, January 22, 1890; *Pandectes françaises,* 1890.2.223.) *Quaere,* whether or not such strictness applies in separation actions? A guardian (*tuteur*) should attend conciliation on behalf of his ward, but a *curateur* should not attend with a minor under limited guardianship. The rule that the parties shall be unaccompanied at the hearing, is a serious hardship upon aliens unfamiliar with the French language and laws. While no stenographic report is kept of the hearing, yet a record (*procès verbal*) is made by the clerk in the judge's minute book and a party may say or do things, or omit to say or do things, or be charged with having done so, which materially affect the case without his realizing the consequences.

If the president is made aware by the attorneys that one or other party cannot attend but desires a hearing, he will usually set a new date for the conciliation or go with the clerk and other party to the house of the party unable to travel. If the plaintiff fails to attend at *conciliation,* this constitutes a discontinuance. If the defendant does not come, the president notes the default on the record and signs an order either allowing the plaintiff to serve a summons for trial or adjourning the hearing until a later date indicated therein. By article 238 of the Civil Code he cannot adjourn the hearing indefinitely, nor for more than twenty days, nor repeatedly. He cannot subordinate leave to sue to the condition that another conciliation shall be held at the end of six months and that this also shall be a failure. (Paris, May 26, 1869; *Dalloz,* 1869.2.247.) If a twenty days' adjournment is ordered and at the second hearing the plaintiff still insists on bringing suit, the president is obliged to accede to the prayer, even though he may consider the complaint frivolous.

At conciliation the president hears the plaintiff, then the defendant, and endeavors to reconcile them. If the attempt at reconciliation is effective, the *procès verbal* usually mention that fact but there is no duty to do so. (Cassation, March 9, 1838; Dalloz, *Code de Procédure Civile annoté,* ed. 1922, article 878, note 9.) The action thereupon stands discontinued. The cause of action also ends; unless perchance it can be shown that the reconciliation was expressly conditional or was a sham or was given under constraint.

If reconciliation is not effected, the president endorses an order granting leave to sue for divorce or separation upon the petition used at the *ex parte* hearing and immediately following the *ex parte* order which authorized the citation for conciliation. The petition is then returned to plaintiff's *avoué.*

The president at conciliation may correct irregularities made at the *ex parte* hearing. Irregularities in the method of service of process under articles 68 and 69 C. C. P. will be waived by attendance of the defendant at conciliation without express oral protest. If any substantial formalities in relation to conciliation are unobserved the procedure will be void. For example, the conciliation procedure is void if the plaintiff has given a false address as that of the defendant and leaves the latter in entire ignorance of the procedure, although being in correspondence with him. (Grasse, November 11, 1912; *Recueil des Alpes Maritimes,* 1913, p. 117; *Recueil des Sommaires,* 1914, no. 3378.) The absence of a conciliation hearing renders a divorce or separation judgment void, and the objection may be raised at any stage of the procedure, in first instance or an appeal. (Algiers, February 1, 1897; *Journal Clunet,* 1898, p. 352.) This means that the parties cannot omit the step of conciliation by agreement or waiver.

Suppose defendant attends at conciliation. In this case it is of especial importance to note that an objection to the jurisdiction or venue must be expressly stated to preserve it. An objection to the competence *ratione materiae* can be raised at any stage of the proceedings, even before the Court of Cassation. This is also true of any substantial irregularities which the Code declares to involve *"nullité."* But mere irregularities must be objected to at the earliest opportunity, else they are cured or waived.

Since a defendant does not present and file any written instrument at conciliation, an objection to the competence, jurisdiction or venue has to be stated orally. If the minutes of the clerk do not show that the objection was duly made it is not possible later to contend the objection was in fact made without bringing a special proceeding to correct the record. A letter which contradicts the minutes, subsequently written by the president himself, cannot be used to contradict the minutes when the minutes themselves have not been rectified by the clerk. (Cassation,

June 1, 1891; *Sirey,* 1891.1.129.) An alien who desires to contest the jurisdiction must do so when he attends at conciliation. (Cassation, May 11, 1915; *Dalloz,* 1916.1. 200.) He must state the objection before he replies to the plaintiff's remarks. An objection to the venue, *compétence ratione loci,* must also be so preserved. (Paris, June 13, 1894; *Le Droit,* July 21, 1894.) A mere verbal reservation at conciliation of the right to object to the jurisdiction when the case comes before the tribunal is insufficient to preserve the objection. (Paris, March 15, 1892; *Sirey,* 1892.2.72.)

A conflict of authority still exists as to whether or not the president can himself at conciliation decide for or against the jurisdiction. For the affirmative, it has been held by the Court of Appeal of Grenoble, May 2, 1891 (*Dalloz,* 1892.2.561) that he can and that an appeal lies from his order asserting jurisdiction directly to the court of appeal, not to the tribunal of first instance. In fact, it has been held in an action between Swiss parties that an objection to the jurisdiction *ratione personae* made at conciliation is waived if no appeal is taken from the president's order giving leave to sue and is also waived by defendant's asking for inspection of plaintiff's documents and conclusions. (Mortain, January 22, 1908; *Journal Clunet,* 1909, p. 736.) The Court of Cassation, January 14, 1928 (*Dalloz hebdomadaire,* 1923, p. 102) held that an objection to the venue, *compétence ratione loci,* is waived unless appeal is taken from the non-conciliation order granting leave to sue, signed at the *conciliation* hearing attended by defendant. This decision would probably also apply to jurisdiction *ratione personae,* as the rules of procedure to contest jurisdiction and venue are the same. *Per contra,* the Court of Appeal of Lyon, March 17, 1891 (*Pandectes françaises,* 1891.2.318) held that the president should simply note an objection to the jurisdiction and should sign the order giving leave to serve summons for trial notwithstanding the objection; that there is no appeal to the court of appeal from the conciliation order on the jurisdictional issue, but the defendant should renew his objection by answer and let the tribunal decide. It has been lately held also that, on an appeal from the order of non-conciliation, the court of appeal cannot decide the jurisdictional question. (Dijon, June 14, 1920; *Gazette du Palais,* July 16, 1920.) It is considered with unanimity, however, that an appeal by plaintiff would lie from an order declining leave to sue for lack of jurisdiction.

Suppose the defendant fails to attend at conciliation. In this case if the citation never reached him or reached him too late to attend, then all authorities agree the jurisdictional objection may be raised by answer. Several authorities state also that a defendant can so object even when his default was deliberate. Some courts and writers consider, however, that in such case the defendant must not only raise the objection by answer but also by appeal from the president's order, *ordonnance de non-conciliation.* For example, the Tribunal of Nice, March 12, 1890 (*La Loi,* March 21, 1890) held that an objection to the venue was waived because this must be stated at conciliation and is "covered" when the judge has pronounced his decision and this judgment has become final. In the Gould case, the Tribunal of Versailles and Court of Appeal of Paris gave as one reason for asserting jurisdiction that defendant, being duly served, defaulted at conciliation, and failed to appeal from the president's order, but this reason was not mentioned by the Court of Cassation when it in turn sustained the jurisdiction. In view of these conflicting lines of cases, an alien defendant should attend conciliation if this is at all possible and should orally object in due season to the jurisdiction or venue. He should preserve his objection by answer and preferably also by appeal from the president's order.

A number of provisional remedies exist which the president has authority to grant at the conciliation hearing. The additional provisions of the order on such matters are prepared by the clerk while the parties are before the president. The request for provisional remedies is not made in writing but is made orally and without notice. The president under article 238 C. C. may change or cancel at conciliation the provisional remedies awarded *ex parte* by the president when plaintiff presented his or her petition. Conciliation is the usual moment at which the questions of temporary alimony, custody of children, residence, delivery of personal effects, conservatory measures, etc., are debated and settled *pendente lite,* though they may be later modified. Nevertheless, a defendant has an uphill task to obtain alteration later, if he intentionally defaults at conciliation. It is astonishing that such important matters should be handled before the president by the parties themselves without their legal advisers. These provisional remedies will be considered in the next chapter.

The socalled "non-conciliation order" gives plaintiff twenty days in which to serve summons for trial. If the writ is not served within this period, the provisional remedies *ipso facto* lapse. Nevertheless, the action is not on that account discontinued and the summons can be served at any time thereafter; that is to say unless and until the action itself shall have been dismissed after three years for laches.

Foreign law plays but a small part in relation to conciliation. Aliens whose national law knows no such preliminary as this are nevertheless subject to it in France. The president usually does not attempt to decide for or against the jurisdiction, but notes the objection, gives leave to sue, and leaves questions of competence, jurisdiction and venue to be decided by the tribunal. He awards provisional remedies according to the French law as a *modus vivendi pendente lite.* Conciliation is not considered so much a legal debate as an attempt at friendly adjustment and reconciliation.

Chapter XX

PROVISIONAL REMEDIES

By article 236 of the Civil Code the president of the tribunal of first instance at the *ex parte* hearing grants leave to the plaintiff to live apart from defendant during the litigation and if plaintiff is the wife indicates a specific place. Under article 238, C. C. he has power to award provisional custody of the children and require delivery of plaintiff's personal effects by defendant. Defendant has no notice and usually no knowledge of this hearing or of the terms of the order until the citation is served upon him. The only thing that can justify at all the award of such relief *ex parte* is its essentially revocable character. Provisional remedies are settled with rather more permanence, but only for the litigation period, at the conciliation hearing, which a defendant usually attends. It is not easy to obtain a later change, although this is legally possible.

The powers of the president at conciliation are much more extensive than his powers at the *ex parte* hearing. Besides separate residences, delivery of effects and custody of the children he can at conciliation award many other provisional remedies, such as alimony, suit money, attachment, sealing, receivership, etc., under article 236 and 238, C. C. and in virtue of his implied powers based upon other legal provisions.

After the president's order at conciliation has been rendered and the summons and complaint, together with a copy of the order, have been served upon the defendant, the tribunal has power over the provisional remedies in view of article 240 of the Civil Code. The tribunal can at such time award the same remedies by preparatory judgment as could the president earlier by order (*ordonnance*). It has even wider authority than the president, for the tribunal can take "all other urgent measures." Judgment of the tribunal is obtained either before trial upon application with written notice to the other side or at the *audience* (trial) of the suit upon oral application or written application made in the answer or reply or in the formal conclusions filed with the clerk. When a case is on appeal before the court of appeal, that court has power also over the provisional remedies and this to the exclusion of the tribunal. The Court of Cassation has no power to award or change the provisional remedies. It can only affirm or quash orders or judgments.

Aside from the foregoing, it is possible to obtain provisional remedies from a justice of the peace in a special action separate from the matrimonial action in course. But the authority of this petty judge under the law of July 12, 1905, is very limited. For example, as to alimony he can make no award of over six hundred francs a year. Furthermore, the justice of the peace can only supplement, not change the relief awarded by the president, tribunal or court of appeal. It is possible for the president or tribunal to supplement the provisional relief, e. g., alimony, awarded by a justice of the peace, but not to cancel or change it. (Paris, July 6, 1921, cited by Boyer, p. 99.) Besides the justice of the peace, the president of the tribunal of first instance has power in a special capacity, as so-called *juge des référés* (*i.e.,* judge of delegated matters) under article 806 of the Code of Civil Procedure, to award provisional remedies. An application made under article 806, C. C. P., is also a separate proceeding which may proceed concurrently with the divorce or separation action. This article applies to all "urgent cases" and a hearing may be secured on a few hours' notice. The award is stated by article 809, C. C. P., to be "without prejudice" to the merits of any controversy over the accessory relief, but otherwise the president's powers under article 806, C. C. P., are without express restriction. In particular the president is not limited thereunder to the powers enumerated in article 238 of the Civil Code which relates to matrimonial actions for divorce or separation. Formal notice of application and conclusions by the applicant's attorney are necessary to obtain relief in a hearing at *référé,* whereas at conciliation or *ex parte* in the principal action an oral request is sufficient and no notice to the other side need be given that such relief will be asked. (Carpentier, *Divorce et séparation de corps,* vol. 1, sec. 1385).

In view of the several possible concurrent actions or proceedings and multiplicity of judges and courts having power over provisional remedies, conflicts of authority are rather frequent. The manner of solving such conflicts requires some explanation. The *ex parte* and conciliation orders of the president under articles 236 and 238 of the Civil Code may be supplemented, cancelled or modified by the president acting under article 806 of the Code of Civil Procedure or by the tribunal acting under article 240, C. C., or by the court of appeal when the case is before it. An order of the president under article 806, C. C. P., may be modified, cancelled or supplemented by the tribunal or court of appeal when the divorce or separation action is pending before the one or the other respectively, but an order of the tribunal or court of appeal cannot be cancelled or modified, but only supplemented by the president acting under article 806, C. C. P.

A serious divergence of views obtains, however, as to the respective powers of the tribunal and court of appeal when the former is seized of the divorce action and the latter of an appeal from the president's order whether granted *ex parte* or at conciliation or as *référé*. Three lines of cases exist. 1. The beginning of the action before the tribunal has no effect upon the incidental appeal. 2. If the appeal has been taken before service of summons is made, the court of appeal retains cognizance of the appeal, but not otherwise. 3. The beginning of the action before the tribunal divests the court of appeal of cognizance over the president's order and the appellant must seek relief against the order from the tribunal, not from the court of appeal. Since in any event the tribunal has power to modify or cancel the president's order notwithstanding the pendency of an appeal, the parties usually go for this purpose before the tribunal rather than continue with or take an appeal from the president's order. Nevertheless, since the tribunal's order only modifies the president's order *in futurum,* an appeal may still be useful to undo the past effects of the president's order; e. g., to escape the duty of paying arrears of provisional alimony awarded by order of the president.

An award made by the president at conciliation of custody *pendente lite* of the children under article 238, C.C., is never *res judicata* but is always provisional only. (Orleans, February 14, 1912; *Le Droit,* May 1, 1921.) This principle would apply to all provisional relief awarded by order or by preparatory judgment.

Consider next in detail the various provisional remedies that may be awarded by one or several of those judges or courts.

The purpose of the law in providing for separate residences during divorce or separation litigation is to prevent the domestic friction and trouble which would inevitably arise during the litigation if the parties were obliged to remain together while suing each other. It is the practice to indicate a particular residence to the wife, but simply to authorize the husband to live apart from her without ordering him to reside in a given place. The wife's desires are taken into consideration in selecting a place for her. The parties are at liberty to settle by agreement where and how the wife shall live during the action. (Cassation, February 6, 1889; *Sirey,* 1891.1.379.) Nevertheless, the judge or court may disregard the agreement or earlier order and fix a different place for good reasons and upon application of either party. It is not necessary to specify a precise house in which the wife shall live, but only the town, village or general locality. She may be permitted to reside abroad, e. g., in Belgium. She may be allowed to dwell with another person, such as her father or mother. A plaintiff wife may be ordered to remain in the home and the defendant husband to leave it. (Cassation, January 18, 1892; *Sirey,* 1892.1.68.) But the president at the *ex parte* hearing cannot by order eject the husband. Furthermore it is not lawful at any time to require the husband to leave the home if the premises are used by him not alone for residence but for business purposes as well. (Paris, November 19, 1856; *Sirey,* 1857.2.257.) The parties may be ordered to live separately in the same building if it can be adapted thereto. If the wife wishes later to change residence or to take a prolonged trip, she must obtain leave of the court upon notice to the husband and special application. For example, an American wife ordered to live in the Hotel Majestic in Paris, should apply for and will be given leave to make a visit to the United States during the litigation. Nevertheless, for short absences no leave is required.

The party leaving the home for a separate residence in pursuance of judicial authorization is permitted by article 238 of the Civil Code to remove personal effects. A wife leaving the home may take her jewels, she may even take furniture. She is entitled to remove such personal belongings as she may desire and the court or judge will order an inventory to be taken of and seals to be affixed upon any wardrobes, trunks, etc., left by her at the home. (Cassation, February 15, 1859; *Sirey,* 1859. 1.201.) If the president's order rendered at the *ex parte* hearing or conciliation does not specify the nature of the personal effects to be removed, the parties may agree upon the list or bring the matter upon notice before the president for his decision. In no event must the removal amount to a liquidation of the matrimonial property régime. If the party remaining in the home obstructs the removal or declines to allow the same, an application will be granted for a mandatory order (*i.e.*, injunction) to compel delivery.

Whereas in the laws of the United States the custody of children during a marriage is jointly vested in the two parents, this is not the case in French law. Speaking of parental authority, *patria potestas,* article 373 of the Civil Code says: "The father alone exercises this authority during the marriage." The children are consequently in the father's custody, although, of course, the mother has clear rights in relation to them. Administration of the children's property during their youth belongs also to the father under article 384, C. C., who enjoys the "usufruct" thereof without accountability for the profits until the child reaches eighteen or is emancipated. In principle the authority of the husband over the person and property of the children is not affected by the pendency of a matrimonial action between the parents. But this is a rule which is frequently put aside, although the president or court ought not to deprive the husband of either custody of the person or administration of the property of his child unless, independently of the divorce or separation action, the facts would support a judgment depriving him thereof. The judicial authorities have, however, a wide discretional latitude over provisional custody under article 238, C. C. It is the interest of the children, not of the father, which controls their decision. The district attorney and any relative has a statutory right to intervene in the suit in this connection. Custody may be awarded to a third person, a school, a *pension,* if the court is so minded.

It frequently happens that the parties agree upon the custody, right of visit, etc., *pendente lite.* Such an accord will usually be confirmed in the order of the president if the matter is brought to his attention, but the accord may be disregarded or modified by the judge or court, either upon his or its own motion or upon application of a principal or intervening party. It is not lawful for the parents to agree to disregard the order or to vary the award or to carry out a different system of custody, visits, etc. In the Gladys Deacon case, the Court of Appeal of Paris, November 22, 1892 (*Dalloz,* 1893.2.523), held that an agreement made between two Americans litigating divorce in France dividing between them the custody of the children, would not be set aside at the husband's request when the facts showed that he had sent to the United States the two children entrusted to him and intended to send there the two left with the wife if he could get hold of them and that the wife's custody had been well conducted.

When custody of a child is given to one spouse, the other always has a right of visit. The law does not precisely state how this right shall be exercised, but the order must set forth practical conditions under which such a right can be usefully enjoyed. An award of custody does not *per se* deprive the father of the other rights of *patria potestas;* he can still decide what school the children shall attend, to what church they shall go, etc. Furthermore, the father is not deprived of the administration of the property of the children by the mere award of custody to another person. He can be deprived of administration and of the other parental rights for good cause only. This total deprivation is rarely ordered, even when provisional custody is given to the wife. No rule of law or practice exists that boys shall be given to the husband, girls to the wife nor is there an age limit below which an infant shall not be separated from its mother. All these aspects are left to the discretion of the judge or court.

Article 238 of the Civil Code gives to the president or tribunal power to award alimony *pendente lite* in favor of either party, although in practice usually a wife only receives such assistance. An award of temporary alimony is not of right, but only of grace. If a wife is successfully earning her own living, or has a separate income, she will not usually receive an award. This is not always true, for a French wife having a separate income of fifty thousand francs a year from *paraphernal* property has been awarded twenty-five hundred francs a month alimony besides. (Orleans, April 3, 1889; *Dalloz,* 1889.2.184.) But an award will not be denied a wife for the reason that her parents have resources or that she holds a power of attorney from the husband by the use of which she could obtain funds. The fact that the wife deserted the husband and is presumptively in the wrong, is not a reason for denying her alimony. (Aix, Frimaire 29, Year XIII; *Sirey,* XIII 2.68.)

Alimony is usually awarded, if at all, in the conciliation order. It is generally given to begin at the date of the *ex parte* order allowing the wife a separate residence. When the wife is defendant, the alimony is payable from the date of the order which indicated for her a separate residence; not from the date of the wife's counter-claim for divorce. (Seine, July 21, 1892; *Le Droit,* August 4, 1892.) Nevertheless, if the common residence of the spouses has been maintained until the date of the conciliation hearing, the alimony will begin only from the date of the order rendered on that occasion. Unless the order is revoked or changed, alimony will remain payable until the divorce or separation judgment is recorded, or until a judgment declining this relief is no longer subject to appeal or review. Yet alimony may be made payable until the property regime is liquidated. Such a provision is not usually included in the judgment of the tribunal or order of the president, but is sometimes found in the judgment which concludes the action.

Payment of temporary alimony is to take place in the manner settled in the order or judgment. For example, it may be made payable quarterly or annually, either directly to the alimony-creditor or to him or her through a third person, either collectible by the alimony-creditor or deliverable by the alimony-debtor. A wife may be authorized to collect herself the revenues produced by the dowry and separate property belonging to her but administered by the husband, and to do so without the passage of these revenues through his hands. (Cassation, March 31, 1908; *Dalloz,* 1908.1.277.)

Article 301 of the Civil Code limits alimony awarded by a judgment of divorce or separation to one-third the income of the losing party. This article does not apply to temporary alimony. The amount of the latter is left to the discretion of the president or court. Usually the temporary alimony is also within this one-third figure, but there is no reason why it should not exceed this if most of the husband's income is derived from property administered by him but belonging to the wife. Article 208 of the Civil Code says simply that alimony shall correspond in amount to the needs of the alimony-creditor and fortune of the alimony-debtor. This article applies to all kinds of alimony, temporary and permanent, between husband and wife, parent and child, etc. Whereas the status of persons cannot be the subject matter of private contract, this is not so of all their pecuniary interests. An agreement between husband and wife during the litigation to settle temporary alimony is perfectly lawful. (Perigeux, February 21, 1907; *Le Droit,* March 5, 1907.) But this is always subject to change by judicial authority under article 209, C. C. The Code provision for alimony is one of public order and cannot be waived by the parties. (Bordeaux, July 26, 1855; *Dalloz,* 1859.5.24.) If the parties settle the amount of alimony, manner of payment, etc., by agreement, this may be varied by the judge or court, but after an alimony order has been made, the parties are not at liberty to fix a different figure. Alimony may be ordered paid by an alimony-debtor who has no capital (*fortune*) but only earnings. An award can be increased or decreased in virtue of article 209 of the Civil Code by later order or judgment, if circumstances alter.

Temporary alimony is quite frequently awarded in litigation between aliens. In the Hart case, an American wife asked five thousand francs suit-money to enable her to sue for divorce in America, jurisdiction for divorce having been denied in France. The Tribunal of the Seine, January 23, 1883 (*Journal Clunet,* 1883, p. 292), refused this request for suit-money, but awarded one thousand francs a month alimony for two months, a ticket to New York and five hundred francs for traveling expenses, which was substantially what the husband had offered. The Tribunal of the Seine, August 18, 1881 (*Journal Clunet,* 1881, p. 526), in the Stern case awarded an American wife six thousand francs suit-money to sue in America and four thousand francs a month alimony for eighteen months. The husband was also ordered to surrender the wife's jewels and clothes within three months. This was an independent action for provisional remedies, no divorce or separation action having been brought. The award is the most liberal on record. In the litigation of French couples and of aliens of other nationalities than American, the awards of temporary alimony are small: for instance, one thousand francs a month between Greeks (Seine, February 14, 1898; *Journal Clunet,* 1898, p. 909); one hundred francs a month between Russians (Seine, July 13, 1911; Paris, January 26, 1914; *Journal Clunet,* 1917, p. 602).

An important difference exists between French law and Anglo-American law in regard to the nature of temporary alimony. In French law temporary alimony is of a different nature also from permanent alimony, which latter will be considered in a later chapter. Temporary alimony is not in French law a donation or contribution from one spouse to the other. It is in principle an advance or loan which is to be eventually reimbursed to the alimony-debtor by the alimony-creditor. In practice it is taken into account and debited against the alimony-creditor upon the liquidation of the property regime. Temporary alimony is legally an advance on account to be repaid to the alimony-debtor from the revenue of the alimony-creditor's property or share of community upon liquidation thereof. (Cassation, January 7, 1890; *Dalloz,* 1891.1.256.) If, however, the alimony-creditor has no property, then the alimony is not a debt but a donation; namely, an irrecoverable and gratuitous contribution for support under article 212 of the Civil Code. If the wife's revenues collected by the husband are less than the alimony he is ordered to pay her, the husband can recover a *pro rata* amount only. The Court of Cassation, July 28, 1889 (*Dalloz,* 1890.1.421) held that a wife who has received a lump sum as paid-up temporary alimony must pay it back later if the revenues collected during the litigation by the husband from her property equaled or exceeded the alimony. The judgment or order awarding alimony, naturally, does not say in advance which character it is to have. This is determined by the outcome of the eventual liquidation of the property regime of the couple. Temporary alimony, in other words, is usually merely an advance from the husband to the wife to be charged against the revenues which he continues to derive from her property during the litigation. Temporary alimony settled by an agreement governed by French law would also be of this nature, in the absence of express clause to the contrary.

No express authority is found in the codes to award suit-money, *provision ad litem,* in matrimonial actions. Nevertheless, the power to award alimony is not the only power over financial matters given to the president or court. By implication there is deemed to be power to give suit-money. Some authorities consider that this is but a variety of alimony or consequence thereof. *Provision ad litem* is not the same as the legal aid or assistance which poor persons may secure. If legal aid is granted, suit-money will be awarded for unusual expenses only, that is to say for those expenses not covered by the aid. The amount of suit-money ordered will be set at a figure not only sufficient to pay attorney's fees according to schedule fixed by authority of law, but also the reasonable *honoraires* of counsel. The amount of suit-money is intended to cover the probable costs of the litigation without taking into account the expenses of an appeal. Supplements may be later obtained. Suit-money does not vary according to the fortune of the debtor, as does alimony. An important rule of practice exists as to suit-money, namely, that this will be awarded only in advance of incurring the expenses, not to reimburse past expenses. (Paris, February 22, 1864; *Sirey,* 1864.2.223.) This rule was applied to deny suit-money in a case in which divorce was pronounced *de plano* for adultery. (Seine, March

15, 1887; *Journal des Avoués,* 1887, p. 227.) The case was ready for judgment on the merits when the application for suit-money was made. Since past expenses were not to be covered thereby and future expenses would be slight, no award was made and the judgment for divorce was pronounced. This case has been inexactly cited by certain authors for the proposition that in case the ground for divorce is a peremptory one, no suit-money is to be awarded. It does not really mean that. Furthermore, an award of suit-money cannot be made conditional upon the outcome of the trial. In some cases, suit-money has been granted to permit suit abroad, but in others the courts have declined to make an award. But in cases between aliens in which this has been declined, alimony has generally been granted sufficient in amount to enable the wife to reach her own courts, where it is inferred she could apply for suit-money.

Article 242 of the Civil Code mentions various conservatory measures in relation to the properties of the spouses which may be ordered at conciliation or later in the action. The article says the president acts subject to reference to the tribunal. The authors are not in entire harmony as to the meaning of this reference. The consensus of opinion is that the president's order does not have to be confirmed by the tribunal, but that the president may, if he desires, refer the matter to the tribunal for decision. It is, of course, entirely permissible for the parties to agree upon the inventory, appraisal and custody of their property for provisional purposes during the litigation although they are not at liberty thereby to change their marriage regime either directly or indirectly. The accord is subject to the control of the judge or court and may be changed by the judicial authorities for cause upon application of either party. If the parties do not settle these matters amicably the president or court will decide on a contested application. Thus, it is quite usual for the president at conciliation to appoint a notary to inventory the community property and the separate property of the wife in the husband's hands.

Wives married under the community regime often ask also at the outset of litigation that seals be affixed to the personalty of the community in order to prevent the husband from selling this without the consent of the wife or court. A wife married under a regime different from that of community may obtain the sealing up of personal property belonging to her which is under the husband's administration. Article 242, C. C., says that the seals may be removed only after an inventory and appraisal has taken place, whereupon the holder of the property becomes *ipso facto* judicial custodian thereof. Nevertheless, a husband when he so becomes custodian does not have to give bond. It is also possible for good cause to have the seals continued after inventory.

It is sometimes possible to obtain an order requiring the deposit of securities in which the litigants are interested with the public custodian (*caisse des dépôts et consignations*), but this will not always be granted, because it is the general rule that a husband is not to be deprived even temporarily of the administration of property, which he is entitled to conduct in virtue of the law or marriage contract.

During the taking of the inventory by the notary it not infrequently happens that evidence of importance to the action is found. If letters are discovered, the president will delegate a justice of the peace to read them and to include in the inventory those only which relate to the property affairs of the couple. Compromising letters or papers affecting the merits of the action will not usually be returned to the husband as head of the community, but will be placed in the hands of a receiver who will produce them at the trial if the court so orders.

It is a difficult question to answer under what circumstances a receiver (*sequestre*) can be obtained to take custody *pendente lite* of community property or of separate property of the wife over which the husband has administration and control. Article 1961 of the Civil Code enumerates the cases in which a receiver may be appointed, and it does not mention that this may be done during or by reason of an action for divorce or separation. In consequence it has been held by the highest court that a husband cannot be deprived of administration of community property in favor of a receiver. (Cassation, March 26, 1889; *Sirey,* 1890.1.253.) Nevertheless, under exceptional circumstances this has been done. These cases are based upon the doctrine that apart from the enumeration of article 1961, C. C., there is implied power in the courts to name a receiver. For instance, a third person has been appointed receiver in order to ensure the payment of alimony and suit-money. (Douai, April 6, 1853; *Sirey,* 1855.2.714.) The courts will more readily appoint the husband than a stranger receiver of the community property, since this will make him responsible to the court without obstructing his administration. Likewise, a wife married under a community regime may be made receiver of her separate property, but this is less easy to obtain because the measure deprives the husband of his right of administration in favor of the wife. It should be remembered that under the *régime dotal* (dower system) the husband administers the wife's *dot,* but she administers her own *paraphernal* property. The separate property of the wife is administered by the husband in the community regimes. In the regime of separation of property there is no occasion for a receiver unless a husband in fact administers the wife's property by authority of marriage contract or power of attorney. In lieu of receivership, the wife can sometimes obtain an order requiring the husband to give bond.

Can the wife or husband as a conservatory measure require that a community business be sold to keep it from being ruined during the litigation? It seems that this can be ordered when the poor management of the husband is leading to great depreciation in value of the business. Alternatively, a receiver could be appointed to conduct it. Can a husband or wife sell a community business during the litigation without the consent of the court or other party? It has been held that the husband during a separation action cannot sell a community business without the wife's consent. (Rennes, July 3, 1841; *Sirey*, 1841.2. 548.) The attitude of French law is that the principal or capital of the community ought to remain in *statu quo* during the litigation so far as is reasonably possible, while yet the freedom of administration is to be preserved. This attitude is dictated by the fact that in property matters between the spouses article 252, C. C., provides that the judgment of divorce shall operate retroactively to the date at which suit was begun, namely, to the date of service of the citation for conciliation. Nevertheless, there is no absolute provision preventing all alienations, but only a provision rendering certain alienations voidable at the request of the wife if made during the suit in fraud of her rights. (Article 243, C. C.) The courts will not issue a general injunction restraining *pendente lite* the husband from selling or disposing of property under his control, but they will entertain, even before judgment of divorce or separation and regardless of the outcome of the principal action, a separate action to annul fraudulent conveyances.

In order to secure the rights of the wife pending liquidation of the regime and to prevent fraudulent alienations by the husband, it is possible for the wife to levy an attachment upon property in the hands of third parties but accessible to the husband, or in the hands of the husband. An attachment may be ordered notwithstanding the fact that this measure interferes with the husband's right to administer the property. (Cassation, March 14, 1855; *Sirey,* 1856.1.655.) A receiver may be appointed to administer the attached property. (Seine, January 29, 1889; *Le Droit,* February 8, 1889.) Nevertheless, no attachment will be ordered or continued if property already still under seal has been inventoried and appraised at an amount sufficient to pay the wife her share of the community property or her separate property upon the eventual liquidation. (Paris, March 2, 1886; *Sirey,* 1886.2.161.)

The power to award provisional remedies is not limited to the foregoing. It is sufficiently broad to do full justice between the parties, whatever may be necessary. It is to be noted, however, that there is no order or judgment in France which corresponds to the writ of the *ne exeat regno.* The French courts will not hesitate to order personal acts to be done by an order equivalent to a mandatory injunction but enforceable by exemplary damages not by imprisonment for contempt in case of violation. They are not limited to forbidding the doing of acts.

Concerning the relation of these provisional remedies to aliens, the legal situation is unsettled. Several of these remedies relate to French public order. For example, this is true of the support of persons physically in the country, of the disposal of French realty or business, and of the custody of children in France. Article 3 of the Civil Code makes French law apply expressly to realty in the country. Article 3, C. C., also states: "Laws of police and public order are binding upon all those who inhabit the territory." It would seem, therefore, that *lex fori* would be applied to the exclusion of *lex nationalis* in relation to several, if not to most, of the provisional remedies. A foreign law which differed from the French in regard to public order or morality would be disregarded. A provision of foreign law which "could compromise the general interest of the French state" would be contrary to French public policy. (Lyon, December 22, 1911; *Journal Clunet,* 1912, p. 508.) According to Pérraud in a note to this judgment, a foreign law will be contrary to French public policy when "there is between the foreign legislation and the French legislation an absolute and decided difference upon points which affect characteristic institutions of French civilization or public morality such as it is commonly and presently understood." (P. 513.) Nevertheless, so far as a foreign law does not violate French public policy, it will be allowed sole or concurrent voice with French law over aliens and their families and personal property in the French Republic. To illustrate these principles, it has been held in a separation action between Italians that Italian law is to be applied with French to decide which parent should be awarded provisional custody of the children. (Cassation, December 26, 1917; *Journal Clunet,* 1918, p. 714.) But French law, not American or Turkish, was applied to decide custody in an action between an American wife and her Turkish husband. The court awarded the children *pendente lite* to the wife, not to the husband who was entitled thereto by Turkish law. (Seine, November 29, 1904; *Journal Clunet,* 1905, p. 187.) In relation to suit-money, French law alone is to be considered. (Paris, February 3, 1892; *Journal Clunet,* 1892, p. 1020.)

Needless to say, a French court does not on these accessory matters go out of its way to apply foreign law. A prayer to have foreign law applied would have to be expressly made by a party. Since in the United States parents have joint custody of the children, this fact might be usefully invoked in France by an American wife to support her claim to custody. Since also an American wife has a wider latitude than a French wife in reference to separate residence or domicile, this might be used as an argument to induce the president to allow an alien wife wider latitude than would be allowed a French wife in selecting a place in which to live during suit; also it might be used to found a claim to separate domicile. Nevertheless, a British or American wife, under a system of separation of property, could not require the sealing up, attachment or receivership of her husband's property unless she could show that she had an interest therein or that her property was confused with her husband's. Since such a wife is legally entitled to collect her own income from her separate property, she would not so often as would a French wife be in a position to require temporary alimony.

Chapter XXI

PREPARATORY PROCEDURE

The president's order signed at the close of the conciliation hearing permits the plaintiff to sue defendant for divorce or separation, unless leave to do so has perchance been refused. The plaintiff is supposed by article 238 of the Civil Code to bring suit within twenty days thereafter, but the only result of failure to do so is that the provisional remedies *ipso facto* lapse. The writ (*ajournement*) which begins the action may be served thereafter, yet the provisional remedies do not thereby *ipso facto* revive. A new order is required to reinstate them. The twenty day provision of article 238, C. C., has no application to provisional measures given when suit for the principal relief must be instituted abroad. (Douai, January 4, 1888; *Jurisprudence de la Cour d'Appel de Douai,* vol. 46, p. 249.) After the conciliation hearing the procedure in matrimonial actions is practically the same as that in other actions. (Article 239, C. C.)

The *ajournement* is a writ of summons to attend before the tribunal which is combined with a statement of claim or complaint. It is a variety of *assignation.* It usually repeats *verbatim* the petition, but it may, however, change or enlarge the same without departing from the grounds alleged. The necessary contents of this instrument are set forth in article 61, C. C. P., as follows: (1) The date, the names, profession and domicile of plaintiff, the name of his attorney-at-law, and the office address at which he elects domicile; (2) the name, dwelling place and license number of the bailiff, the name and dwelling place of the defendant and the name of the person with whom process was left for defendant; (3) the nature of the relief prayed and a "summary exposition" of the allegations (*moyens*); (4) the tribunal and return day. If any one of these is lacking or insufficient the *ajournement* is void. For example, the plaintiff's real domicile must be stated; the party's name with the words "living in London" are insufficient, and the election of the domicile at the attorney's office does not add thereto the necessary information for defendant. (Seine, December 9, 1886; *Journal Clunet,* 1887, p. 312.) The *avoué* of plaintiff signs the *ajournement* and selects the bailiff to serve this process, no particular bailiff being indicated by the president, as was necessary for service of the citation. A copy of the president's "non-conciliation order" is ordinarily served with the *ajournement,* but it may be served separately.

The allegations of the cause of action in the *ajournement* are not required to conform to any set style of pleading. They are presented in more or less narrative form, and not as a series of counts or paragraphs in numbered sequence. The papers are not printed, but may be typewritten or may be in longhand. The pleading usually sets forth the facts and then concludes that these warrant divorce or separation on one or more grounds of the Code. A plaintiff cannot pray for divorce or separation in the alternative, nor subsidiarily for separation if divorce be not granted. It has, nevertheless, been held that in the case of aliens lacking capacity or liability to divorce, a prayer for divorce is to be deemed a prayer for separation, the greater containing the lesser. (Colmar, April 7, 1915; *Journal Clunet,* 1926, p. 74.) Ordinarily, however, no such rule obtains. No conditional prayer is permissible.

Wide latitude is given to amend the pleadings during the action. Thus, according to article 239, C. C., the plaintiff may at any time change his prayer from divorce to separation, but not from separation to divorce. It has been decided, however, that a husband who started suit for separation thinking he was a Spaniard, and hence unable to divorce, might change to divorce when he found he was French. (Paris, May 27, 1915; *Journal Clunet,* 1919, p. 1064.) The plaintiff may add to his *demande* (complaint) allegations of fact of the same general nature as those already alleged, but cannot add other grounds. Additional grounds and different sets of facts could be presented nevertheless in another action and then the two actions could be consolidated.

Concerning joinder of causes of action, it is not possible to sue simultaneously for divorce and separation, but an action for annulment may be combined with either and will be decided first. An action for *séparation de biens* may be combined with a divorce or separation action. An action for damages under article 1382 of the Civil Code, by reason of loss of the marriage, namely, breach of marriage viewed as a contract, may be joined with a divorce action, even when alimony is also asked under article 301, C. C. It is possible to unite with a divorce action a cause of action for damages for maladministration by the wife of a business owned by the husband. (Caen, January 30, 1918; *Recueil Caen,* 1919, p. 59.) An action for damages for libel may be joined with one for divorce growing out of it. (Cassation, February 20, 1912; *Le Droit*, March 16, 1912.)

The question of parties plaintiff and defendant has been treated earlier. Suffice it here to mention that there is no joinder of an accomplice as co-respondent, though such person can intervene to protect his good name.

When the action is started, the plaintiff's attorney is required to notify the district attorney's office, as provided in article 239 of the Civil Code. This is in harmony with the general rule expressed in article 83 of the Code of Civil Procedure that in all litigation concerning status the district attorney must be informed and heard.

The *ajournement* calls upon defendant to enter an appearance within eight days plus the distance periods from the date of service. The defendant must make his own computation of the time, service being complete when the process is served personally or by substitution in France, as indicated in the Code of Civil Procedure. In the case of an alien or Frenchman served at the *parquet,* the service dates from the time process reached the district's attorney's office, not that at which it reached the defendant through the consulate.

In order to appear, the defendant gives a special power of attorney to an *avoué* practicing before the particular tribunal, authorizing him to conduct the case and electing domicile at his office. The power need not be notarial, but it must be special not a general authority to conduct any and all litigation. The election of domicile is not a submission to the jurisdiction, for the jurisdictional objection if duly presented at conciliation may be raised by answer. It is not necessary to limit the power to a special appearance to contest the jurisdiction, nor is it customary or proper to do so. The giving of an unrestricted power is not a waiver of the jurisdictional objection.

The defendant's attorney informs the plaintiff's by written notice that he has been retained and files the power with the clerk of the tribunal. The notice to the plaintiff's attorney constitutes the appearance. (Article 75, C. C. P.) The recording of the power is not the appearance and has no effect if the notice to the attorney has not been given. The recording of the power is not a waiver of objection to the jurisdiction. It is not necessary to mention procedural or jurisdictional objections in the notice in order to preserve them.

In a divorce action, if the defendant fails to appear and was not personally served with the process in France, the tribunal before entering judgment by default against him may, and usually will, order publication of a notice in the press intended to acquaint defendant with the existence of the suit. (Article 247, C. C.) However, no duty has been imposed by law upon the court to render such an order and the provision does not apply to suits for separation. This publication measure is not a system of service of process by publication, but is a publication of notice regarding pendency of action. The notice need not reproduce or summarize the terms of the *ajournement* nor even say that the suit is for divorce. In fact the notice is supposed to be phrased discreetly, in order that the public shall not know the nature of the litigation. The court in its discretion selects the newspapers, number of papers and insertions. The notice is not usually published in the *Journal Officiel,* nor in the *Bulletin des Annonces légales.* The judgment which orders this publicity is probably not subject to appeal by plaintiff, and failure to require publicity is not an objection to the judgment of divorce or separation.

After appearance the defendant has fifteen days in which to serve an answer and to file this with the clerk of the court. (Article 77, C. C. P.) All papers after appearance are served upon the attorney, but judgments must be served both upon the party and his attorney. Apart from this *réponse* (answer) there is no separate pleading such as a common law demurrer or a motion in lieu of demurrer, nor is there a system of summons before a master for directions as in modern British practice. The answer in French law comprises issues raised by the common law demurrers, pleas in abatement, dilatory pleas, pleas to the merits or traverses and denials, and also counterclaims. Several defenses are called *exceptions* and resemble in some ways demurrers or special pleas. (Articles 166 to 192, C. C. P.) An *exception* in French law is not the reservation of an objection to a ruling of the court. It is a part of the *résponse,* but must precede any plea to the merits or any counterclaim.

Exceptions are of three sorts: *fins de non-procéder,* such as lack of jurisdiction, copendency of action and *connexité* (*i.e.,* necessity of consolidation); (2) *fins de nonrecevoir,* such as lack of necessary character or capacity to sue, limitation and abandonment of action; (3) *fins de nullité,* such as illegality of proceedings. A distinction is made in terminology between defenses which lead to the extinction of the action and those which merely delay it or which lead to annulment of steps of procedure. Thus, exceptions are either peremptory or dilatory. Defenses to the merits are called *moyens.* The Civil Code, however, sometimes confuses *exceptions* and *moyens.*

Perhaps it would be well, at this point, to mention that there are three ways in which jurisdiction or venue may be contested by answer: (1) by *déclinatoire,* (*i.e.,* by *exception* in the answer) followed by appeal to the court of appeal in case the tribunal rejects the objection and by petition for review to the Court of Cassation in case the court of appeal does not sustain the *exception;* (2) by *déclinatoire,* followed by a petition to the Court of Cassation *"en indication de juges"* (*i.e.,* to indicate the proper judges) under the ordinance of August, 1737; (3) by *déclinatoire,* followed by suit before another tribunal and application to the common court of appeal or Court of Cassation for *"règlement de juges"* (*i.e.,* to choose between the judges) under article 363, C. C. P. (Note under Cassation, June 1, 1891; *Sirey,* 1891.1.29.)

Exceptions to the jurisdiction or venue must be decided summarily before the merits and sometimes must be decided by judgment separate from that on the merits. (Article 172, C. C. P.) An objection as to competence may be raised at any stage by application to the court. (Article 170, C. C. P.) Exceptions and pleas to the merits may be combined in the answer, but care must be taken to raise them in a certain order and to state that the merits are contested only conditionally and on the hypothesis that the *exceptions* shall not be sustained. An *exception* to the jurisdiction or venue must be stated before any other exception or defense. (Article 169, C. C. P.) Various sorts of *exceptions* may be interposed: for example, to require the plaintiff to provide security for costs (article 166, C. C. P.); to contest the jurisdiction or venue (article 168, C. C. P.); to obtain consolidation with another action or to obtain dismissal for copendency of another action (article 171, C. C. P.); to obtain the annulment of the procedure for illegality (article 173, C. C. P.); to obtain inspection of documents in the opponent's possession which he intends to use in evidence (article 188, C. C. P.).

Some exceptions can be interposed only by the parties. *Res judicata* is a defense that can be invoked only by a principal party, not by the district attorney or the court itself, for no question of public order is involved. Other exceptions, e. g., lack of competence, may be interposed by the parties or *ex officio* by the judicial authorities.

Mention should be made that a bare traverse or denial in an answer of plaintiff's allegations is not always sufficient in French law to place these in issue and to compel plaintiff to prove them. The denial must be explained by defendant, by stating what are the true facts. For example, an allegation of adultery *flagrante delicto,* supported by evidence of a police report, is not put in issue by a mere denial which is unaccompanied by a prayer for leave to falsify the report. This was the decision in the Gould case.

A defendant in his answer to a divorce action may counterclaim either for divorce or for separation (article 239, C. C.), or indeed for annulment of marriage, but no counterclaim asking for a divorce can be made in an action for separation. A counterclaim may be interposed by *conclusion* (notice) of one attorney to the other at any stage of the proceedings before the tribunal or on appeal before the court of appeal (article 248, C. C.), but not when the case is before the Court of Cassation. Different suits for divorce or separation may be copending between the two parties, or a suit for separation may be brought by one and one for divorce by the other. Unless consolidated, these various actions may be tried separately. Each party may win or lose, as a French court can at the same time award divorce to both or divorce to one and separation to the other or relief to neither.

Article 78 of the Code of Civil Procedure allows a plaintiff eight days after service of the answer in which to reply if he so desires. After expiration of the time to reply either side may serve notice of trial. (Article 80, C. C. P.) The case is put upon the trial calendar by the clerk forthwith after receipt of a *placet* (notice of trial) from the attorney of the diligent party. If the defendant fails to serve an answer in due season the plaintiff may without further delay serve a notice of trial. (Article 79, C. C. P.)

Usually a considerable time elapses in contested divorce or separation actions after a reply and before a notice of trial is served. In the interval there are a number of incidental proceedings to be conducted preparatory to trial. But if three years pass between steps in the litigation, the action may be dismissed upon application of the diligent side. (Article 397, C. C. P.) Laches *pé-*

remption) cannot be waived or renounced by stipulation in advance, but can be waived after they have occurred. If the non-diligent side makes a move in the action before the application is made, the laches are cured or effaced and the case can no longer be dismissed for lack of diligence.

The various incidents of the proceedings are settled by orders (*ordonnances*) of the president or judgments of the tribunal. Judgments are either preliminary, preparatory, interlocutory or definitive. Preliminary judgments are those rendered to protect the person or property of the parties during the proceedings. Preparatory judgments are those which advance the solution of the controversy, e. g., which order an *enquête* (inquiry). An interlocutory judgment decides the case or issue subject to some condition; e. g., unless the parties become reconciled within six months divorce will be granted to the plaintiff. Such judgment is later followed by a definitive judgment. "*L'interlocutoire ne lie pas le juge*" (*i.e.*, the interlocutory does not bind the judge), is a French maxim. It means that the court is not bound to decide the case along the lines indicated by an interlocutory judgment, but the eventual result is forecast unless the court changes its mind. A definitive judgment passes upon the merits of the case or of some decisive issue; it is absolute. The word definitive (*définitif*) in this relation does not signify final, although the same French word means final in the French sense. Final in the English and French senses are not quite the same thing, as will be seen later.

The exceptions tending to oust the jurisdiction or to delay the case are decided by the tribunal at a special hearing before the merits of the case are tried and before notice of trial is given. (Article 172, C. C. P.) *Cautio judicatum solvi* (*i.e.*, security for costs) must be asked by *exception* but it is a matter usually taken up for decision at a special hearing. Article 16 of the Civil Code imposes the duty upon an alien plaintiff litigating against a French defendant to give security, but this does not apply to an action between two aliens. An alien owning sufficient land in France is not required to give bond. No amount is fixed by law for security; the court in its discretion sets a figure.

Before notice of trial is given, any written evidence intended to be used at the trial must be discovered to the other side as required by article 188 of the Code of Civil Procedure. The documents are either delivered by one attorney to the other or are left with the clerk of the court for inspection at the court house only. An order may be procured for the production and inspection of specific written evidence in the other side's possession which has not been voluntarily disclosed and which the opponent does not intend to use in the case. (Cassation, June 17, 1879; *Dalloz,* 1880.1.427.) The maxim *nemo tenetur edere contra se* is not an obstacle to compulsory discovery. If the evidence is in the hands of a third person an action *ad exhibendum* will lie.

Pleadings may be amended before trial by mere notice of one attorney to the other. If the amendments are deemed objectionable by the other side, the matter is taken before the president. Most of these incidental matters are settled informally between the two *avoués* for the parties. Particulars may be required and non-pertinent allegations struck out on application with notice, although neither is often required or granted since the pleadings are not subject to strict rules as to form or contents.

It is necessary, however, to apply to the tribunal for a preparatory judgment in order to be able to take testimony. If oral evidence is considered necessary by the party's *avocat,* the facts which the party desires to prove are stated in a *conclusion* (notice) served by his *avoué* upon the other side. (Article 252, C. C. P.) The facts alleged must be admitted or denied within three days. If the facts are relevant and decisive and are denied and the law does not forbid the evidence, then the court in its discretion may authorize proof thereof to be taken by deposition upon commission. (Article 253, C. C. P.) The court can also of its own motion order an *enquête* (inquiry). (Article 254, C. C. P.) Proof is required or allowed only of facts which the court indicates, and not of facts which are neither alleged (*articulés*) by the parties nor indicated (*retenus*) by the court. The facts to be proved must be concisely stated in the application for an order. A plaintiff will, nevertheless, be allowed to prove the actual facts if in his *demande* (complaint) he indicated the general nature of the offensive acts and the period of time within which they occurred, even though he did not set forth therein the details nor fix the exact dates. (Rennes, February 4, 1813, cited by Carpentier, *Divorce et séparation de corps,* 1899, vol. 1, sec. 2456.)

According to article 255 of the Code of Civil Procedure, the court appoints a judge of its own bench to act as commissioner to conduct the inquiry. This is held privately at the commissioner's chambers in the presence of the parties and their attorneys. It is possible for the court to issue letters rogatory to another French court to conduct the inquiry. A French court will not delegate a foreign court to take testimony in a separation action, because the latter would not apply the French rules of *enquête*, which rules are mandatory, under penalty of illegality. (Jonzac, September 15, 1874; *Journal Clunet,* 1877, p. 44.) It has been held, however, that none of the French *enquête* rules are obligatory in the sense that a departure therefrom means *nullité* of the procedure; hence a *commission rogatoire* may be sent to Russia in a legitimacy action and the *enquête* held *ex parte* under Russian procedure is valid in France. (Douai, December 19, 1894; *Journal Clunet,* 1896, p. 581.) The Tribunal of the Seine, November 7, 1895, (*Journal Clunet,* 1896, p. 141) in a divorce action between two Americans issued letters rogatory to the French consul in San Francisco and required him to take testimony there within six months. Ordinarily, however, the inquiry is to begin within eight days following the judgment which authorizes the taking of the testimony. (Article 257, C. C. P.) The tribunal in its judgment or the judge commissioned to conduct the inquiry sets the date of the hearing. Without good cause the proceedings should not be adjourned after they have once been begun and should not be adjourned at all beyond eight days without court order. (Article 278, C. C. P.) A writ of subpoena is theoretically still available to compel the attendance of a witness, but in practice arrest of the person in civil causes is never resorted to since the repeal of articles 126 and 127 C. C. P. in 1867. A fine of one hundred francs only is imposed for non-attendance. Consequently if a witness does not desire to testify, there is no effective way to compel him to do so.

Bodington says this of the French manner of taking testimony: "Witnesses giving their testimony under *enquête* are expected to *parler d'abondance,* that is to narrate uninterruptedly the circumstances to which their evidence relates. In this narrative personal knowledge is intermingled with hearsay and opinion." (Bodington, French Law of Evidence, 1904, p. 2.) The judge may interrogate the witness and will put to the witness any questions which the parties may reasonably desire. (Article 273, C. C. P.) If a party objects to the pertinence of a question, the commissioner decides provisionally and without prejudice, and the party can renew the objection before the tribunal at trial. If the objection was not sustained by the commissioner but ought to have been, the question and answer will be disregarded by the tribunal. If the objection is erroneously sustained by the commissioner, and the testimony excluded, the tribunal may order the witness to be heard again. Article 276 of the Code of Civil Procedure says: "A party can neither interrupt the witness in his deposition, nor interrogate him directly." This, however, is not the practice in criminal prosecutions. "The elaborate machinery of examination-in-chief, cross-examination and reëxamination is unknown" in France and "the spectacle of counsel wrangling over the relevancy of particular documents or the admissibility of a particular question to a witness, and obtaining then and there the ruling of the judge, is one which is rarely, if ever, witnessed in a French court." (Bodington, p. 2.) A witness may not make use of written notes. (Article 271, C.C.P.) At the close of the testimony the deposition is read to the witness, is corrected and is signed by him. It is then joined with the other depositions, which, together with his report, are filed with the clerk of court by the commissioner.

Usually there cannot be two inquiries for the same party, but there may be one inquiry ordered at the request of a party and another ordered by the court of its own motion. Whenever an *enquête* is ordered, a *contre-enquête* (counter-inquiry) for the other side is of right. Another application and judgment, however, are required for this purpose. The counter-inquiry takes place separately from the inquiry and witnesses for the one party are not examined at an *enquête* held at the instance of the other unless called by both sides. The two inquiries cannot be conducted simultaneously. But a party who is both plaintiff on the claim and defendant on the counter-claim may conduct the *enquête* and *contre-enquête* at the same time. (Dijon, December 11, 1911; *Gazette des*

Tribunaux, March 13, 1912.) The facts established at the counter-inquiry cannot be controverted by testimony taken at a second inquiry, nor can an inquiry be adjourned until the nature of the testimony to be taken or actually taken at the counter-inquiry is disclosed. A summary inquiry held before the tribunal at the *audience* (trial) is void. (Colmar, April 22, 1807, cited by Carpentier, *Divorce et séparation de corps,* 1899, vol. I, sec. 2525.)

A special hearing before a commissioner is also held in case any written evidence is sought to be falsified or the identification of any signature or writing becomes necessary. Elaborate provisions for such proceedings are contained in articles 193 to 251 of the Code of Civil Procedure. When a party is to be interrogated (examined before trial) a procedure similar to that of *enquête* is followed. (Articles 324-336, C.C.P.)

When notice of trial is filed a case receives a calendar number and it comes up for trial when reached. A weekly and daily cause list is made. This is posted on the bulletin board of the court chamber and is inspected from day to day by the attorneys and counsellors. A convocation to attend the court, called an *avenir* is given by the one party to the other one day before the case will be reached. This notice calls upon the other side to file *conclusions* (points) of fact and of law.

Conclusions are set out in an instrument separate from the pleadings. The instrument is not a mere notice but resembles somewhat a short brief. It is a pleading in its nature. It is filed with the clerk. As soon as *conclusions* have been filed there is joinder of issue, *litis contestatio,* and the action is therefore a contested one no matter whether counsel argue at trial or not. The filing of an answer does not make the case contested, but the filing of *conclusions* does do so. Conclusions are the final claims and contentions of the litigants. They are not necessarily a repetition of the respective allegations or prayer in the complaint or answer. They may be different, broader or narrower than the contentions in the earlier pleadings, but they may not differ from them to the extent of enlarging the causes of action or defense or changing their nature. *Conclusions* may be amended as of right at any time before the court has declared the trial closed.

A distinction is drawn in French law between matters of procedure which relate to the substance of the action, the merits, and those which relate purely to form. Matters of procedure *qui faciunt ad litis decisionem* are governed by the law which applies to the merits, those *qui ordinationem litis rescipiciunt* are governed by *lex fori.* In other words, procedure *decisionae litis* in divorce and separation actions in France in the case of two aliens will be subject usually to *lex nationalis;* procedure *ordinationae litis* will be subject to French law. For reasons of public policy French law may, nevertheless, be exclusively applied in certain cases. Furthermore, the courts will apply French law unless a party suggests the applicability of foreign law. Possibly in some cases an attempt might be made to apply both legislations concurrently. Laches would be governed by French law. (Weiss, *Manuel de Droit International Privé,* 1914, p. 662.) Would this also be true of prescription? The manner of taking evidence in France will be governed by French law, since this is a matter of procedural form. (Weiss, *Manuel de Droit International Privé,* 1914, p. 664.) The Tribunal of the Seine, December 22, 1911 (*Journal Clunet,* 1912, p. 508) applied *lex nationalis* to the substance of procedure in relation to article 1575 of the German Civil Code. By this provision of German law a defendant when sued for separation and found guilty of conduct warranting this, has a right to require that divorce be pronounced against him instead of separation. No corresponding provision exists in French law. In an action for separation in France between two Germans, the defendant invoked article 1575 and the French tribunal accordingly in view of German law pronounced divorce notwithstanding plaintiff's prayer for separation and objection to divorce.

Chapter XXII

EVIDENCE

The burden of proof is upon the plaintiff to prove his cause of action, but the burden is also upon a defendant to prove his traverse or affirmative defense. A defendant cannot simply deny the allegation and sit idly by and yet require plaintiff to go forward with proof. A mere denial is considered frivolous, unless explained and justified. All *exceptions* require proof by the defendant. Thus, a defendant who sets up his legal freedom from liability to be divorced must prove it, for capacity, not incapacity, is presumed. (St. Etienne, February 4, 1891; *La Loi,* 1891, p. 214.) A French court, of its own initiative, requires an alien plaintiff to prove the foreign law on grounds. In relation to foreign defenses, the court applies French law unless one or the other party suggests the applicability of foreign law to the matter.

The Civil Code in articles 1315 to 1369 contains various rules of evidence in relation to proof of civil obligations and of payment. Several of these rules apply by analogy to controversies in which no question of contract or payment is involved. They relate, however, chiefly to the probative value of writings. They do not always apply in matrimonial actions. Rules requiring written evidence in certain circumstances do not prevent oral testimony on the aspects relevant to the divorce or separation action. For example, a will must be in writing but oral evidence is admissible of a pardon expressed in a will even if the will itself is not produced. A scarcity exists of texts on evidence in general in French law. Article 1353 of the Civil Code says *inter alia:*

Presumptions which are not established by law are left to the learning and prudence of the judge, who shall only admit presumptions which are serious, exact and consistent and in cases only in which the law allows oral evidence, unless an instrument is impeached for fraud or deceit.

This article practically means that all evidence in relation to which there is no written text of law is left to the judge to consider or to reject in his discretion. The word *présomptions* in this article means inferences or rebuttable presumptions, as any known fact may support a rebuttable presumption of another fact in French law. (Article 1349, C. C.) Irrebuttable presumptions *juris et jure*, such as *res judicata pro veritate habetur*, are mentioned in articles 1350 and 1352 of the Civil Code.

The preference of French law for written over oral evidence is striking. In the early history of French courts the maxim *témoins passent lettres* (*i.e.*, witnesses are superior to writings) prevailed, but in 1566 the *Ordonnance de Moulins* enacted a statute of frauds, now article 1341 of the Civil Code. Since that time oral evidence has come to be regarded adversely. A mere written statement of a third person is admissible as proof of a ground for divorce under article 1353, C. C., for what it is worth and without opportunity for cross examination. (Cassation, March 1, 1916; *Sirey*, 1919.1.39.) Consequently affidavits sworn by alien witnesses before a foreign notary or before a consul abroad will be received in evidence in France.

Many actions of divorce and separation go to trial without the hearing of a single witness. In fact witnesses are not heard at all in any action unless an application is made to the court and preparatory judgment is rendered ordering the taking of testimony on commission, by *enquête*. Article 253 of the Code of Civil Procedure states that an inquiry may be held "if the facts are admissible, are denied and the law does not forbid the proof." But the court will not order an inquiry unless it considers that the facts if proved will be conclusive and will control the outcome of the action. The tribunal can refuse to order an *enquête* either because the facts are not pertinent or are not sufficiently grave, though pertinent. (Cassation, March 1, 1918; *Sirey,* 1919.1.21.) Furthermore, a fact of adultery mentioned by a witness but not alleged in the *assignation* (complaint) cannot be invoked by plaintiff. (Cassation, January 10, 1911; *Sirey,* 1911.1.223.) Facts not alleged in the complaint cannot be set up as grounds for relief but may be considered in evidence to establish the gravity of the grounds already alleged. (Piérard, vol. 1, Sec. 276, p. 539.)

Proof must be legally possible, else no order to take testimony on the point will be made. For instance, an offer to prove unnatural acts alleged to have been committed privately by defendant upon plaintiff was not considered sufficient basis for an *enquête* because such acts leave no trace and it was not suggested that they were witnessed by others or that conversations concerning them were overheard. (Orleans, March 4, 1903; *Dalloz,* 1903. 2.67.)

The civil law of evidence is by no means so highly developed as is the common law. For instance, according to Bodington, under the head of relevancy one would search the codes in vain for a provision excluding "hearsay" or "opinion" evidence or "evidence as to character" (Bodington, p. 2). This statement is perhaps somewhat too broad. It has been held that the mere repetition by a witness of what he heard a party say is not available as proof. (Dijon, January 6, 1913; *Recueil Dijon,* 1913, p. 22; *Recueil des Sommaires,* 1913, no. 4468.) Yet, it has been also decided that a witness may repeat what someone else told him and that such indirect or hearsay evidence is admissible for what it is worth (Pau, January 3, 1893; *Gazette des Tribunaux,* January 4, 1893.)

Certain persons are not competent witnesses in French law. A child under fifteen can testify but is not sworn. Article 268 of the Code of Civil Procedure says no person can be a witness who is a relative in direct line by blood or marriage to one of the parties or to his spouse, even if divorced. In divorce and separation actions this rule is slightly different, for article 245, C. C., permits blood relatives except descendants and servants to testify. The incompetency extends however to sons and daughters-in-law. (Caen, May 4, 1910; *Dalloz,* 1911.2.232.) Letters written by persons who are incompetent to be witnesses, e.g., children of the parties, are inadmissible in evidence.

Article 283, C. C. P., as limited by article 245 of the Civil Code, provides also for the possible challenge and exclusion of various classes of witnesses, namely of certain blood relatives and relatives by marriage, of the presumptive heir or donee of the party, of any person who has eaten or drunk with the party at his expense subsequent to the judgment which has ordered the *enquête,* of anyone who has given a certificate in regard to the facts in issue, of any person sentenced to a degrading and corporal punishment or to punishment for theft. A witness who is so challenged is heard at the inquiry in accordance with article 284, C. C. P., but the court later decides whether to retain or to strike out the testimony. A document injurious to a third person cannot be excluded on that account from evidence, but the name of such person will be ordered effaced from the record. (Paris, January 8, 1912; *Le Droit,* June 29, 1912.)

Expert evidence is available in France in a divorce or separation action. For example, a doctor may be appointed by the tribunal to examine the parties to determine whether the husband is impotent or the wife sterile.

(Douai, July 1, 1913; *Le Droit,* October 11, 1913.) Whether or not it is lawful to require a wife to submit to medical examination to determine her virginity has been decided both ways. (*Pro:* Douai, April 3, 1912; *Le Droit,* April 30, 1912; *Contra:* Limoges, July 30, 1911; *La Loi,* December 1, 1911.)

Expert evidence regarding foreign law is given by written *certificat de coutume* (*i.e.,* certificate of foreign law) signed by a member of the bar of the country whose law is to be proved and whose membership therein is certified and his signature authenticated by his consulate in France. Members of the bar of any American state or members of the federal bar, are allowed to certify as to the law in all the states, because numerous states are unrepresented in France by persons who are members of their respective bars. Such certificates are susceptible of rebuttal by contrary certificates from other lawyers. In some actions numerous certificates are submitted on both sides. Unfortunately some American lawyers are not careful in drafting certificates. Certificates which are incomplete expositions of American law are not unknown. Certificates are usually extremely short and are general statements of law, not specific statements addressed to the facts of the case in which they are to be used; consequently they are peculiarly susceptible to wording in an ambiguous manner. As a means of proving foreign law they are unreliable and the French practice of accepting them as evidence without cross examination is subject to criticism.

A certificate of custom will be required to show what are the foreign grounds and defenses, etc., and to show that a foreign judgment is valid in the country where rendered.

Under article 1358 of the Civil Code there is a survival in France of ordeal by oath; that is to say one party is at liberty solemnly to call upon the other to swear to the truth or falsity of a decisive allegation. The reply will bind both parties. (Article 1363, C. C.) It seems, however, that this decisive oath cannot be required in divorce or separation actions. (Grenoble, July 19, 1838; *Sirey,* 1839.2.415.) Nor can the court of its own motion require a party under article 1366, C. C., to take a so-called supplemental oath (*serment supplétif*) of a similar nature. A party may none the less be compelled to answer interrogatories. (Rouen, February 23, 1891; *Jurisprudence de la Cour d'Appel de Rouen et de Caen,* 1891, p. 221.)

Formerly admissions were not considered admissible evidence in matrimonial causes, by reason of the maxim *nemo propriam turpitudinem allegans auditur.* This is no longer law. The Court of Cassation, April 29, 1862 (*Sirey,* 1862.1.945) held that an admission of adultery on the part of a defendant in a separation action, although insufficient of itself to prove the reality of the facts alleged, might nevertheless be taken under advisement by the court and might render an inquiry unnecessary, particularly when the admission was not entirely voluntary and was corroborated by other facts already established in evidence. The rule, therefore, appears now to be that an admission is evidence but requires corroboration. Admissions must usually be taken as a whole. It has been held, nevertheless, that when, before a police officer, a wife admitted adultery but at the same time said that her husband knew of and tolerated the offense, the qualification might be disregarded though the fact of adultery would be deemed established. (Seine, May 28, 1891; *Le Droit,* June 15 and 16, 1891.) An admission of adultery by the husband and also by his accomplice, would be held to suffice for establishing the offense.

Letters addressed to the parties by third persons and letters written by the parties to each other may serve as evidence of any of the grounds of divorce or separation save that of penal condemnation, for which a certified copy of the judgment is required. Letters, however, are inadmissible in evidence if illegally procured. For instance, letters obtained by fraud or violence will be excluded by the court. If a letter belongs to a third person, it cannot be produced by the party who holds it without his consent. There is a wide divergence of views as to who in the law owns or controls a letter. Three principal opinions obtain: (1) that the letter belongs without restriction to the sender; (2) that it belongs to the receiver; and (3) that the sender retains a veto power over the use of the letter if it is confidential. The weight of authority seems to favor the second view. A husband has somewhat of an advantage in respect to securing letters because he is the head of the family. In view of this fact it has been held that he may lawfully intercept letters written to his wife. (Tarbes, December 14, 1892; *Gazette des Tribunaux,* March 18, 1893.) But a wife cannot introduce in evidence a letter written by her husband which she took from a servant who was about to mail it. (Rouen, November 13, 1878; *Sirey,* 1879.2.80.) To piece together torn letters found by the wife in a waste basket is not a fraudulent acquisition and such letters may be used against the husband. (Paris, January 20, 1897; *Le Droit,* February 24, 1897.) This will be the case also when the wife finds the letter in an unsealed envelope in her husband's clothes hung up in a closet. (Cassation, March 25, 1890; *Sirey,* 1890.1.168.) Even a collection of copies of letters sent and received by the husband may be used in evidence, provided they fell accidentally into the wife's hands, but copies are always viewed by the courts with considerable reserve.

No special rules of evidence exist as to proof of violence, cruelty and gross insults. Adultery may be proved either by written or by oral evidence. Presumptions or inferences may be invoked, since circumstantial evidence to prove adultery is not objectionable. No third person need have actually seen the act of misconduct committed. A criminal judgment of conviction for adultery in a prosecution which was defended will be considered conclusive evidence of guilt in a civil action for divorce or separation. An acquittal will be conclusive proof of innocence in the case of the wife, but not of the husband, since in his case to be criminally punishable the adultery must have been accompanied by introducing the concubine within the home, while the qualification is not necessary for the civil liability. The penal acquittal may have been due to absence of aggravation. A police report that defendant was found in adultery *flagrante delicto* by the police officer and two witnesses will be considered conclusive proof. A person charged may contest the veracity of a police report by bringing a special proceeding called *inscription de faux* under article 1319 of the Civil Code, which is the only proceeding available to correct errors in authentic instruments. A police report with two witnesses obtained even when a police commissioner acted *ultra vires,* because the adultery was not committed in the home, is admissible if it was not obtained by violently breaking into a house. (Caen, December 31, 1889; *Dalloz,* 1891.2.280.)

Article 194 of the Civil Code states that no person can lay claim to being a husband or wife unless he or she can produce an extract from the register of civil status mentioning the marriage solemnization. This article applies wherever one party is French, for even foreign marriages of Frenchmen or women are necessarily recorded in France under article 171, C. C., within three months after their return to France. Article 194, C. C., does not apply to two aliens. In their case evidence sufficient by their national law or *lex loci celebrationis* will suffice as proof of marriage. Even a common law marriage of the state of New York has been sustained in France. (Seine, January 17, 1924; *Journal Clunet,* 1925, p. 401.)

It should be borne in mind that it is not necessary in France to submit proof of every allegation in the complaint or defense. Allegations not contradicted are deemed admitted. This usually obviates the need of establishing a *prima facie* case or of submitting corroborative evidence, save in matters of adultery. All that is necessary is to convince the court that the allegations are well founded, and this is frequently accomplished simply by argument of counsel based upon a few letters or on the pleadings. Proof cannot be established by investigations made by the judge of his own initiative out of court. The report of an inquiry held in an action for separation which was terminated by a reconciliation is admissible in evidence in a second action based upon the old and also upon new facts. (Paris, June 19, 1839; *Sirey,* 1839.2.370.)

Whereas the manner of taking evidence is a matter of form governed by *lex fori,* evidence *per se* is, according to the French rules on the conflict of laws, a matter of substance in the litigation. Consequently in a divorce action between aliens the rules of evidence to be applied are those of *lex nationalis.* (Weiss, *Manuel de Droit International Privé,* 1914, p. 662.) In practice, however, French rules of evidence are applied, because foreign rules are almost never invoked. It would be indeed a rash American or British litigant who would try to induce a French court to apply the common law rules of evidence. Nevertheless *lex nationalis* may be, and on occasion is, invoked in relation to evidence. The Court of Cassation, October 30, 1905 (*Journal Clunet,* 1906, p. 410), held that the manner of proving the religion of an alien whose capacity to divorce in his national law depends upon his faith, is to be determined in France by the foreign law. In Austria, a Jewish wife can sue for divorce but a Catholic wife cannot. Faith is indicated by the entry of one's name upon a special register established by law for each creed. An Austrian Catholic, who alleged conversion to Judaism but could not supply an extract from the Hebrew register showing entry of the name, was denied the right to sue in France. In the Knibloe case, an affidavit of defendant made before the United States consul in France was admitted in evidence to help establish the fact of domicile in New York, although proof by affidavit is not known to French law. It was supposed by the court to be proof under American law. (Havre, November 17, 1923; *Journal Clunet,* 1924, p. 1000.) The Tribunal of the Seine, June 5, 1891 (*Journal Clunet,* 1892, p. 194), declined to allow proof of the offensive acts alleged in an action between two Russian Jews, although defendant had waived objection to the jurisdiction, because Russian law allowed divorce only for adultery, impotence, sterility and loss of civil rights, whereas the facts alleged did not fall within these grounds, and hence were irrelevant and inadmissible.

Chapter XXIII

TRIAL

Until 1927 in divorce and separation actions of aliens in Paris it was the practice for the *avocats* to waive *audience,* that is to say, the case was not argued in open court when reached on the calendar. Counsel for both parties agreed upon a draft judgment which they submitted informally with the papers to the president. The three judges then passed upon the case in chambers and usually granted the judgment as desired. This is still the practice in Paris so far as French parties are concerned and it saves a great deal of time since the calendar is congested. "Consequently, in the large majority of cases which come before the French Civil Courts, the trial of the case consists merely of the arguments of counsel on either side, followed by the argument of the *Procureur de la République,* no witnesses are heard, the *dossiers* of either party, consisting of the documents of procedure and the documents of proof produced by them, are handed in to the court, and it is upon these documents that the court forms its opinion of the case and delivers its judgment." (Bodington, p. 6.)

Mention has been made that both plaintiff and defendant are required to file a pleading called *conclusions* (points) before the *audience* (trial). If the plaintiff or defendant fails to do so he defaults. Consequently there are two kinds of defaults in French law, default for non-appearance and default for non-conclusion. (Article 149, C. C. P.) In both cases a default judgment will be rendered against the defaulting party. This will result from failure to file points, even though a defendant has appeared and answered and gone on with the case right up to the time to *conclure.* When both sides have given their conclusions there is joinder of issue, *litis contestatio,* and thereafter the case proceeds without default as a contested action even though counsel may refrain from attending trial or submitting evidence.

When the case is called the clerk reads aloud the conclusions of the parties. The tribunal can dispense with oral argument if it desires. If audience is not waived counsel for the plaintiff addresses the court and refers to the evidence, all of which is by that time in written form. He is followed by counsel for the defendant and by the district attorney. There is no requirement that the parties shall be present in person at the trial.

The reading of the conclusions and the oral arguments of counsel usually take place in open court, but in matrimonial actions article 239 of the Civil Code permits the court to order *huis clos,* secrecy of session. Trial is always before the court without a jury. No reference is made to a referee or master to hear and determine. Newspaper reports in divorce and separation actions are forbidden whether the trial be secret or open. The penalty for violation is a fine of from one hundred to two thousand francs, as set forth in the law of July 29, 1881. No printed briefs or records are used before the French courts, but usually a short manuscript analysis of the facts and law is prepared by counsel on a double sheet of paper, which is used as a cover for the written evidence of the party and which is read by the court when it considers the evidence in chambers.

At the close of the oral argument of counsel for the parties and the district attorney, the court declares the trial ended. It thereupon usually reserves decision and examines the papers in executive session. In a clear case a decision may be arrived at by the judges without leaving their seats. In a difficult case the court will instruct one of its members to prepare a report. A case is ordinarily discussed in chambers by the judges and a conclusion is reached as to the relief to be awarded. Special rules obtain as to how a decision shall be reached by the court when there is no majority, but only a plurality of the judges for a given solution. For instance, if there are three divergent solutions, the one rallying the fewest supporters is to be abandoned and the judges who voted for it must vote for one of the other two. (Article 117, C. C. P.) The youngest judge votes first. When no other way is open to secure a majority, an extra judge is called in who participates without having heard the trial. No dissenting opinions are rendered publicly and the vote of the judges is recorded only in the private minutes of the court. The judgment is in all cases read in open court by the president.

When the judges no longer require the *dossiers* (files), the documents are returned to the attorneys by the clerk. Practically all that remain on record in court are the judgments and minutes of the clerk. Consequently no certified copies of testimony or of pleadings can later be secured, the original papers being in the files of the respective attorneys.

Chapter XXIV

JUDGMENTS OF DIVORCE AND SEPARATION

French judgments are divided into three parts. The *qualités* (recitals) set forth the name of the court and number of the chamber which rendered the judgment, the date, names, occupations and dwelling places of the parties, the names of the attorneys and counsellors and the contentions and points of law and fact of the parties. (Article 141, C. C. P.) The attorney for the winning side prepares this part. It is settled by the president on notice, if the proposed text is not approved by the losing side, otherwise it is simply delivered to the clerk. The *motifs* (opinion) state the reasons of law and fact upon which the award is based. The president prepares the *motifs* without the intervention or control of the rest of the bench. Hence it sometimes happens that the reasons do not entirely harmonize with the result. "Sometimes a President whose views have not been followed by his court allows himself the artful satisfaction of so presenting the reasons for the judgment as will cause it to be reversed on appeal." (Foignet, *Manuel élémentaire de procédure civile*, 1912, note 12.) A French judgment is not an instrument upon which the entire court has necessarily passed; the *dispositif* only is the work of the court itself. The *dispositif* is the award. It is prepared by the court. The clerk combines the three parts and adds the executory formula. He then delivers the *grosse* (first certified copy) to the attorney for the winning side.

When a divorce or separation is asked because defendant has been condemned to a degrading and corporal punishment, the court is required upon proof thereof to award an immediate judgment. In all the other cases if the court makes up its mind to grant the relief, it may nevertheless grant an interlocutory judgment and defer definitive judgment for not exceeding six months. (Article 246, C. C.) An interlocutory judgment, if rendered, indicates the eventual result and continues the provisional remedies. This interlocutory judgment is *nisi* in character. At the expiration of the six months, if no reconciliation has been effected, either party may summon the other to attend court and hear judgment of divorce or separation pronounced against the party already indicated as the losing side in the interlocutory judgment. The court at the end of the period of stay cannot decline to grant the definitive judgment, or stay the action further, or reopen the trial. The tribunal of first instance alone, no court of appeal, can stay the rendering of judgment of divorce or separation for the six months period. The tribunal may pronounce divorce or separation *de plano,* that is to say unconditionally upon the record as it stands, or it may render an interlocutory judgment conditional upon further proof before the definitive relief is awarded. In such case the judgment is really preparatory only in character and is followed by another *audience* and judgment on the merits after the proof has been supplied.

With some exceptions, the rules of law in France applicable to judgments in general apply to those of divorce and separation. A judgment refusing divorce terminates *ipso facto* and by implication the provisional remedies previously awarded by order or judgment. The judgment of divorce or separation not alone pronounces divorce or separation, but usually also settles various accessory matters in a permanent or rather in a semi-permanent manner. That is to say the accessory relief lasts until changed by a later judgment, which the French courts have always power and jurisdiction to render.

French definitive judgments of divorce pronounce unconditional dissolution *de plano* of the marriage. This is true even if divorce has been awarded to one and separation to the other. This latter type of judgment does not mean that the one spouse will be divorced, and the other still married. Both will be divorced by the divorce award of the judgment, but the fact that separation was awarded to the losing side in the divorce action means that both spouses will forfeit the financial advantages stipulated in the marriage contract, instead of the winner of the divorce retaining those stipulated in his or her favor. Divorce may be pronounced simultaneously against both parties. For example, a wife who conspires with a servant to commit adultery with the husband is guilty of a gross insult to her husband and the husband who commits the adultery is also guilty; accordingly divorce will be pronounced against both parties. (Seine, November 16, 1897; *La Loi,* December 31, 1897.)

French judgments of divorce and separation often purport to dissolve "the community having existed between the spouses." They always name a particular notary or the president of the chamber of notaries to liquidate the matrimonial property regime, under the control of a designated judge of the bench. The clause quoted is not an adjudication that a regime of community did actually exist between the parties. It is simply a dissolution thereof in case such regime did exist. The notary appointed can wind up other regimes than those of community. This provision in the judgment is made in pursuance of article 1449 of the Civil Code which says that divorce and separation both involve necessarily separation of the property of the couple. The liquidation by the notary is of particular importance to French spouses because it is a statutory consequence that certain advantages are forfeited by the losing party and the forfeited gifts, etc., are to be actually returned and the advantages relinquished, as certified and indicated in a notarial instrument to be approved by the court. Many aliens fail to invoke the notary's or court's intervention in the winding up of their financial affairs, particularly when their property lies outside France and they are married under a regime of separation of property. Nevertheless the provisions of French judgments do not differ in this respect for aliens and for French. A notary is always designated and is permanently available to assist the parties should occasion arise.

Concerning alimony, article 301 of the Civil Code reads:

> If the spouses have not stipulated any advantages in favor of each other, or if those stipulated do not appear to be sufficient to secure the support of the spouse who has obtained the divorce, the Tribunal may award such spouse an alimentary pension, charged upon the property of the other, in an amount which cannot exceed one-third of the revenues of the latter. This pension shall be revocable in case it should cease to be necessary.

Although article 301, C. C., speaks of divorce only, it applies to separation as well. (Seine, September 6, 1886; *Pandectes françaises*, 1887.2.141.) It has been held that alimony cannot be awarded when divorce has been pronounced simultaneously against both spouses. (Cassation, November 24, 1886; *Dalloz*, 1887.1.335.) Permanent alimony usually dates back to the time of service of the conciliation order and any temporary alimony repayable by the party is taken into account at the liquidation of the property regime. Permanent alimony continues after the death of the alimony-debtor to be payable out of his estate. (Seine, September 6, 1886; *Pandectes fran-*

çaises, 1887.2.141.) Unlike temporary alimony, permanent alimony is not in the nature of an advance on account, but in the nature of damages to make good the loss occasioned by bringing about a rupture of the marriage and an ending of the marital rights. (Cassation, December 15, 1909; *Dalloz,* 1911.1.25.) Alimony is not granted upon any theory that article 212, C. C., imposes a continuing duty of assistance upon ex-spouses after dissolution of the marriage. Yet permanent alimony will be reduced or terminated at the request of the heirs if the creditor inherits from the debtor *un gain de survie* (right by survivorship) equal to the alimony pension amounting to one-third the revenues of the debtor. (Lyon, January 4, 1892; *Pandectes françaises,* 1893.2.198.) This practice is more consistent with the theory of assistance between married persons under article 212, C. C., than it is with the theory of damages for breach of contract. Remarriage of the alimony-creditor or alimony-debtor will not *ipso facto* or necessarily end the alimony. It is generally considered, however, that alimony cannot be increased if the debtor becomes more wealthy or the creditor poorer.

Permanent alimony is usually payable monthly. It is a significant fact that in actions between aliens, an award of permanent alimony is rather rare. This is probably because of the practice of adjusting such matters out of court by contract between the parties and also because a French award is revocable and would be difficult to enforce extraterritorially in the United States and Great Britain.

A wife can obtain besides general damages, namely alimony, special damages under article 1382, C. C., in reparation of the injury occasioned by reason of her "loss of a home," upon whose continued existence she had the right to rely, and of her "loss of a brilliant position in life" which she had assisted to establish. (Rhône, December 1, 1926; *Dalloz hebdomadaire,* 1927, p. 147.) Article 301, C. C., authorizing alimony does not exclude the possible application of article 1382, C. C.; consequently an award of both damages and alimony may be made. (Bordeaux, January 3, 1912; *Recueil des Sommaires,* 1912, no. 994.)

In a separation judgment, a provision may be inserted in view of article 311 of the Civil Code forbidding the wife to use the husband's name or granting her leave not to use it. Mandatory non-user of the ex-husband's name by the ex-wife follows by operation of law and no clause requiring non-use is inserted in the divorce judgment itself.

By article 302 of the Civil Code the custody of the children is usually awarded to the winning party, but custody may be divided or given to the losing party or even to a third person as the best interest of the children may require. Article 303, C. C., states that no matter to whom the custody is awarded both parents remain liable to contribute toward the support of the children in proportion to their respective abilities. The party who does not receive the custody has nevertheless a right of visit. This should be expressly defined in the definitive judgment or in a later supplemental one. The administration of the property of the children belongs during marriage to the father, but he is deprived thereof as a consequence of divorce against him. (Article 302, C. C.) This deprivation applies also by analogy to separation. The award of custody may be changed by a later judgment. Even when the award is without express time limit it is essentially provisional and revocable. (Paris, July 17, 1886; *Dalloz,* 1887.2.211.)

The divorce or separation judgment usually awards costs to the winning party, but these may be divided.

Generally in the case of aliens or persons domiciled outside France the court will also indicate the commune in whose marriage records the judgment is to be recorded.

The court in the definitive judgment may award provisional accessory relief of the various kinds already described, as well as the semi-permanent relief mentioned in this chapter. A French court has always power to change or supplement or revoke the accessory relief contained in a divorce or separation judgment, without express reservation of such a right and without purporting in the judgment to have given the relief provisionally only or temporarily. It is, of course, not an easy matter to obtain at a later time such modifications, but this may be secured for good cause.

Every French judgment whether provisional, preparatory, interlocutory or definitive must be *enregistré* (stamped and registered) in order to be used. The *grosse* (first certified copy) in each case is presented by the attorney desiring to use it at the *enregistrement* office for registration and stamping. The charge for so doing is one hundred and fifty francs for judgments of the tribunal of the first instance, and two hundred francs for judgments on appeal. Since a judgment cannot be served until registered this formality is of special importance and is usually very promptly performed.

Copies of French judgments must in every case be served upon the losing party. Service is made by one or other of the methods available for service of process, except that a judgment taken upon default of appearance is served by a bailiff designated by the court instead of by a bailiff selected by the attorney for the winning side. If it is not personally served, an extract of the judgment is published in the same way as is a notice of pendency of action. (Article 247, C. C.) Publication is required even though the *ajournement* came to the defendant's knowledge and even though a copy of the default judgment served by substitution actually reached him.

Chapter XXV

CONTESTING JUDGMENTS

French judgments and orders may be contested in several different ways before the same or before an appellate court. An appeal may be taken to a court of appeal on the facts and law. A petition may be submitted to the Court of Cassation for review on questions of law. *Opposition* may be made to open a default judgment before the court that rendered it. A new trial may be asked of the same court in a *requête civile* (respectful petition).

In French law a judgment has the "authority" (*autorité*) of *res judicata* as soon as it is rendered, and before the expiration of time to oppose it or to appeal, but it has not the "force" (*force*) of *res judicata* (*chose jugée*) until the "ordinary" recourses of opposition and appeal have been exhausted. The distinction apparently means that the judgment having "authority" of *res judicata* can be used as a shield until overthrown, but until it acquires the "force" of *res judicata* it cannot be used as a sword. The fact that a judgment is still revocable does not prevent its use and execution. In fact, it is a question whether some French judgments are ever theoretically really irrevocable, in view of the right to apply for a new trial within two months after discovery of decisive evidence suppressed by the other side, or discovery of fraud or forgery. A judgment is called "final" (*définitif*) when it is no longer subject to opposition or appeal, although it may still be subject to cancellation as a consequence of new trial or review. Finality relates rather to form than to duration or permanence. It is called "irrevocable" only when both the "ordinary" recourses of opposition and appeal as well as the "extraordinary" recourses are exhausted, that is to say when there is no longer a right to petition for review or new trial. "A judgment is irrevocable only when all recourses, ordinary and extraordinary, have been exhausted." (Foignet, p. 182.)

An action to annul a void judgment probably does not lie in France. This was held in an action brought in Paris to annul a judgment of the Tribunal of Haipong (Cochin China) and cancel its recording in France (Seine, January 5, 1899; *Gazette des Tribunaux*, January 6, 1899.) Loysel formulated this maxim: *Voies de nullité n'ont lieu en France contre les jugements.* After a judgment is recorded and the time to appeal or open a default or petition for review has expired there seems to be no possible way directly to contest validity of the preliminary procedure or the judgment itself on grounds of illegality save by a new trial before the original court.

Nevertheless, Piérard says that an *action en nullité* can be brought against a judgment by a party or by any interested person. (Piérard, Vol. II, Sec. 850, p. 623.) Equitable relief might be awarded in exceptional cases against a judgment, such as an injunction to prevent its enforcement. A party cannot usually attack collaterally a judgment rendered against him, but if a judgment has lapsed and become void after recording, it ought to be possible to institute an action to compel the public authorities to strike out the mention of divorce or separation from the marriage record. This would render the judgment obsolete in fact. It is possible however that the judgment could be cancelled by an action to declare it void, as Piérard indicates. If a person's rights are affected by a void judgment, the *exception de nullité* may be interposed by way of defense. For example, the Tribunal of Tunis, June 2, 1920 (*Journal Clunet,* 1923, p. 113) annulled the second marriage solemnized in France of an Italian woman whose first marriage had been dissolved by a default judgment of divorce secured in France against her Italian husband. It did so upon proof by the second husband that the divorce was void because the wife had concealed from the first court her Italian nationality, there being no divorce in Italian law.

Turn now to each of the recourses directly available against a judgment. Article 247 of the Civil Code allows opposition to be made to a default judgment of divorce or separation taken on failure to appear when there was no personal service of the writ. Opposition is made by defendant's attorney serving a notice upon the plaintiff's attorney and upon the clerk of the court. This can be done only within one month from the date of personal service of the judgment upon defendant, or in case of non-personal service within eight months plus the distance periods following the last act of publicity. (Article 247, C. C.) This article does not apply to definitive judgments taken on default for failure to conclude, nor at all to interlocutory, provisional or preparatory judgments. Opposition may also be made to judgments which are not within article 247, C. C.; namely in virtue of the ordinary rules of the Code of Civil Procedure. Default by these rules can only be opened until the day of execution (article 158, C. C. P.) in case of non-appearance, or until expiration of a week from the date of service of the judgment in case of default for non-conclusion (article 157, C. C. P.). A belated opposition will nevertheless be allowed when the plaintiff husband fraudulently prevented the wife from preserving and reading the judgment served upon her. (Paris, March 19, 1920; *Gazette du Palais,* March 26, 1920; Cassation, February 16, 1921; *La Loi,* April 27, 1921.)

An opposition made in due season automatically opens the default and allows the case to proceed as if answer had just been filed, the notice of opposition being drafted to constitute an answer. The judgment is not automatically cancelled by the filing of notice, but stands in suspense awaiting confirmation or revocation by a second judgment which will be rendered upon a hearing of the opposition. The procedure is well illustrated by the Gould case already described.

As to appeal one may say in general, that all contested orders of the president and nearly all judgments of the tribunal are subject to appeal to the court of appeal. An interlocutory judgment, however, is not subject to appeal. (Cassation, July 24, 1922; *Dalloz*, 1925.1.161.) Article 248 of the Civil Code grants in divorce and separation actions a right of appeal to be taken within the time indicated by article 443 of the Code of Civil Procedure, namely, within two months from the date of service of the judgment in case of judgments rendered not by default and within two months from the date at which opposition is no longer possible (*i.e.*, default cannot be opened) in the case of judgments rendered by default. It is not possible, however, to appeal until at least eight days after service of the judgment. A respondent cannot waive the expiration of the time to appeal or stipulate an extension thereof, as such periods are considered matters of public order. (Cassation, March 25, 1879; *Dalloz,* 1879.1.270.)

An appeal from a judgment of divorce or separation is taken in the same way that an action is begun. That is to say the appellant engages an attorney, different from the one used before the tribunal, namely an attorney entitled to practice before the court of appeal. This second *avoué* thereupon prepares an *assignation* (complaint) which recites the judgment and the party's objections or assignment of errors thereto. This is served upon respondent. Service is made in the manner indicated in articles 68 and 69, C. C. P., through a bailiff selected by the appellant. If the respondent has his domicile and residence abroad within the meaning of article 69, C. C. P., the *assignation* on appeal, called an *acte d'appel* (instrument of appeal), is served at the *parquet* (district attorney's office) of the tribunal which rendered the judgment, not at that of the tribunal of the place where respondent has his presumed domicile. (Douai, April 28, 1899; *Journal Clunet,* 1902, p. 843.) The respondent engages similarly a new *avoué* and in the usual way enters an appearance or defaults. The time within which respondent must appear is the same as that given a defendant in first instance. Consequently, when the return day is erroneously fixed in the appeal at sixteen days, instead of one month in the case of an English respondent, the appeal is void. (Paris, May 13, 1898; *Journal Clunet,* 1899, p. 105.) Likewise, the *acte d'appel* will be void if the appellant gives as his domicile the address of a London solicitor; he should give his true domicile. (Paris, October 26, 1907; *Journal Clunet,* 1908, p. 168.)

It is the theory of French law that every litigant is entitled to two trials before different courts. An appeal is really a second trial before a bench of five judges in which the first judgment is simply evidence for the winning side. But it is not a new trial as if the first had not taken place. Thus, new facts may be alleged and new evidence be offered by either party on appeal. (Cassation, June 15, 1836; *Sirey,* 1837.1.89.) But a party who neglected to take testimony as authorized by judgment of the tribunal, cannot ask for an *enquête* on appeal. New causes of action cannot be presented on appeal nor can a prayer for greater relief be considered. Nevertheless, a prayer for additional suit-money may be introduced for the first time into the *assignation* (complaint) on appeal and this is not deemed a new prayer within the prohibition. (Cassation, July 14, 1806; *Sirey,* 1806.2.563.) *Exé-*

cution provisoire (provisional execution) may be asked on appeal, as it is not considered a new demand but an accessory remedy. (Rennes, July 30, 1894; *Dalloz,* 1896. 2.281.) The defendant in a divorce action is expressly allowed by article 248 of the Civil Code to counterclaim for the first time on appeal. This right has been extended by implication to actions for separation. As a corollary a defendant can request leave to hold an *enquête* in relation to the counterclaim. (Cassation, May 27, 1897; *Gazette des Tribunaux,* July 29, 1897.) It is possible for the appellant to contest the jurisdiction on an appeal from a default judgment, when the delay in raising the objection is due to the delay in receiving from the consulate the *ajournement* which started the action. (Paris, May 21, 1884; *Journal Clunet,* 1884, p. 624.)

An appeal in matrimonial actions, and even the time for appeal, operates as a stay of all procedure affecting the merits. Judgments for divorce and separation cannot be carried out before the time to appeal has expired. (Agen, January 20, 1807, cited by Carpentier, *Divorce et séparation de corps,* 1899, vol. II, sec. 3028.) Appeals from definitive judgments of divorce or separation vest jurisdiction in the court of appeal and thereafter the case is never sent back to the same lower court for retrial. The appeal has a so-called *dévolutif* (transmissive) effect, that is to say all incidental matters, such as changes in the provisional remedies, are thereafter decided by the court of appeal, not by the lower court. In fact, on an appeal from a preparatory judgment, the court of appeal can evoke (*évoquer*), *i.e., certiorari,* the entire case on the merits, provided it is ready for trial, and can then itself decide the case without there ever having been a judgment on the merits in the court below. (Article 473, C. C. P.) The parties in this way would be denied one degree of jurisdiction. The practice is unusual and is utilized only when the decision upon the incident under appeal is so bound up with the merits that the decision upon the incident will of logical necessity control the decision upon the merits.

French law considers that there are only two judicial degrees, the tribunal as first instance and the court of appeal as second instance. The Court of Cassation is not considered a degree or an appellate court, but is looked upon as a special and exceptional judicial body of limited jurisdiction to which recourse can be had only of grace. In substance, however, the Court of Cassation is an appellate court and one to which there is access as of right. Nevertheless, it is necessary to obtain the consent of the Court of Cassation before review will be permitted.

In practice the chamber passing upon the petition thoroughly considers the questions of law involved in the *pourvoi* (petition for leave to review). Its hearing upon the petition is really a review of the judgment attacked and its decision denying leave to review is as authoritative as an exposition of law as that of the chamber which decides upon an allowed review. Review can be secured only upon matters of law, not of fact. A judgment can be quashed only (1) for violation of law; (2) for lack of competence, jurisdiction or venue; (3) for non-observance of the requisite formalities; or (4) for inconsistency between two or more judgments of different courts in the same cause. Various restrictions or limitations are imposed upon the right to petition for review. For example, judgments of default cannot be reviewed so long as they may be opened or appealed. Some preparatory judgments can be reviewed only with the definitive judgment on the merits. Judgments of separation, rendered in first instance, cannot be reviewed if no appeal was taken; but judgments of divorce rendered by the tribunal may be reviewed notwithstanding failure to appeal.

CONTESTING JUDGMENTS

Article 248 of the Civil Code says *pourvoi* to the Court of Cassation shall be taken within the time indicated by the Code of Civil Procedure. The latter code provides that the time in case of a judgment not taken by default, is two months from the date of service of the judgment, and in the case of a default judgment two months from the date of expiration of the time to open the default. By reason of article 249 of the Civil Code the right to petition for review of divorce judgments cannot be waived, except judgments of conversion of separation into divorce; but it can be waived as to separation judgments.

Whereas, a petition to the Court of Cassation does not stay most actions, article 248 of the Civil Code expressly derogates from this rule in the case of actions for divorce and separation. The filing of the petition for review automatically stays the action until the petition is either allowed or disallowed, and if allowed the action is further *ipso facto* stayed until the review is decided. This stay applies to judgments granting relief as well as to those refusing it. The *pourvoi* upon a preparatory judgment stays all proceedings which would affect the merits. This has been held in the case of a petition to the Court of Cassation against a judgment ordering an *enquête* and the inquiry cannot proceed until the petition is decided. (Cassation, November 23, 1891; *Dalloz,* 1892.1.291.) It does not prevent the carrying out in the interim of a judgment awarding custody of the children and alimony. (Rennes, July 30, 1894; *Dalloz,* 1896.2.281.) The stay, however, has the effect of rendering void any recording of the judgment of divorce upon the register of civil status and any remarriage of a party on the faith thereof, which recording and marriage take place before the *arrêt* of the Court of Cassation is rendered and even though the judgment is affirmed by it.

Even the time within which to file a petition acts as a stay. Nothing can be done either under a judgment of divorce or separation until the time given by law in which to take a *pourvoi* has expired. Anything done before that time will be void, even should no recourse be actually had to the Court of Cassation.

The civil chamber, when review has been allowed, hands down a judgment (*arrêt*) which either affirms or quashes and annuls (*casse*) the judgment of the lower court. When the judgment is quashed, the case is remanded for retrial to a different court of appeal than the one which rendered the judgment. The second court of appeal is supposed to follow the law as laid down by the Court of Cassation. Sometimes, however, it follows the law held by the original tribunal or first court of appeal, or reaches still another legal conclusion of its own. If the same case comes on review three successive times to the Court of Cassation, then all the latter's chambers will unite upon a decision. The fourth court of appeal to which the case is then remanded is obliged by law to follow the ruling of the Court of Cassation. Even such three-chamber decisions are not binding precedents in another cause!

Apart from recourse to a court of appeal and to the Court of Cassation, a judgment may be annulled by the court that rendered it by special proceedings for a new trial called *requête civile.* This procedure, under article 480 of the Code of Civil Procedure, cannot be used when the objections could have been raised by appeal or review. (Lyon, June 14, 1893; *La Loi,* October 6 and 7, 1893.) The remedy of a new trial is available in some cases even against judgments final in the French sense and recorded. Apparently, in relation to divorce and separation, the remedy is only available against contested judgments of a court of appeal or default judgments of such a court which can no longer be reopened.

Judgments reviewed in this fashion may be *rétractés,* that is, they may be withdrawn or cancelled, upon any one of the following grounds enumerated in article 480, C.C.P.: (1) Personal fraud of a party; (2) illegality (*nullité*) for violation of essential formalities of procedure; (3) adjudication upon matters not raised by the pleadings; (4) award of greater relief than that prayed; (5) failure to pronounce upon a prayer; (6) conflict between two judgments in the same cause; (7) inconsistency between the various awards of relief in the same judgment; (8) failure to notify the district attorney of the pendency of action; (9) discovery that evidence used in the case was forged; and (10) discovery of new evidence of a decisive character concealed by the winning party.

The *requête civile* proceeding can, with certain exceptions, be instituted only within two months plus the distance periods from the date of service of the judgment which it is desired to contest. (Article 484, C.C.P.) The exceptions to this time rule are found in article 488, C.C.P.; namely, when forgery, fraud or newly discovered evidence is the basis of the petition the time does not begin to run until the facts became known.

Formalities for whose non-observance *nullité* is expressly stated by the law to be the consequence must be pointed out at the earliest opportunity, the legal proceedings quashed and the case continued from the stage previously reached. If an illegality is not contested by appeal or review, it is usually deemed cured or waived, and only such illegality as has not been *couverte* (covered) by the parties may be invoked as a reason for quashing a judgment by *requête civile.* (Article 480, C.C.P.) What illegalities are waived by failure to raise the point by appeal or review is not stated in the Code, nor settled in practice. Possibly lack of competence *ratione materiae* would be an objection not "covered" by the acquistion of the character of finality by a judgment.

The filing of a petition for a new trial does not operate as a stay. (Article 497, C.C.P.) The proceedings looking toward the new trial are conducted in the same manner as in an action. If the petition is granted the judgment is cancelled and the original case proceeds from the stage which it had reached before the overthrown judgment had been rendered. (Articles 501, 502, C.C.P.) "By reason of its rarity, this remedy has given occasion for very few decisions." (Carpentier, *Divorce et séparation de corps,* 1899, vol. II, sec. 3123.) Indeed, before it can be brought, the written opinions of three French *avocats,* that the petition is well founded, are required. (Article 495, C.C.P.) Furthermore, security for costs and for possible damages must be given. (Articles 494, C.C.P.) If the petition is denied, the party is fined. No judgment can be attacked twice by *requête civile,* nor can the judgment which rejects the petition be subjected to such attack. (Article 503, C.C.P.) Apart from this procedure of *requête civile,* there is no possibility of an application for a new trial or for a re-argument after the *audience* is closed, although a court may of its own instance order the taking of further proof or re-argument if it so desires.

There would seem to be no estoppel against invoking the remedy of *requête civile.* For example, remarriage in the interval or voluntary execution of the divorce judgment would probably not prevent such attack upon the judgment. Under article 249, C.C. divorce judgments cannot be "acquiesced" in, that is to say voluntarily accepted, consequently there can be no estoppel against attacking these. The remedy of new trial is expressly stated to be available to either party. (Article 480, C. C. P.) Yet no instance can be cited in which a French judgment of divorce or separation has actualy been cancelled under these proceedings.

Chapter XXVI

RECORDING AND PUBLISHING JUDGMENTS

Judgments for divorce and separation must not only be entered in the court records, but must be also recorded in the register of civil status. Under the law of April 18, 1886 (article 252, C. C.) failure to record within two months after the judgment became definitive caused the judgment to lapse and become void. This provision concerning lapse was repealed by the law of June 26, 1919, but the necessity of recording and the two months' period were retained. Delay is punishable by a fine upon the attorney, but the judgment does not become void for failure seasonably to record. It is necessary to obtain a special judgment ordering the officials of the borough hall to record the judgment of divorce or separation if the two months have passed without the observance of the recording formality. This is the case whether delay is due to the fault of the party or to that of officials.

Recording consists in copying the award into the French register of civil status and noting the fact of divorce or separation on the margin of the marriage certificate.

Article 251 of the Civil Code reads:

The award of the *jugement* or *arrêt* shall be transcribed upon the register of civil status of the place where the marriage was solemnized. An entry is made of the *jugement* or *arrêt* on the margin of the certificate of marriage in accordance with Article 49 of the Civil Code. If the marriage was solemnized abroad, transcription is made in the register of civil status of the place where the spouses had their last domicile, and mention is made on the margin of the certificate of marriage if this has been transcribed in France.

These provisions fit the case of aliens or French spouses married in France and French spouses married abroad who have recorded a certified copy of the certificate of marriage in France as required by article 171 of the Civil Code. The rules do not find easy application in the case of aliens married abroad, as these have had no occasion to record a copy of their marriage certificate in France.

Under article 251 of the Civil Code in the case of marriages solemnized in France, judgment of divorce or separation is recorded in the place where the marriage record is kept. In the case of a French couple married abroad one would suppose that the judgment should be recorded where the certified copy of the foreign marriage entry was filed in France, but the rule is otherwise. The recording in such case is made on the register of the commune in France which was the domicile of the couple at the time when the judgment was rendered. (Circular of the district attorney of the Tribunal of the Seine, July 25, 1887; *Journal Clunet*, 1892, p. 644.) Probably, entry of the judgment on the margin of the certificate of marriage would also have to be made where the certified copy of the foreign marriage record was filed. When the husband has no known domicile or residence in France at the time of the judgment, it is recorded in the register of the commune of the domicile of the wife, not as one might suppose in the register of the place where the French marriage record is or should be located. When the husband and wife have separate domiciles, as they have when separated judicially, the judgment of divorce should be recorded in the registers of the communes of both domiciles, except when it is simply a judgment of conversion of separation into divorce. (Carpentier, *Divorce et séparation de corps,* 1899, vol. 2, sec. 3181.)

RECORDING AND PUBLISHING

In the case of aliens married outside of France, the judgment is recorded in the register of civil status of the commune which the plaintiff gives as that of the defendant's domicile or residence in France. If there be none, then the register of the commune is selected in which the court sits. When there is no marriage record in France the formality of mentioning it upon the margin cannot be complied with and is not required. No attempt is made in the case of aliens to record French judgments with the French Ministry of Foreign Affairs or to transmit the judgment abroad for recording with the French consulate or foreign record office where the marriage was solemnized or where the parties are or were domiciled or resident. (*Questions et solutions pratiques,* no. 71; *Journal Clunet,* 1892, p. 640.) No publicity takes place abroad even when required by *lex nationalis* for its own domestic judgments. In view of these difficulties it is now the practice to ask the court to indicate in the judgment itself where it shall be recorded.

Recording is effected under article 252 of the Civil Code by the attorney for the winning party. If the attorney for the successful litigant fails to do this within fifteen days after the judgment has become final the attorney for the unsuccessful litigant may do it. A general power of attorney in favor of an attorney, simply retaining him to conduct the litigation, is not enough to enable him to record the judgment. A special power is required and a judgment recorded by an *avoué* who lacks such authority is void. (Nancy, January 14, 1886; *Sirey,* 1888.2.53.) In view of this rule of law, the power originally given by a client is usually made to contain a grant of express authority to record any judgments in the action. The rule is not, however, always rigorously applied. Thus a woman who contests a judgment of divorce on the ground that she has never ordered it recorded or given a power to that effect, but who has obtained the *grosse* of the judgment through legal aid, and thereby showed her intention of utilizing it, will be presumed to have given a power and the *transcription* (recording) will be deemed regular. (Toulouse, November 15, 1913; *Gazette des Tribunaux du Midi,* December 21, 1913; *Recueil des Sommaires,* 1914, no. 1932.)

When the time for appeal or petition for review has expired, the attorney files a petition with the clerk of the *commune* asking that the judgment be recorded and delivers to him the first certified copy (*grosse*) for this purpose. This copy is eventually returned by the clerk with the fact of recording and the date noted thereon. The attorney is also required to deliver to the clerk, before the clerk can proceed, various certificates indicated in article 548 of the Code of Civil Procedure. First is required a certificate of the attorney himself stating the date of the service of the judgment upon the losing party. If the judgment was taken by default, the certificate must also state whether service was personal or not. If it was not personal then the certificate must give the date of the last act of publicity. Second, there must be supplied a certificate of the clerk of the tribunal or court that no notice of opposition or appeal has been entered. If an appeal has been taken, then a certificate of the clerk of the court must be obtained that no notice of petition for review to the Court of Cassation has been entered. In case petition was taken to the Court of Cassation, a certified copy of any *arrêt* (judgment) of that court confirming the lower courts' judgment must be procured. If the petition for review was discontinued, as may be done in a separation but not in a divorce case, a certificate to this effect from the clerk of the Court of Cassation will be necessary.

RECORDING AND PUBLISHING

From these papers and certificates the clerk of the borough will be able to decide whether or not recording is seasonable and warranted. If the judgment is prematurely recorded, the recording will be void and the judgment inoperative. In such a case, a second judgment ordering the clerk to rectify the record must be obtained before the judgment of divorce or separation can be properly recorded. (Cassation, August 5, 1896; *Gazette du Palais,* 1896, p. 503.) A marriage of a divorced person is invalid when the judgment was prematurely recorded in reliance upon an erroneous certificate of the clerk of the Court of Cassation that no petition for review was on file. In the leading case in this sense, the marriage although considered void was held to be *putatif,* that is, the woman though unmarried retained the property advantages she would have enjoyed had it been valid. (Nice, March 6, 1894; *Dalloz,* 1894.2.509.) The Court of Appeal of Aix, January 23, 1895; (*Sirey,* 1895.2.217; affd. by Cassation, August 5, 1896; *Gazette du Palais,* 1896, p. 503) evaded actually declaring the marriage void and gave two months in which to record the divorce judgment, considering that the failure to record in the season was due to *force majeure,* since the erroneous recording prevented a correct recording in time. Nevertheless, the belated recording would not operate *nunc pro tunc,* hence the marriage would be still void and could be annulled. A second marriage ceremony after proper recording of the divorce judgment would be necessary to render the parties man and wife.

The clerk of the commune is obliged to record and annotate on the register of civil status on the fifth day following receipt of the papers, not before and not later. If he fails or refuses to do this a second judgment is necessary to enable or compel him to carry out these formalities. The judgment of divorce or separation remains inoperative until properly recorded whether the delay be due to the party, his attorney, or the clerk; but if it be the fault of the attorney or the clerk, he will be liable to the parties in damages for any prejudice caused by his neglect.

Judgments for divorce and separation, unlike other judgments, are subject also to certain special rules of publicity, quite apart from the publication mentioned in the case of those taken in default and apart from the recording and annotation just described. Article 250 of the Civil Code requires that an extract of the judgment shall be posted for a year on the bulletin boards of all civil and commercial courts and in the offices of all attorneys and notaries in the judicial district in which the couple were domiciled. An extract must also be inserted such number of times as the court shall order in a paper selected by it, appearing in the judicial district. The extract must state the date of the judgment, name of the court and the names, occupations and dwelling-places of the parties. When a party is in trade in France, the judgment must likewise be read at the bar of the tribunal of commerce of the place in which the party's name is entered in the register of commerce. The law does not indicate a fixed time within which this publicity must be begun or ended, nor does the judgment or order of the court do so. This is left to the attorney of the winning side. The divorce or separation will not be or become invalid by reason of failure to perform these formalities or by reason of defective publicity, but third persons injuriously affected by such absence or incompleteness will be entitled to recover damages from the parties and their attorneys.

Chapter XXVII

DURATION OF JUDGMENTS

A judgment which is no longer subject to possible opening of default or appeal to the court of appeal or cassation is spoken of as having the "force" of *res judicata; il est passé en la force de la chose jugée.* A judgment of divorce or separation when it has been duly served, recorded and published usually becomes final in the French sense, but is subject always to possible future change in the accessory relief and even to cancellation by new trial proceedings in a limited set of circumstances. However, a very important exception exists. Article 156 of the Code of Civil Procedure provides that judgments taken on default for non-appearance "shall be deemed not rendered" unless they are "executed" within six months of their service upon the defaulting party. By "execution" is meant in the case of judgments for divorce or separation certain acts of a nature likely to bring home to the losing party knowledge of the existence of the judgment. It is not necessary, however, that defendant shall actually learn of the fact of execution. A summons to pay costs, to appear before the notary to liquidate the matrimonial regime, to cease bearing a husband's name, these collectively would be sufficient acts of execution to comply with article 156, C.C. However, a mere protest for non-payment of costs would be insufficient and a default judgment of separation so executed could not be converted into divorce, for it never became final and opposition was still possible against it. (Pontoise, December 15, 1892; *Le Droit,* January 6, 1893.)

Placarding of the judgment on the bulletin boards of the civil and commercial courts and in notaries' and attorneys' offices would not be sufficient execution to save a judgment from lapsing. But an attempt to attach personalty at the defendant's domicile is sufficient execution, even when the bailiff reports that by reason of the small value of the property found the attachment was not carried out, because it would have been oppressive to have done so. (Nimes, July 30, 1889; *Gazette des Tribunaux,* August 15, 1889.) The requirement of article 156 C.C.P. applies to judgments of a court of appeal, as well as to those of tribunals of first instance.

It is difficult to harmonize the requirements of article 156 C.C.P. with those of article 247 C.C., which latter allows eight months plus the distance periods in which to open a default judgment not personally served and two months more in which to appeal therefrom. Must the judgment be executed under article 156, C.C.P. before it has become final under article 247, C.C.? Doctrine is divided on this matter. Carpentier considers that article 156, C.C.P. does not at all apply to divorce or separation judgments. (Carpentier, *Divorce et séparation de corps,* 1899, vol. 2, sec. 2938.) The *Instructions de la Chambre des Avoués de Paris* (Instructions of the Attorneys' Association of Paris) say: "Perhaps to avoid all possibility of criticism, one would do well, in this case, to execute the judgment by demanding the payment of costs, forcing in this way the defendant to open his default or to renounce the right to do so by payment." Bioche, *Journal de Procédure civile et commerciale, 1886,* vol. 51, p. 184.) Jurisprudence, however, holds that article 156 C.C.P. must be observed. Thus, in the *affaire* Cochet, the Tribunal of the Seine, February 1, 1894 (*Gazette des Tribunaux,* February 9, 1894) decided that a default divorce judgment lapsed for failure to execute within six months and the lapse carried with it that of the *assignation* (complaint) which began the suit, otherwise the provision of law would be futile and without practical interest. A note to the report of the decision reads: "At the same sitting the Tribunal rendered several decisions in the same sense. We call the attention of attorneys to the importance of this point of law solved by the judgment above reported in the matter of procedure in divorce actions."

Inasmuch as under article 548, C.C.P. no certificate that the judgment has been executed is required for recording, a judgment may be found recorded upon the register of civil status and nevertheless have lapsed for *non-execution.* It has been held that a default judgment not executed within six months is non-existent, and another suit may be instituted for the same grievances. (Seine, March 22, 1890; *Le Droit,* April 3, 1890.) A judgment that has lapsed under article 156, C.C.P. is not a bar to another action on the same facts and grounds. Lapsing under article 156, C.C.P. can be set up for the first time on appeal in a divorce action since the defendant cannot lawfully acquiesce in the failure to execute the judgment, and acquiescence cannot revive the lapsed judgment or give it authority of *res judicata* which it lost by the mere expiration of the six months without execution. (Amiens, January 26, 1926; *Dalloz hebdomadaire,* 1926, p. 226.)

This situation is of particular moment to aliens, since many foreign defendants default after service of process upon them and not all French *avoués* or foreign advisers are careful about observing article 156, C.C.P. The ostensible and recorded judgment satisfies the ignorant client and the collateral legal matters, such as execution and publication, are sometimes omitted. It is to be apprehended that quite a few French divorces between aliens suffer from this latent defect and are really void by reason of non-observance of article 156, C. C. P.

DURATION OF JUDGMENTS

A judgment for divorce comes to an end upon remarriage of the parties to each other, but under article 295, C. C. as amended by law of March 26, 1924, the parties cannot remarry each other (unless there are children) if either has been married to another and divorced in the interval. A second marriage is, of course, necessary to reunite a divorced couple, but this is not the case with couples merely separated.

So far as the separated parties are concerned reconciliation *ipso facto* ends the judgment. (Article 311, C. C.) Reconciliation may be established by any evidence in so far as the relations between the couple are concerned, but the judgment of separation ceases to be operative *vis-à-vis* third persons only upon the performance of certain formalities. Until the formalities are observed a wife enjoys the enlarged capacity provided by article 1449 C. C. in favor of separated women. In order that the separation shall come to an end so far as third persons are concerned, the reconciliation must be declared before a notary and an extract of the declaration must be published as indicated for the judgment itself in article 1445 of the Civil Code. The declaration of reconciliation is in turn recorded in the register of civil status and is mentioned in the margin of the marriage record. (Article 311, C.C.) A wife cannot waive the benefit of a recorded judgment of separation when the husband asks its conversion into divorce, for the judgment benefits both parties even when it is only against one. (Cassation, May 3, 1910; *Sirey,* 1911.1.135.)

A French judgment of separation comes to an end also so far as the principal relief is concerned when it is superseded by or converted into a judgment of divorce under article 310 of the Civil Code. The accessory relief will not be affected by the conversion, unless a change is expressly made therein. Article 1444, C.C. which provides that every judgment pronouncing separation of property must be executed within fifteen days else it becomes void, does not apply to judgments of separation of the persons, although separation of property is an inevitable consequence. (Bordeaux, February 4, 1811; *Sirey,* 1811.2.163.) Similarly, article 1444, C.C. will not apply to judgments of divorce.

Chapter XXVIII

CONVERSION OF SEPARATION INTO DIVORCE

Article 310 of the Civil Code says *inter alia:*

When a separation of the persons shall have lasted three years, the judgment shall of right be converted into a judgment of divorce upon the demand of either spouse.

It is legally possible for a separated couple to divorce otherwise than under article 310, C.C., namely by one party bringing a separate action under article 234, C.C. upon new grounds alone or upon new grounds coupled with the old grounds. In fact, both procedures may be combined, or they may be conducted separately but concurrently. There is no *litispendence* between an action of conversion instituted by one party and an action for divorce brought by the other in which the plaintiff in the conversion action counterclaims for divorce. (Aix, May 21, 1885; *Gazette du Palais,* 1885.1.782.) The defendant in a conversion action is not allowed to counterclaim for divorce on new grounds, but he may bring a separate divorce action and then ask for a stay of the conversion action to enable the judgments in both actions to be rendered at the same time.

The period of three years begins from the date when the separation became final, not from the date when judgment was rendered or when suit was begun. It is clear that a judgment is final within the meaning of law when recorded. Is separation final any earlier? Since judgments of separation may be acquiesced in, they may become final before recording so far as the parties are concerned. Hence the three years may begin to run from the date of a notarial instrument of liquidation of the regime made in execution of the separation, if this instrument is earlier in date than the recording. (Cassation, November 28, 1887; *Sirey,* 1890.1.113.) But in case of a default judgment of separation insufficiently executed under article 158, C.C.P. to prevent opening the default, there can be no conversion until three years after the time to open the default or appeal has expired. Publication of the judgment, liquidation by default and notarial protest for non-payment of costs served at the *parquet* (defendant's domicile and residence being unknown) are not sufficient execution to start the three years running. (Amiens, January 8, 1885; *Gazette du Palais,* 1885.1.493.) Such acts of execution would, however, suffice to prevent lapsing under article 156, C.C.P. The three years mentioned in article 310, C.C. must have expired before the action for conversion is started in order for conversion to be granted. The conversion will not be pronounced if the three years would expire only at the time of the rendering of the conversion judgment.

An action for conversion is begun by service of an *assignation* (*ajournement*) in virtue of an *ex parte* order of the president of the tribunal. (Article 310, C. C.) The petition for leave to sue does not have to be presented, according to the weight of authority, to the president by the plaintiff in person. No conciliation hearing occurs. The president in his order names a judge to report upon the case, indicates that notice shall be given to the district attorney and sets a date for the trial. The date for the hearing is eight days plus the distance periods after service of the writ. The trial is held in the court chambers at a private session.

The law of June 6, 1908, has made conversion mandatory at the request of either party. Before that time it was simply permissive, that is the tribunal could refuse to convert. Conversion of a separation pronounced under the old law may be granted after enactment of the 1908 law notwithstanding previous refusal under the old law. (Cassation, April 7, 1910; *Dalloz*, 1910.1.256.) The ground upon which separation was awarded cannot be modified in the judgment of conversion; hence in a separation action based upon cruelty and gross insults, the plaintiff cannot reserve the right to allege adultery in case the defendant should later attempt to convert the separation into divorce. (Cassation, December 15, 1896; *Le Droit,* February 15 and 16, 1897.) When the separation was awarded against both spouses, it is not permissible to convert this into a divorce against the husband alone. Divorce cannot be pronounced in favor of the party who lost the separation action, but only against him, although the divorce may be prayed for in the second action by either the winner or loser of the first suit. This is the case even though during the three years the winning party may have committed offensive acts constituting new grounds for divorce. In such cases, the losing party should sue for divorce by separate action and not sue for conversion.

The judgment of conversion cannot modify the alimony awarded in the judgment of separation. (Article 310, C.C.) While the question of modification of the other accessory relief has not been expressly dealt with by the law, the prevailing view is that none of the accessory relief can be changed by the conversion judgment. In other words, the power granted to the courts in article 310, C.C. is limited to conversion itself. A separate proceeding may be brought, of course, to change the accessory relief.

The judgment of divorce upon conversion must be served, published and recorded in the manner already described for judgments of divorce.

SEPARATION BECOMES DIVORCE

The principles of private international law mentioned in relation to grounds for divorce apply equally to conversion under article 310, C.C. If the action is between two aliens unable to divorce by *lex nationalis* the conversion of their separation into divorce will be refused them in France even though the separation was by French judgment. If the applicant is French, the right to convert will outweigh any disability or non-liability of the other party by reason of foreign law. For example, a French woman became Italian by marriage. She later obtained a separation in France. As an Italian she could not divorce her husband, an Italian. Upon her restoration to French nationality by decree she was allowed at the end of three years to convert her separation into divorce. (Seine, July 3, 1914; *Journal Clunet,* 1919, p. 1069.)

Chapter XXIX

CONSEQUENCES OF DIVORCE AND SEPARATION

In France, apart from the effects of the judgment of divorce or separation expressly stated therein, various legal consequences result by operation of law in view of the change in status.

The temporary separation of the couple during the divorce or separation proceedings, and the payment of alimony *pendente lite,* modify to some extent the respective rights of the parties and this more particularly in relation to the wife's capacity and liability. A husband cannot be held for debts contracted by the wife during the litigation beyond the amount of the temporary alimony. If the wife spends the alimony otherwise than for her support and that of any children in her care, creditors, even those for necessaries supplied to her, have no recourse against the husband. If the husband voluntarily authorized the wife to live apart from him during the suit, debts incurred by the wife for support will be the joint and several obligation of the two spouses. But if the separate residence was ordered by the court or if the wife left her husband of her own accord, her creditors can look only to her share of the community property or to her separate property at the liquidation of the regime. The temporary separation suspends during its duration the duties of obedience by the wife and life in common, but apart from the foregoing the marital rights and duties remain substantially the same. Thus, contracts made by the wife during temporary separation without the husband's or court's consent may be annulled at her instance after divorce.

(Seine, November 29, 1888; *Pandectes françaises,* 1889. 2.6.)

It is not entirely clear in French law to what extent a judgment of divorce or separation is binding upon third persons. It is a general principle of French law that judgments are *in personam,* not *in rem. Res inter alias judicata aliis neque nocet neque prodest.* (Article 1351, C.C.) Nevertheless Piérard says: "Judgments of divorce and of separation of the persons create a situation which is established *erga omnes* and is opposable to all persons, to third persons as well as to the parties." (Piérard, vol. 1, Sec. 244, p. 461.) A third person may intervene in an action for divorce or separation by consolidating with it a separate action brought by him to protect his interests, but he cannot act against the divorce or separation by the procedure of *tierce opposition.* (Cassation, November 7, 1838; *Journal du Palais,* November 9, 1838.) A third person would have no standing to contest directly the validity of the divorce or separation or to take part in the trial of these personal issues, but he could set up invalidity of the judgment as a defense in another action or he could under some circumstances contest the judgment collaterally.

It seems to be the law, however, that neither the parties nor the children after the parents' death have an action under article 187, C. C. to attack on grounds of illegality a divorce which has become final or to assert the illegality of a second marriage contracted on the faith thereof.

Turning now to the statutory consequences of divorce and separation, it must be remarked at the outset that these judgments operate as to third persons and as to the persons of the parties to the suit from the date of recording, but operate retroactively, to the date of the complaint in the litigation, between ex-spouses as to their property relations. Article 252, C. C., reads:

> The *jugement* or *arrêt* when it has become final operates retroactively between the parties in its effects upon their properties to the day of the complaint. But it shall produce effect in relation to third persons only from the date of recording.

The date of the complaint is the date of the service of the *assignation* (*ajournement*), not of the citation for conciliation. (Cassation, May 27, 1921; *Dalloz,* 1923.1.65.) Nevertheless, it has been held that an inheritance vested in the wife between the date of the service of the *citation* and of the *assignation* does not fall into community, but remains separate property of the wife. The *masse portageable* (estate of the community) is determined as of the date of the service of the citation, although the husband must be made a party to the proceedings for the liquidation of the decedent's estate from which the inheritance is payable. (Paris, January 7 and 8, .1914; *Dalloz,* 1914.2.137.) But the retroactive effect of a judgment for divorce will not validate alienations made by the wife during the proceedings without her husband's consent. (Cassation, April 8, 1893; *Sirey,* 1894.1.5.)

Consider the statutory consequences of divorce. After divorce, the ex-wife has her own domicile, but the domicile of a divorced wife remains that of the husband until she changes it. (Law of November 27, 1891, article 12.) Also by article 299 (2) of the Civil Code "as a consequence of divorce, each spouse resumes the use of his own name." But article 299, C. C., paragraph 2, is not of public order. Hence a divorced spouse can expressly or impliedly renounce for moral or pecuniary reasons the benefit of this provision. It has been held that a husband can waive article 299 (2) C. C. during the divorce action as the consideration of a waiver by the wife of alimony. (Bourges, October 21, 1921; Cassation, February 20, 1924; *Gazette du Palais,* March 20, 1924.) Divorce does not *per se* change nationality, but an ex-wife, French before marriage, may recover French citizenship after divorce by presidential decree. The winning party in a divorce action is entitled to the custody of the children, unless the court otherwise orders. (Article 303, C. C.) The successful litigant is also entitled to the enjoyment of the property of the children during part of their minority, no matter to whom custody is awarded. (Article 386, C. C.)

Divorce does not of itself entitle the winning party to alimony, but an award may be expressly made in the circumstances stated in article 301, C. C. Apart therefrom there is no longer a mutual duty of aid or assistance. Parties cannot before divorce surrender claim to permanent alimony or waive it. It is not lawful to make a liquidation by anticipation of the respective property rights or to violate the rule of public order that ante-nuptial contracts are not changeable by agreement during the marriage. After divorce the parties can probably compromise upon the alimony, the alimony-creditor may renounce it, and the alimony-debtor may purchase the claim by a cash payment or by an annuity. Contractual alimony, like judicial alimony, would be changeable by a court. But there is on this point some contrary authority.

Divorce ends the right of parties to inherit from each other as compulsory heirs. (Article 767, C.C.) *Quaere,* whether or not foreign dower would be considered lost under article 767, C. C. upon divorce or retained as an advantage under article 300, C. C.? An alien wife has no dower in her husband's realty in France. This was decided in relation to a Virginian wife by the Court of Cassation, April 4, 1881. (*Journal Clunet,* 1882, p. 86.) Wills are not *ipso facto* revoked by operation of law upon divorce, but legacies made before divorce by one spouse in favor of the other lapse in view of the judgment.

CONSEQUENCES

A divorced wife is no longer under any disability of coverture, save matrimonial capacity under article 296 of the Civil Code. This article provides that a divorced wife cannot remarry any man except her former husband until three hundred days after the date at which a separate residence was taken up or after the date of the first preliminary or preparatory judgment in the action. If the wife gives birth, however, after the transcription of her divorce, the period of delay comes to an end at once. (Law of December 9, 1922.) Formerly, by article 298 of the Civil Code the losing party guilty of adultery could not marry his or her accomplice, but this article was abrogated by law of December 15, 1904. Divorced persons cannot remarry each other if either has been married and divorced from another in the interval, unless there are children of the first union. (Article 295, C. C.) Upon remarriage to each other the parties are required to adopt the same matrimonial property regime as the one they had before, but all the terms of the old marriage contract need not necessarily be revived.

The relationship of alliance, that is the relationship which arises by reason of marriage between one spouse and the family of the other, is not ended by divorce. Such relationship will continue as an impediment to marriage within the degrees indicated by law. But the duty of support owed by sons- and daughters-in-law to their respective fathers- and mothers-in-law under article 206, C. C. ceases upon divorce. (Cassation, July 13, 1891; *Sirey,* 1891.1.311.)

Divorce produces dissolution of the property contracts made in view of the marriage. (Piérard, vol. II, Sec. 748, p. 464.) The winding up of the property regime in France takes place in the manner indicated by the Civil Code according to the system governing the parties. Divorce does not operate quite like death in all cases; that is to say, in case of a wife awarded divorce, rights of survivorship do not vest in possession at divorce but are preserved and vest at the death of the ex-spouse. (Article 1452, C. C.) The same principle applies to rights of survivorship of a winning husband. The rule extends to contractual *préciput,* namely, to the contractual right to receive a certain sum or property at the death of the spouse. (Article 1518, C. C.)

By article 1441, C. C. any community of property between the spouses is dissolved by divorce. The liquidation is carried out without reference to any settlement or contract made during the marriage, even with a view to the divorce, because any contract made before divorce or separation concerning the partition of the community property has no legal value and is contrary to articles 1389 and 1453 C. C. Such contract would be contrary also to article 1395, C. C., which says of contracts of marriage: "They cannot be in any wise changed after the solemnization of the marriage." In French law, marriage from the property standpoint is a partnership, whatever be the chosen property regime. Upon divorce this comes to an end and must be wound up. On this occasion, article 299 (1) C. C. provides:

The spouse against whom divorce shall have been pronounced shall lose all the advantages which the other spouse may have made him, either by contract of marriage, or after the marriage.

Article 300, C. C. reads:

The spouse who shall have obtained the divorce shall retain the advantages made to him by the other spouse, even though they were stipulated to be reciprocal and reciprocity does not take place.

Upon liquidation of the regime before the notary a computation is made of all advantages theretofore given and received respectively. Those advantages which are within article 300, C. C. are retained by the winner. The losing spouse is required under article 299, C. C. to pay over the value of the advantages forfeited or is debited the corresponding amount in compensation. According to Treilhard, the provision of article 299, C. C. was not inserted in the Code "because the spouse placed himself among the ranks of the ingrates, hence should be treated as such," but because a party who violates a contract should not retain its benefits. The revocation of the Code is by operation of law and no express provision to this effect in the judgment is necessary. It is not permissible for the parties to agree before or during the marriage that the forfeiture of article 299, C. C. shall not take place in case of divorce or separation.

By the term *avantages* is meant more particularly gifts. The half share in the community property obtained by operation of law by marrying under this regime or without pre-nuptial contract is not meant. The half share is kept by the winner and is not forfeited by the loser. A life insurance policy in the losing spouse's favor would be a gift within the meaning of article 299, C. C. and would be forfeited as such. The forfeiture does not apply to wedding presents not enumerated in the pre-nuptial contract of marriage nor to gifts received from the parents of the winning spouse in consideration of the marriage. Nor would the forfeiture operate to divest the title of a third person who before the action was instituted had received the property in good faith by donation from the losing party. (Coulon, *Le Divorce et la séparation de corps,* 1890-97, vol. 5, part one, p. 195.) But the value thereof would be debited against the losing party on accounting. It is to be noted that gifts made between the spouses during marriage are always revocable in view of article 1096, C. C. This article harmonizes with the provision in this sense of article 299, C. C.

CONSEQUENCES

An ex-wife is in the same position as a widow in relation to protecting her property rights *vis-à-vis* the ex-husband and his creditors. She must therefore claim her statutory lien (*hypothèque légale*) under article 2121, C. C. upon his realty to secure her *reprises* (claims), in view of the law of March 23, 1855, and do so within a year after divorce in order to have priority of security going back to the date of the marriage. (Seine, July 13, 1892; *La Loi,* August 10, 1892.) Alimony awarded under article 301, C. C. is entitled to the security of a statutory lien in virtue of article 2121, C. C. (Cassation, December 15, 1909; *Dalloz,* 1911.1.25.)

Article 243, C. C. now reads:

Every obligation contracted by the husband for which the community is responsible, every alienation made by him of realty belonging thereto, after the date of the order mentioned in Article 235 shall be declared void if it is proved in addition thereto that the same have been made or consented to in fraud of the rights of the wife.

This provision suspends to some extent during the proceedings the husband's powers as administrator of the community under article 1428, C. C. and an action will lie after judgment to set aside fraudulent alienations. (Cassation, June 26, 1866; *Sirey,* 1866.1.334.) It is also possible before trial, in view of article 243, C. C., to take steps to set aside any alienations of the community property made by the husband in fraud of the wife's rights. But alienations made by the husband during proceedings, in good faith and without fraud against the community, are not void or voidable.

Separation from bed and board naturally involves much less radical legal consequences than divorce. A judgment of separation excuses the wife from future obedience and frees the couple thenceforth from living together. The duties of fidelity, aid and assistance remain unaffected.

Separation has no effect upon the nationality of the wife. The separated wife has a domicile of her own under article 102 of the Civil Code, as amended by law of February 6, 1893. A separated wife continues to bear the husband's name, unless forbidden from so doing or permitted not to bear it by provision of the judgment. The separated spouse in whose favor judgment was rendered retains the right to inherit from the other as compulsory heir. (Article 767, C. C.) The losing spouse is deprived of this right. Custody of the children goes to the winning party by analogy with article 302, C. C. Administration of their property also goes to the winning side, by analogy with article 386, C. C. and because custody of the children and administration of their property should not be severed. However, some contrary authority exists on the administration question.

Article 1441 of the Civil Code says separation dissolves the marital community. Article 311 of the Civil Code expressly confirms this by saying that separation of the the persons involves separation of their property. Hence, whatever regime existed between the parties during their life together is dissolved and is liquidated by the notary. According to article 1449 of the Civil Code the separated wife is no longer under the disabilities of coverture, except that consent of the husband or of a court is still necessary if she wishes to sell her realty. Much divergence of views has existed as to whether or not article 300, C. C. retaining, and 299, C. C. forfeiting, the advantages apply by analogy to separation. These articles speak of divorce alone and they do not purport to apply to separation. After much hesitancy, the Court of Cassation finally decided on May 23, 1845 (*Sirey*, 1845.1.321) that the law in divorce and in separation is the same.

A French judgment of divorce or separation between aliens or in relation to an alien, will naturally produce in

France all the effects expressly stated therein even though the alien's own country may decline to recognize it. To what extent will the statutory consequences of the internal French law apply to aliens? The implied consequences of the judgment in France when aliens alone are involved will not be those of French law, unless public policy so requires. That is to say, a French divorce between aliens will produce in France the foreign implied effects. *Lex nationalis* in principle governs the effects of divorce or separation. If one spouse is French while the other is alien, French effects will be applied to the former, foreign effects to the latter. But should there be irreconcilable conflict between the two effects, French effects will prevail. If there should be an irreconcilable conflict over the effects of a divorce between two foreign laws, the parties being of diverse alien nationalities, the national law of the winning party would probably be applied. The law in force on the date judgment becomes final governs effects. So, an Italian formerly French can convert his French separation into divorce, under article 310, C. C., although in the interval he has become Italian and by Italian law there is no divorce. (Seine, January 7, 1885; *Journal Clunet,* 1885, p. 177.)

The Court of Appeal of Paris, June 15, 1904 (*Le Droit,* August 4, 1904) confirmed these principles in relation to Americans. Two United States citizens domiciled in Paris were divorced there. The ex-wife continued to use the ex-husband's name contrary to article 299 of the Civil Code. The ex-husband sued to prevent this by an injunction to be enforced by exemplary damages for every day's violation. The court referred to the law in America, which it found allows an ex-wife to use the ex-husband's name or not, as she pleases. But the court also found that by American law the effects of a French divorce in France would be governed by French law, not by American. Consequently the French court applied article 299, C. C. on *renvoi* and forbade the use of the name. In a separate phase of the Gould case, Mr. Gould obtained in France a similar injunction to prevent his wife from using the Gould name, upon proof that by New York as well as by French law, she was not allowed to use it.

Various other French cases illustrate the application of *lex nationalis* to the effects of divorce or separation. For example, the Tribunal of the Seine, April 5, 1895 (*Journal Clunet,* 1895, p. 602) held that the law of February 6, 1893 amending article 1449 of the Civil Code and enlarging the capacity of women separated judicially from their husbands, does not apply to an Italian wife separated by a French judgment if her national law does not concede to separated women a capacity of equal breadth. A British ex-wife divorced in France cannot claim a statutory lien (*hypothèque légale*) upon her husband's realty in France under article 2121, C. C., to secure her property claims, since there is no such lien in English law. (Seine, April 28, 1911; *Journal Clunet,* 1912, p. 844.)

The Court of Appeal of Paris decided, February 13, 1872, (*Sirey,* 1872.1.112) that article 296 C.C., forbidding remarriage by the ex-wife for three hundred days, is based upon public policy and hence applies to an alien divorced woman in France. This will be the case whether the divorce took place in France or elsewhere, but applies only to remarriage in France. Nevertheless a different attitude has been taken by the government officials. A letter of the Minister of Justice to the district attorney of the Court of Appeal of Pau, November 30, 1898, (*Journal Clunet,* 1898, p. 218) stated that there could be no objection to the remarriage to each other of New York spouses divorced in France even before the expiration of ten months, because their capacity is governed by New York law, in which no period of delay is indicated. The Minister pointed out that article 296 C. C. is not (in his opinion) based upon public policy, although he admits the Court of Appeal has held that it is. He added that a violation of article 296 C. C. would not render the marriage void, but only make the mayor who proceeded with the marriage solemnization in violation of the article liable to a fine. In practice, alien women do remarry in France not only their former husbands but other men at any time after the recording of their divorces. It is manifest, therefore, that foreign law will receive preferential and often exclusive application in relation to the implied effects of divorce and separation in France so far as aliens are concerned.

To what extent will a French divorce affect a foreign agreement made before it in relation to the property rights of the alien parties? The Tribunal of Chambéry, June 26, 1869 (*Dalloz,* 1869.2.154) held that the financial advantages stipulated in favor of a spouse in a pre-nuptial contract made in Savoy (Italy) under Sardinian law, which law provides that such advantages cannot later be revoked for ingratitude, are not revoked in France by operation of law as a consequence of a French judgment of separation rendered after the annexation of Savoy to France, although such advantages would be so revoked under the French Civil Code. It would seem, therefore, that article 299, C. C. forfeiting advantages would not operate to forfeit in France, either as to French or aliens, advantages irrevocably acquired under foreign national law. However, here again, the *renvoi* doctrine may play a decisive part, particularly when the parties are aliens. If in the foreign law the effects of divorce in the place where rendered are considered to be governed by the law of that place, then French law would be applied and the advantages would be forfeited under article 299, C. C. *Quaere,* whether or not this solution would be limited to advantages having relation only to property in France? This subject of the effects of French judgments upon aliens is extremely complicated and unsettled in French law.

Chapter XXX

MEASURES OF ENFORCEMENT

Article 554 of the Code of Civil Procedure says:

> If difficulties arise upon the execution of judgments or in case of emergency, the local court shall provisionally adjudicate, and remand the case on the merits to the proper court for execution.

This article must be read with article 472, C. C. P. which states that the proper court for execution of a judgment confirmed on appeal is the tribunal of first instance. This would be the proper court also when there was no appeal taken. The court of appeal is the proper court for enforcement, or another tribunal of first instance indicated by the court of appeal, when the judgment in first instance has been reversed. The tribunal is the authority that enforces an order of the president.

Ordinarily a default judgment cannot be executed until a week after it has been served. (Article 155, C. C. P.) The *grosse* (*i. e.,* first certified copy) of every French judgment is sufficient to enable it to be carried out by all public officers whose aid is asked. But it is not possible for a certified copy of the president's order awarding custody of the children under article 238, C. C. to be issued by the clerk, because it is only provisional and not *res judicata*. (Orleans, February 14, 1912; *Le Droit*, May 1, 1912.) No executory clause is attached to such orders or to other provisional orders; consequently to enforce them against persons or property an application must be made to the tribunal for a judgment to this end.

Whereas an appeal or opposition to a judgment usually operates as a stay of execution until it is decided, there are certain judgments and orders or provisions thereof that may be enforced at once notwithstanding pendency of appeal or of other recourse against them. Naturally, if the recourse is successful and the judgment or order is annulled, then the effects of the execution carried out meanwhile must be effaced and conditions restored to their former status. Article 238 of the Civil Code provides that the order of the president at conciliation shall be *exécutoire par provision,* that is to say, shall be carried out provisionally until set aside or modified. By articles 457 and 458, C. C. P. a court of appeal may only order provisional execution "if provisional execution has not been pronounced in the case and it is one in which this is lawful." The president's *ex parte* order and other orders and judgments of the tribunal are not expressly mentioned by law in this relation. In regard to provisional enforcement they would be governed by article 135 of the Code of Civil Procedure only. Article 135, C. C. P., states that provisional execution shall be ordered without bond when there is an authentic title, acknowledged promise or a condemnation under a judgment which is not subject to appeal. Provisional execution by this article may, but need not, be ordered, and if ordered, it may be ordered with or without requirement of bond. Provisional execution is authorized by this article in various sorts of proceedings, such as proceedings for sealing, inventory, ejectment, receivers and alimentary pensions and provisions. In these permissive cases, the president or court cannot order immediate execution unless this is asked for by a party.

Article 135, C. C. P., is not considered limitative and hence a president or court will occasionally order provisional execution in proceedings not included in the enumeration. For example, it has been held that a change in the custody of the children may be ordered to be carried out at once upon entry of judgment, without waiting for registration or service thereof, and this may be done even if the spouse awarded the custody has not asked for such favor. (Poitiers, July 9, 1889; *La Loi,* January 22, 1890.) Custody awarded by a judgment of divorce has also been granted with a provision for immediate execution of this accessory award, on the theory that the latter aspect was urgent. (Paris, January 21, 1895; *Dalloz,* 1895.2.168.) The suggestion that provisional execution may be ordered whenever there is urgency has been adversely criticized. (Carpentier, *Divorce et séparation de corps,* 1899, vol. 1, sec. 1665.) There can be no *exécution provisoire* of an order for payment of a *provision ad litem* (Rennes, July 30, 1894; *Dalloz,* 1896.2.281.) A tribunal could not order provisional execution of the judicial separation itself, since separations are not specifically enumerated in article 135, C. C. P. Provisional execution applies to accessory relief, not to divorce or separation, the principal relief sought in the action.

It is a general principle that French courts can select whatever method of enforcement suits their inclination, even when the method selected is not the one asked or desired by the parties. Thus, an award of custody of children in favor of the husband was enforced against the Princess de Beauffremont by exemplary damages for every day's delay in surrender, although the husband to compel compliance with the custody award had prayed for attachment and receivership of his wife's property. (Cassation, March 18, 1878; *Sirey,* 1878.1.193.) Actual compliance cannot be avoided by merely paying the damages, for refusal of obedience in a case of surrender of custody of children required by a court is a *quasi-délit,* a misdemeanor. (Bordeaux, March 16, 1894; *La Loi,*

September 14 and 15, 1894.) Arrest of the person is also possible to enforce surrender of custody. (Paris, June 27, 1810, cited by Carpentier, *Traité théorique et pratique du divorce*, 1885, vol. 1, no. 383.) By law of December 5, 1901, removal, concealment or non-surrender by a parent of a child awarded to the other by the court is a felony punishable by imprisonment not exceeding one year and fine not exceeding five thousand francs. An action will lie for the equivalent of a mandatory injunction with a monetary penalty of twenty-five francs *per diem* for non-compliance, directing a wife who has lost her divorce action to return to her husband and to bring back the child. (Gray, December 5, 1890; *Gazette des Tribunaux*, December 14, 1890.) An award of damages of one hundred francs per day has also been granted to compel surrender of custody. (Besançon, July 29, 1890; *Gazette des Tribunaux*, December 14, 1890.) While arrest may be resorted to in penal cases, or cases which amount thereto, nevertheless specific performance is not usually compelled in this fashion in view of the law of July 22, 1867, which abolished civil arrest, *contrainte par corps*, formerly permitted by articles 126 and 127, C. C. P. Refusal to obey is not in civil cases a contempt of court punished by imprisonment. The chief means of enforcement of an award of custody is, therefore, by exemplary continuing damages.

The law of February 7, 1924, makes it a felony voluntarily to neglect payment of judicial alimony for three months; this applies to temporary but not to permanent alimony awarded under article 301, C. C. For either of these awards, however, attachment of property or garnishment of salary may be ordered, or a receiver may be appointed to collect the debtor's revenues. Authorities are not in accord whether or not a levy of execution is allowed to collect arrears. But a court can order the debtor to pledge a specific capital asset or assign a given revenue to the payment of alimony. (Cassation, January 38, 1828; *Sirey,* 1828.1.278.) A creditor of temporary alimony has no statutory lien under articles 2117 and 2121 of the Civil Code nor the lien of a judgment upon the debtor's realty under 2123, C.C. (Seine, February 1, 1894; *Le Droit,* October 29 and 30, 1894.) Alimony provisionally awarded in favor of children of the litigants can be sued for on their behalf by a guardian and collection secured by attachment. (Orleans, February 14, 1912; *Le Droit,* May 1, 1912.) Both alimony and suit-money have a special legal affectation in favor of the party beneficiary and cannot be attached in the husband's hands and diverted from their destination by creditors of the wife. (Seine, November 28, 1889 and January 9, 1890; *Le Droit,* January 10, 1890.) It is not possible to obtain a stay of action until alimony or suit-money is paid.

A divorced wife may be obliged to discontinue the use of her ex-husband's name by an action for an injunction enforceable by exemplary damages.

An action lies to compel a divorced spouse to proceed with the liquidation of the property regime. Such action does not have to go through the preliminary formalities of conciliation before the justice of the peace or the president. If necessary a receiver will be appointed to take possession of property detained by an ex-spouse. In fact an ex-spouse who conceals and withholds community property is probably liable to punishment for theft. If a party who has been divorced or separated by judgment refuses or fails to attend before the notary and to account for the community property or the separate property of the other under his administration, the liquidation can proceed before the notary without him. Upon submission to the judge of the notary's report and of the draft instrument of account, appropriate legal means will be indicated by the tribunal in favor of the well-conducted party to enable him or her to recover the payment of sums estimated and held to be due. For example, a money judgment would be awarded based upon which an attachment, garnishment or execution could be levied upon property of the accounting party in France.

It is entirely permissible while a divorce or separation action is in progress to bring an action separate therefrom and seeking merely separation of property. (Albi, December 12, 1893; *Gazette des Tribunaux*, February 1, 1894.) Such separation of property does not operate retroactively to the date at which the action was begun, as does the separation of property which accompanies a divorce or separation of the persons. Separation of property without divorce or separation of the persons is more readily obtained than is divorce or separation and usually with greater celerity. The course of bringing a separate action for the more limited relief is sometimes followed in order to protect the interests of the wife when the outcome of the divorce or separation action is in doubt or is delayed or when it is desired to accelerate the solution of the property questions. It is also possible, either during the pendency of the divorce or separation action or thereafter, to bring an action to set aside fraudulent conveyances of the husband of community property, in view of article 243 of the Civil Code as amended by law of April 18, 1886.

The methods of enforcement in France of a domestic judgment of divorce or separation between aliens are generally considered to depend upon *lex fori* not *lex nationalis*. The manner of enforcement certainly depends upon *lex fori* alone. The same rules apply as in the case of the enforcement of foreign judgments. So far as matters of substance are concerned, a French judgment of divorce or separation between aliens is deemed to be like a foreign judgment between them which has been given *exequatur* in France.

Chapter XXXI

RECOGNITION IN CIVIL LAW COUNTRIES

Comparatively little occasion has as yet arisen in foreign countries to pass upon the validity of French divorces and separations. Fortunately, however, the law upon recognition of foreign judgments is sufficiently clear in most of them to enable one to state what it is with reasonable accuracy.

To begin with, in Belgium and Switzerland French judgments have a special standing by virtue of treaty. These countries will respectively recognize as *res judicata* a French divorce of Belgian subjects or of Swiss citizens bona fide domiciled in France if the divorce was given for reasons approved by their national law. Since there is no such thing as a perpetual separation in Swiss law, Switzerland, like Germany, would not admit the validity of a French separation of Swiss spouses. Belgium, however, would treat separation judgments in the same way as divorce judgments.

During the ten years in which France was a party to the Hague Convention, her divorce and separation judgments when rendered in conformity with that treaty and between nationals of the signatory powers were entitled to recognition in the other treaty countries, namely when the parties were domiciled in France and national law was applied to their status and capacity. It is still an open question what difference, if any, the withdrawal of France has made in this respect. Probably the Convention countries would still apply tests similar to those of the treaty, but this is not certain.

The lack of reciprocity by France might now be a reason for refusal of recognition of French judgments in some countries. Thus the *Kammergericht* of Berlin, February 16, 1910 (*Journal Clunet*, 1911, p. 286) held void a New York divorce between Germans and declined to recognize the contract to pay alimony which had been made a part of the judgment. The reasons given were that as "reciprocity is not guaranteed," as the judgment contained a prohibition upon the remarriage of the guilty party and the alimony provision was unchangeable by a later judgment, the effects of the judgment were disapproved. The German courts might readily take a similar attitude toward French judgments, the judgments of Germany not always receiving full faith and credit in the French Republic.

Some other countries would surely decline to recognize French divorces between their nationals for reasons of public policy based usually upon religion. This is the case of Brazil. For example, the Court of Appeal of Rio de Janeiro, decided October 2, 1919 (*Journal Clunet*, 1921, p. 990) that an alien duly divorced in his own country who remarries in Brazil is not guilty of bigamy, but the marriage is void. Nevertheless, an alien divorced and remarried outside Brazil will be considered by Brazilian law to be validly married to the second spouse. (Tribunal of Para, April 5, 1905; *Journal Clunet*, 1906, p. 498.) The Federal Supreme Court of Brazil, by a four to three decision, refused on October 1, 1913 (*Journal Clunet*, 1915, p. 691) to grant *exequatur* to a Portuguese divorce judgment rendered between Portuguese citizens, even so far as property effects in Brazil were concerned. These cases show what would be the standing of a French divorce in Brazil under like circumstances.

Spain, though equally or even more Catholic than Brazil and though not a party to the Hague Convention, takes a very fair judicial attitude toward foreign divorces. Naturally, no divorce rendered in France between Spaniards would be recognized in Spain, but a separation between Spaniards domiciled in France would probably be duly recognized. The Synodal Tribunal of the Diocese of Barcelona, January 24, 1906 (*Journal Clunet,* 1907, p. 190) held that the marriage of Spanish Catholics is indissoluble and that a Porto Rican divorce obtained by the husband domiciled in the territory is void. Consequently the second marriage of the husband, solemnized outside Spain, is mere concubinage and the first wife may obtain a separation (*divorcio*) from him in Spain on this ground. But the Supreme Court of Spain, April 13, 1915 (*Journal Clunet,* 1917, p. 732) recognized the validity of a German divorce between German subjects, the marriage having taken place in Spain and the wife having been born Spanish and the spouses being domiciled in Madrid when the German judgment was rendered. The lower court declined *exequatur* "considering that the German civil courts were without competence to grant dissolution of a canonical marriage, a marriage within the competence of the Spanish ecclesiastical courts." This decision was reversed by the Supreme Court. The ex-husband, who had remarried in Germany, was held by the highest court to be not guilty of bigamy in Spain and not liable to be sued there for separation by his ex-wife. Most of the Spanish-American Republics would take a legal position similar to that of Spain.

Italy is a member of the Hague Convention, but prohibits divorce, so her situation is rather unusual. A French divorce of Italians would be void in Italy. A French separation would be valid if the rules of the Hague Convention had been applied. The Court of Appeal of Bologna (Italy), June 21, 1911 (*Journal Clunet,* 1912, p. 287) granted *exequatur* to a French divorce obtained by two French spouses who, when Italian, had separated in Italy by mutual consent and who later had both become naturalized in France and then divorced. When, however, only one of the spouses changes from Italian to French nationality and then divorces in France, the French judgment will not be recognized in Italy against the Italian spouse. (Court of Appeal of Florence, March 10, 1923; *Journal Clunet,* 1923, p. 1021.) Furthermore, Italy has decided to break up the practice of Italians becoming French in order to divorce and then becoming Italians again. The Court of Appeal of Rome, November 30, 1922 (*Journal Clunet,* 1923, p. 659) held that when Italians become naturalized abroad in order to divorce and do not really remove their domicile from Italy, they will be deemed still Italians and their divorce will be considered void. But persons who have lost Italian nationality without gaining another citizenship are still in a privileged situation. For instance, a Swiss divorce granted on Swiss grounds only in an action between *heimatlos* ex-Italians, was granted *exequatur* in Italy. (Court of Cassation of Florence, May 19, 1913; *Journal Clunet,* 1914, p. 271.)

The Dutch attitude toward foreign divorce is perhaps the most liberal of all the civil law countries. The High Court of the Netherlands, November 24, 1916 (*Journal Clunet,* 1921, p. 278) recognized the validity of a New York judgment of divorce for adultery, rendered in an action between Hollanders domiciled in New York, since adultery is a ground in Dutch law. The Court said no *exequatur* was necessary because the litigation was not to permit execution of the American judgment in Holland, but simply to secure recognition of a consequence of divorce, namely of the change in status. In other words, Holland applied to an American judgment rules similar to those of the Hague Convention, although the United

States is not a party thereto. Dutch courts would do the same for French judgments.

In those continental countries which have adopted the Hague Convention, or which follow its rules, the statutory consequences of a French divorce or separation indicated by the *lex nationalis* of the parties would be applied. In Latin-America where status is governed, not by *lex nationalis* but by *lex domicilii,* the statutory effects of the latter law would govern.

In various civil law countries, recognition would be granted also to provisional remedies awarded by a French court of the domicile or residence notwithstanding revocability of the award in French law. The direct enforcement by *exequatur* of such temporary measures rarely occurs however, inasmuch as reliance is usually placed upon a new superseding domestic judgment or order. A French divorce or separation judgment would probably be given effect in the civil law countries notwithstanding possible revocability by *requête civile,* since in other civil law countries such recourse is not unknown.

Chapter XXXII

RECOGNITION IN ENGLAND

For many years the question of the recognition in England of foreign divorce judgments was unsettled. It is still today incompletely settled. The attitude of English law was long influenced by the decision in Lolley's case, 2 Cl. & F. 567, (1812), or rather by what was supposed to be the rule in that case, namely that an English marriage of Scotch subjects could be dissolved only in England, not in Scotland. Consequently in such case a Scotch divorce would not be valid in England. The rule really applied only to the case of spouses domiciled in England at the time of the marriage. Accordingly, somewhat later, a Scotch divorce between Scots domiciled in Scotland but married in England was sustained. [**Harvey-Farnie**, C. A., 6 Probate Division 35, (1880) ; H. L., 8 A. C. 43, (1882).] The "English marriage" doctrine was subsequently abandoned, or at least basically changed. Under the revised doctrine an English marriage could be dissolved in another country, but only on English grounds. The doctrine even so modified did not long endure.

A foreign divorce judgment may be impeached now only for lack of jurisdiction or fraud or perhaps for denial of justice. A foreign judgment which is not a bar to subsequent proceedings between the same parties in the country where it was rendered, is not a final judgment which can be sued upon in England. [*In re* Henderson, Nouvion-Freeman, (1887), 37 Chancery Division 244; H. L., 59 L. J., Chancery 337, (1889).] The lack of reciprocity is not an objection to the foreign judgment in England. "So far as English law is concerned the rule of competence in matrimonial matters is the same as the rule of recognition of the competence in such matters of foreign courts." (Piggott, Foreign Judgments and Jurisdiction, 1908, vol. II p. 108.) The English courts assume that the jurisdiction of foreign courts is based upon the same principles as their own, and recognize foreign divorces if the English tests of the domicile of the parties in the foreign country are satisfied. The English courts seem to show little regard for what really is the foreign law of jurisdiction in any given case. They make a semblance only of inquiry as to whether or not domicile is in fact where it is supposed to be. Recognition is independent of the question as to whether or not the foreign court conformed to the English test of jurisdiction deliberately or unintentionally.

The rule of recognition of foreign judgments of divorce in England is today substantially this: (1) A foreign judgment of a court of the domicile rendered without fraud will be recognized in England, even if the grounds differ from those of British law and regardless of where the marriage was solemnized; (2) a foreign judgment not of a court of the domicile rendered without fraud will be recognized in England if it would be recognized by the courts of the domicile. Several cases involving American divorces illustrate the present rule, but no French divorce appears to have been passed upon. In Bater-Bater, 1906, Probate Division 209, British spouses married in England and were domiciled there. The husband sued before the High Court in London for divorce on grounds of adultery and the wife filed a cross-bill setting up cruelty. The British court dismissed the suit, so the husband went to America and acquired there a new domicile. The wife then sued for divorce in New York, without disclosing the English proceedings, received a decree of divorce and remarried. The second husband later sued in England to annul the second marriage. The High Court refused to grant this relief, holding the New York divorce to be valid. It inquired whether or not the New York court had jurisdiction and had correctly decided according to New York law, and upon finding the affirmative sustained the divorce. Following this, Pemberton-Hughes, 1899, 68 L. J. Chancery 281, held that British subjects married in England and domiciled there at the time of the marriage may without fraud or collusion establish a domicile in Florida and obtain a divorce there on grounds unknown to English law, in particular for the ungovernable temper of the wife. Armitage-Attorney General, 1906, Probate Division 135 recognized as valid a South Dakota divorce between a New York husband and an English woman, the marriage having taken place in England. The domicile of the husband was New York, but the wife had acquired a separate domicile in South Dakota and the husband had appeared in her action for divorce. Upon proof that the New York courts would recognize such a divorce, the British court likewise did so. *Per contra* in Cass-Cass, 102 L.T.R. 397, (1910) a South Dakota divorce between Massachusetts spouses married in Germany was held void in England upon proof that the courts of the domicile, Massachusetts, would decline to recognize it.

Concerning the nature of the domicile meant by English law, it is clear since Lolley's case that a mere "forensic domicile" is insufficient to sustain divorce jurisdiction. At one stage in British legal evolution a foreign judgment would be recognized though rendered by a court not of the domicile but only of the "matrimonial home." Thus in Niboyet-Niboyet, 4 Probate Division 1, (1878) English courts had asserted their own jurisdiction in such a case. But Le Mesurier-Le Mesurier, 1895, Appeal Cases 517, finally disposed of the "matrimonial home" doctrine. Therein a Ceylon divorce between an English husband domiciled in England but living in Ceylon, as a member of the Civil Service, and his wife formerly French, was held to be void. Le Sueur-Le Sueur, 1 Probate Division 139, (1876) indicates that a deserted wife may choose a new domicile without having already secured a decree of separation, but the court refused to take jurisdiction or accept the so-called American view that "the courts of the bona fide domicile of either party may entertain suit for divorce." English law, not foreign law, will be applied by an English court to determine where a party is domiciled.

What conclusion is to be drawn from the foregoing in reference to the validity of a French divorce judgment in England? One may say with confidence that a French judgment would be given full faith and credit if France were the true domicile of the parties, even though the parties were English, the grounds were not those of English law, and though the marriage had taken place in England. A French divorce obtained by parties not domiciled in France would be recognized if the parties were aliens of a country whose courts would in turn recognize the French judgment. British subjects could validly divorce in France, according to the English view, only if domiciled there.

Recognition in England entitles the judgment to be considered not only *prima facie* evidence, but *res judicata* without reinquiry on the merits. What are the other effects which would be given to a French divorce apart therefrom? The statutory consequences of divorce indicated by *lex domicilii* would probably be applied in England, although the consequences of English law or of the French law or even of *lex nationalis* might to some extent be given application. Piggott, indeed, thinks that *lex nationalis* will eventually displace *lex domicilii* in English private international law. Dower, however, in land in England would be governed by British law. Thus, in Collis-Hector, L. R., 19 Equity Cases 334, (1874) a Turk, married to an English woman in England, returned to Turkey and divorced her there. It was held by the British courts that the wife's settlement was not affected in England, although by Turkish law it became void. It seems also that a foreign judgment annuling a marriage is not such a judgment as will entitle the British courts to vary the terms of a British trust settlement. (Moore-Bull, 1891, 1 Probate Division 279.)

The British courts will more readily recognize a foreign separation than a divorce. Separation in English law is not deemed to affect the status of the parties. Consequently, a foreign court of the permanent residence of the spouses, "without reference to the domicile of the parties," may award separation. (Armitage-Armitage, 1898, Probate Division 178.) In other particulars, the English law concerning recognition and effects of foreign separations will be similar to the law applicable to foreign judgments of divorce.

The question of the possible enforcement of a foreign award of alimony is not readily answered in English law. Naturally, the judgment to be recognized at all would have to emanate from a foreign court having jurisdiction. The court of a place where the couple are merely sojourning is considered by British courts to be entitled to award such relief as alimony. Nevertheless, an award of alimony in a French judgment would probably not be enforceable in England because the award is, in France, always subject to modification. In Beatty-Beatty, 131 L. T. 226 (1924), a New York judgment for alimony was enforced in England upon proof that the American court had no power to interfere with the accrued installments though it might vary its order with respect to future payments. The Irish courts in McDonnell-McDonnell, 2 Ir. R. 148 (1920), held that a Montana alimony award payable into court "until further order of the court" was not such a final and conclusive judgment as to be enforceable in Ireland even for the arrears accrued. In the City of Mecca, 1881, 6 Probate Division 106 a foreign judgment *in personam* was denied effects *in rem,* although a similar British judgment would have been of the latter sort. *Quaere,* whether in view of this decision a French divorce would be binding in England *erga omnes?*

For purposes of marriage in England, a foreign divorce judgment between aliens will usually be accepted by the registrar of marriages as sufficient to warrant the issuance of a license, without necessity for any English court proceedings.

Chapter XXXIII

RECOGNITION IN THE UNITED STATES

In no country is the question of the recognition of French divorces of more importance than it is in the United States and probably in none is the legal attitude less certain. Freeman writes: "The decisions in the United States upon the subject of foreign judgments are infrequent. The law on that subject must be regarded as not well settled." (Freeman, A Treatise on the Law of Judgments, 5th ed. 1925, vol. III p. 3047.)

No judgment has any effect of its own force beyond the limits of the sovereignty from which its authority is denied. It is by comity according to the American law that one nation by its judgments is allowed to operate within the dominion of another nation. Comity is not a rule of law, but it is a rule of practice, convenience and expediency. Article 4, section 1 of the United States Constitution says:

> Full faith and credit shall be given in each state to the public acts, records and judicial proceedings in every other state.

This does not apply to foreign judgments, but only to those of sister-states of the American Union. The tendency is, however, in the United States constantly to narrow the difference between the two sorts of judgments. Furthermore, in several states there are statutory provisions which deal with the recognition of foreign judgments. For example, the California Code of Civil Procedure, section 1915, provides that a foreign judgment shall have in that state the same effect as it has where rendered and also the same effect as a domestic judgment and the jurisdiction of the foreign court shall be tested by the foreign law. The New York Civil Practice Act provides that a foreign judgment duly authenticated "is evidence," but the "effect" is to be decided by the court. (Sections 395, 396, C.P.A.) The Uniform Annulment of Marriage and Divorce Act has been adopted by New Jersey, Wisconsin and Delaware only, and Massachusetts and New Hampshire have enacted laws similar thereto. The Act has a provision:

> Nothing herein contained shall be construed to limit the power of any court to give such effect to a decree of annulment or divorce by a court of a foreign country as may be justified by the rules of international comity.

However, there is also an important limitation:

> If any inhabitant of this state shall go into another state, territory or country in order to obtain a decree of divorce for a cause which occurred while the parties resided in this state or for a cause which is not a ground for divorce under the laws of this state, a decree so obtained shall be of no force or effect in this state.

Hilton-Guyot, 159 U. S. 113, (1895) is the leading case in the United States, on the recognition of a French judgment. The United States Supreme Court stated: "Every foreign judgment, of whatever nature, in order to be entitled to any effect, must have been rendered by a court having jurisdiction of the cause, and upon regular proceedings and due notice." The court must be assured also that the judgment is untainted by fraud. Dividing foreign judgments into those *in rem* and those *in personam,* the court declared concerning the former: "A judgment affecting the status of a person, such as a decree confirming or dissolving a marriage, is recognized as valid in every country, unless contrary to the public policy of its own laws." Speaking of judgments *in personam,* and in particular of a foreign money judgment, the Supreme Court held that such judgment would be conclusive evidence on the merits, unless there were lack of reciprocity, in which case it would be presumptive evidence only. The Court found that France reviews American judgments on the merits, and hence, although recognizing the validity of the French money judgment, the court declined to consider it more than *prima facie* evidence. While Hilton-Guyot is of the highest authority in the United States, the decision does not prevent a state from giving greater recognition to a foreign judgment than the minimum indicated by the Supreme Court and to do so notwithstanding absence of reciprocity.

In New York, comity rests upon persuasiveness not upon reciprocity. It is the practice in New York State to give further recognition than that required by the Hilton case regardless of lack of reciprocity. [Johnson-Compagnie Générale Transatlantique, 242 N. Y. 381, (1926).] The Hilton case is called by the New York Court of Appeals, fifty-four pages of "magnificent dictum," and notwithstanding it: "The law of the State of New York remains unchanged and the French judgment should be given full faith and credit." The Court of Appeals in Dunstan-Higgins, 138 N. Y. 70, (1893), said: "It is the settled law of this State that a foreign judgment is conclusive upon the merits. It can be impeached only by proof that the Court in which it was rendered has no jurisdiction of the subject-matter of the action or of the person of the defendant, or that it was procured by means of fraud." (P. 74.)

Concerning the American idea of the jurisdiction of the foreign court, this is to be tested by the law of nations as applied in the place where judgment is sought to be enforced. Jurisdiction so far as recognition is concerned depends upon international law not upon the municipal law of the foreign country where the judgment was rendered. [Rose-Himley, 4 Cranch 241, (1809).] California is an exception and perhaps there are several other states that would apply the foreign tests. It seems to be the American rule that nationality alone is not sufficient warrant for a foreign court to take divorce jurisdiction. [Grubel-Nassauer, 210 N. Y. 149, (1913).] Nor is the fact that the marriage was solemnized within the state sufficient of itself to sustain the divorce jurisdiction. [Barber-Barber, 151, N. Y. S. 1064, (1915).] An equivalent of the "English marriage" doctrine has never obtained in America. Furthermore, consent of the parties is not enough to supply a jurisdiction over the subject-matter otherwise lacking. [Lister-Lister, 86 N. J. Eq. 30, (1915).]

In many if not most states marriage is considered a *res* and jurisdiction for divorce is deemed to exist wherever either party is domiciled. [Cheever-Wilson, 9 Wallace 108, (1869).] In view of the foregoing, it is the view in these states that a court of the place where either party is, or both parties are, bona fide domiciled can pronounce divorce and can do so for causes established by its own laws. By way of exception, New York and a few other Eastern states will decline to recognize a default judgment of divorce rendered upon constructive service in a state or country which is the new domicile of one spouse and which never was that of the couple. Recognition nevertheless will be given in the latter states when the domicile of plaintiff was the last matrimonial domicile. [Atherton-Atherton, 181 U. S. 155, (1900).] Jurisdiction by a court merely of the residence of the plaintiff will not be recognized in New York. [Haddock-Haddock, 201 U. S. 562 (1905); Andrews-Andrews, 188 U. S. 14, (1902).] New York will recognize a divorce rendered by the courts of a foreign country in which both parties were long resident but not domiciled if the award be for adultery committed in such country. [Gould-Gould, 119 Miscellaneous 845, (1922); affd. 201 A. D. 127, (1922); 201 A. D. 670, (1922); affd. 235 N. Y. 14, (1923).]

The New York rule against recognition of foreign or sister-state default judgments of divorce based upon constructive service will not be applied in favor of those who are not citizens of the state. [Kaufman-Kaufman, 160 N. Y. S. 19, (1916).] Nor will the rule be applied when a good reason is lacking. For example, a party who has procured a judgment to be rendered in another state cannot therefore be heard to question the jurisdiction of the foreign court. [Starbuck-Starbuck, 173 N. Y. 503, (1903).] A husband against whom a void divorce has been obtained, cannot first remarry and later sue for divorce in New York. "So here, if plaintiff desired to challenge his first wife's divorce and her remarriage, he should have delayed his second marriage until he had obtained a divorce from his first wife. I think now he is not in a position to invoke such relief." [Kelsey-Kelsey, 204 A. D. 116, (1922).]

The New York Appellate Decision in Beech-Beech, 211 A. D. 720, (1925) stated: "It has been the established policy of the courts of this State to disregard decrees of absolute divorce of foreign jurisdictions granted for causes other than adultery, when it has been possible so to do, without disregarding the provisions of the Federal Constitution." *A fortiori* this would be the case of foreign divorces, since these are under no constitutional protection. The latest American cases show a tendency to try to break up the vicious practice of procuring surreptitious decrees of divorce in western states for extraterritorial purposes. People remarrying in the states of their domicile on the faith of such decrees have been subjected there to prosecutions for bigamy. [People-Dowell, 25 Michigan 247, (1872); People-Baker, 76 N. Y. 78, (1879).]

This attitude might be applied to French divorces procured under like circumstances.

In determining whether or not an American court has jurisdiction the *lex fori* alone is applied to test domicile. But when the question is whether or not a foreign court has jurisdiction, it seems the foreign law on domicile is sometimes to be applied. At any rate foreign law has been considered by American courts in relation to domicile in several will cases. For example, in Dupuy-Wurtz, 53 N. Y. 556, (1873) a testator was held to be still domiciled in New York because under article 13 of the French Civil Code he could not have a true domicile in France without a presidential decree. In Harral-Harral, 39 N. J. Eq. 279, (1884) testator was found domiciled in France because French law recognizes *de facto* domicile and such domicile is meant by a reference from New Jersey law to *lex domicilii.* When a defendant has appeared in a foreign action, the *bona fides* of plaintiff's domicile will not be investigated by the New York courts. [Tiedemann-Tiedemann, 172 A. D. 819, (1916); affd., 225 N. Y. 709, (1919).] Other states, following Andrews-Andrews, 188 U. S. 14, might nevertheless do so. New York may later limit or qualify the Tiedemann case.

Fraud is also a reason for impeaching a foreign judgment. Migration for divorce is a species of fraud which will render a foreign divorce judgment unenforceable in several states. This is the case either by statute, as in Massachusetts, or by decision of the courts, as in New York. In New York a Pennsylvania divorce was disregarded by reason of fraud of the party who was plaintiff in the Pennsylvania action, in declaring that he did not know the defendant's place of residence. ([Dean-Dean, 241 N. Y. 240, (1925).] It should be remembered, however, that one who has obtained a divorce decree cannot by direct petition have it vacated for collusion. [Bancroft-Bancroft, 173 Pacific 579, (California, 1918).] A party is estopped from setting up his own fraud as a way to defeat a foreign divorce, but it is uncertain if this rule would apply to a mere declaratory judgment or would prevent invocation of acts short of fraud which would tend to defeat the foreign judgment.

Some authority exists in the United Staes for the belief that foreign judgments opposed to natural justice or in which a mistake of law or a mistake of fact has occurred will not be given full faith and credit. In Burnham-Webster, 1. Woodbury & Wilmot 172 (U. S. C. C., Maine, 1846) it was held that the *prima facie* obligation of a French judgment might be rebutted by showing that the merits of the claim were not in fact considered by the foreign court owing to some accident, mistake or agreement of the parties or other sufficient excuse. Judge Woodbury remarked: "Nor can much comity be asked for the judgments of another nation, which like France, pays no respect to those of other countries, except as before remarked, on the principle of the parties belonging there, or assenting to a trial there." (P. 179.)

The American courts are beginning to realize the wide divergencies between foreign and American laws and practice. In Gioe-Westervelt, 116 Federal Reporter 1017, (1902) the court remarked: "To one who goes carefully through the documents that make up the record of proceedings in the Italian courts, which terminate in the judgment here sued on, it seems lamentable that a sense of comity ever induced our courts to accept as *res judicata* the judgments of courts in foreign countries, whose systems of jurisprudence are totally different from our own. Truly, the judgment in this case is fearfully and wonderfully made and so far as one can make out from the documents, rankly unjust. Nevertheless, under authorities controlling upon this court, there seems to be nothing to do save to accept it as a finality."

American courts, like British, recognize only final foreign judgments. A judgment considered "irrevocable" in France would be final within the meaning of American law. But would this also be true of a judgment called in France "final" (*définitif*) yet liable to cancellation by review or new trial, if fraud or forgery should later come to light? The answer is highly uncertain. The American rule might be satisfied thereby if it could be shown by proponent that the judgment were not in fact liable to such cancellation, or to put it differently, unless it could be shown by opponent that the judgment were in fact liable to be overthrown or that proceedings for a review or new trial had been begun or were imminent.

The only reported case in America involving a French divorce judgment is Gould-Gould, already cited. The history of this case in France has been given earlier. The case in New York should now be discussed. After the French divorce judgment in favor of the husband had been recorded, the ex-wife brought suit for divorce in New York. The ex-husband set up the French judgment in bar. The special term of the New York Supreme Court dismissed the complaint and the Appellate Division affirmed this dismissal. Mr. Justice Page in the opinion of the Appellate Division laid emphasis upon the fact that the matrimonial domicile of the couple was France, although the testamentary domicile of the husband was New York. The Court of Appeals did not pass upon this particular point, but considered that the prolonged residence of the spouses in France and the commission of the adultery there were sufficient to sustain French jurisdiction for a divorce judgment. The Court of Appeals said: "Under the circumstances of this case, the policy of this state is not offended by the recognition of the judgments of the court of France. Even though it be assumed that we are not required because of the absence of domicile to give effect to their judgments, we are not prohibited from doing so where recognition, in conformity to the principle of comity, would not offend our public policy. If in the instant case the judgments of the courts of France disclosed that the parties were merely sojourning in France at the time the decree of divorce was granted, or that a residence in France was of such limited duration as to lead the Supreme Court to believe that the decree was the result of collusion, or the judgment was rendered for a cause not recognized as sufficient cause of absolute divorce by the law of this state, it may be that the justice presiding would be justified in holding that the decree was contrary to the policy of this state, and in a refusal to give effect to the evidence sought to be established thereby. We leave those questions open." (P. 30.)

The decision in the Gould case apparently means that a French divorce will be recognized when both spouses, although domiciled in New York, have been long resident in France, when the cause occurred during that residence, when the cause was sufficient for divorce in New York and when both parties submitted to the jurisdiction. Not many French divorces between Americans can comply with these requirements, but even so restricted the Gould case has been seriously criticised. Beale characterizes it as a "novel decision." [Haddock Revisited, 39 Harvard Law Review 417, (1926).] It does indeed go beyond the usual rule in America, by recognizing a divorce judgment rendered by a court not of the domicile but only of the residence. It follows as to domicile the English rule of Niboyet-Niboyet, which however was overruled by Le Mesurier-Le Mesurier. It fails to follow Hilton-Guyot on the question of reciprocity. Furthermore the attorneys for Mrs. Gould did not point out to the New York courts that she might have sued Mr. Gould for divorce in France notwithstanding the judgment against her and that the judgment might be still open to direct attack by proceedings for a new trial if the facts warranted this. The point seems never to have been raised that French divorces or separations are never "final" in the absolute and strict sense so long as the recourse of new trial is still open. Consequently it is highly uncertain to what extent Gould-Gould will be followed in other states.

An anticlimax to the principal Gould case may be incidentally mentioned. An attempt to reopen the New York case was made by the ex-wife on the ground that the French judgment had not been recorded within two months after it was rendered. The Appellate Division [Gould-Gould, 202 A. D. 492, (1922)] held that the French judgment would not be disregarded on this account since it had been recorded within two months after the review by the Court of Cassation had terminated, as French law required.

A number of other cases exist in the United States in which foreign, but not French, divorce judgments have been passed upon and sustained. In Sorensen-Sorensen, 202 N. Y. S. 620, (1921) a Danish divorce by royal decree in favor of a deserted husband, and rendered upon personal delivery of process to the wife in New York at the Danish consulate was sustained. Rabbinical divorces awarded in Russia between Russian Jews domiciled there have also been considered valid and a bar to a later action in America. [*In re* Spondere, 162 N. Y. S. 943, (1917); Miller-Miller, 70 Miscellaneous 368, (1911); Leshinsky-Leshinsky, 5 Miscellaneous 495, (1893).] Divorces pronounced by the judicial authorities of the Cherokee nation between Indians have been recognized. [Wall-Williamson, 8 Alabama 48, (1845); Wall-Williamson, 11 Alabama 826, (1847).] In Lie-Lie, 159 N. Y. S. 748, (1916) a Norwegian divorce between Norwegians, granted to the wife after her return to a separate domicile in that country, was considered a good defense to a later action of the husband in New York.

However, there are various cases in which foreign divorce judgments have been considered void and not *res judicata,* although admissible in evidence. A German divorce in favor of the husband was not a bar to a New York action for separation by the wife, when the parties were domiciled in New York at the time the Saxon court purported to dissolve the marriage and the wife was not served with process in Germany. [De Meli-De Meli, 120 N. Y. 485, (1890).] A Swedish ecclesiastical divorce granted under similar circumstances was rejected in St. Sure-Landfield, 82 Wisconsin 346, (1892). Saperstone-Saperstone, 73 Miscellaneous 631, (1911) held that a Russian rabbinical divorce between Russian Jews domiciled at the time in New York was void. An injunction was granted in Greenberg-Greenberg, 218 A. D., 104, (1926) to prevent a New York citizen from proceeding to sue for divorce in Sonora, Mexico, his wife who remained in New York. A declaratory judgment may be obtained by a New York citizen that a Mexican divorce not entitled to recognition in America leaves the marital status unaffected in New York State and an injunction may be obtained to prevent the spouse who secured the divorce from representing as his wife a woman whom he later married in Connecticut. [Baumann-Baumann, 222 A. D. 480, (1928); 228 N. Y. S. 539, (1928).]

Marriage license clerks in America recognize and act upon foreign divorce judgments very readily and issue license to remarry in view thereof. In fact, cases are not unknown in which a *divorcio* rendered in Catholic countries, such as Austria, Italy, Brazil, which is a separation only, has been treated in America as if it were a real divorce, owing to ignorance on the part of the clerks and to intentionally or unintentionally faulty translation of the foreign judgment.

Foreign judgments of separation from bed and board will be more readily recognized and given full force and credit in America than will those of divorce. Separation judgments may be impeached for lack of jurisdiction, fraud and perhaps unfairness. Freeman remarks: "As we have seen, domicile is the test of jurisdiction in the case of divorce if the decree is to be effective internationally. But this is not true if a mere judicial separation is decreed, residence alone being sufficient whether the offense upon which the proceeding is founded occurred within or without the forum." (Freeman, vol. III, p. 3099.) Nevertheless, residence alone is not sufficient without personal service of process within the foreign country, because separation is *in personam,* not *in rem.*

It seems in one case only as yet has a foreign separation been passed upon by an American court, namely in Zaveglia-Notarbartolo, 137 Louisiana 722, (1915). Two Italians were separated in Italy. The husband came alone to Louisiana, purported to become domiciled there and took out first citizenship papers. He then sued to convert the Italian separation into a Louisiana divorce, under a statute provision somewhat similar to article 310 of the French Civil Code. The court named an attorney to represent the absent wife. She appeared in the action. The court declined to award divorce against her because the Louisiana code provision has no application to a foreign, but only to a domestic, judgment of separation. The court indicated that there must be read into the Italian judgment the condition prescribed by Italian law, that no final divorces are allowed in Italy, from which it follows that neither the Italian judgment of separation from bed and board, nor any such judgment predicated thereon by a court of the United States can be made to serve the purpose in question, since no judgment can be given, either directly or indirectly, greater effect beyond than it has within the territorial jurisdiction of the court by which it was rendered.

Foreign judgments of divorce or separation awarding alimony seem to have come up rarely before the American courts. Jurisdiction over the parties is conceded to carry with it authority to adjust the rights as to property within the jurisdiction. [McCormick-McCormick, 82 Kansas 31, (1910).] The courts of a state may subject a defendant's land to the payment of alimony although he is non-resident and not served with process in the state. But a judgment for alimony is *in personam* and in America will be respected extraterritorially only when founded upon personal service of process within the foreign jurisdiction. An order for temporary alimony is not such a final and complete judgment that it can be called a debt of record and cannot be sued upon in the courts of another state, since it is subject at any time to vacation. [Henry-Henry, 74 West Virginia 563, (1914).] De Brimont-Penniman, Federal Cases 3,715, (1873) is a case in which the Federal District Court declined to recognize a French award of alimony rendered in favor of a French son-in-law against his American father-in-law. The court considered that the laws of France upon which the award was based were local in their nature and intended to protect the public against pauperism and they have no extraterritorial significance, but must be executed upon persons and property in France only. In view of the fact that French judgments, both preliminary and definitive, awarding alimony are always subject to modification so far as that relief is concerned, the prospects of collecting French alimony in the United States are not brilliant. Perhaps accrued alimony under the final definitive judgment would sometimes be collectible.

What shall one say of the possibility of enforcement in America of an award of custody of the children in a French judgment? Probably, the French judgment to be recognized as valid would have to be based upon personal service or appearance in France. But since in France an award of custody is revocable, it is probable that an American court would not feel bound by it if the children were in the state. The Utah courts in Cooke-Cooke, 248 Pacific 83, (1926) awarded custody of a child to a wife in her action for separate maintenance notwithstanding a Canadian judgment that she had been guilty of adultery and that awarded custody to the husband.

In Munn-Cook, 8 N. Y. S. 698, (1890) an interlocutory divorce judgment of an English court was not considered entitled to recognition in so far as enforcement of the accessory relief concerning the marriage settlements was concerned because the judgment was not final. Would this be the attitude also as to accessory relief relating to property in a French judgment? It is quite undecided whether or not an American court would recognize the powers of a French notary named to liquidate the matrimonial property regime of the ex-spouses. A party would not be obliged by an American court to place property physically located outside France within the reach of the French notary or court, nor would the notary be entitled, as a sort of receiver, to sue therefor and collect the property in America. A French money judgment approving the notary's liquidation would probably be enforceable in New York; at least so far as the liquidation relates to property in France and possibly also as to property elsewhere, even perhaps as to the value of dower in realty. A Nevada decree of divorce which required the husband to account for the community property was not considered sufficient *per se* to entitle the wife to an accounting in New York in the absence of proof that there was such property in the state. [Tiedeman-Tiedeman, 156 N. Y. S. 111, (1915); reversed by 158 N. Y. S. 851, (1916); 172 A. D. 819; affd., 225 N. Y. 709, (1919).] The reason for the refusal to order an accounting was stated by the Appellate Division to be that accounting is a method of enforcement and enforcement is a matter of *lex fori*. Full faith and credit does not apply in a suit of equity to provisions of a judgment which are incidental to the main relief and are in the nature of execution of the judgment itself. The French judgment ordering liquidation would entitle the parties to a domestic judgment of accounting in relation to property in the state.

Turn now to the implied effects or statutory consequences in the United States of a French divorce whose nature justifies or entitles it to full faith and credit. Does French law or American law apply? In California by statute the effects of a foreign judgment are those both of the foreign and of the domestic law. In New York the effects are left by statute to the courts for decision, and the courts do not always treat the foreign or sister-state divorce as the equivalent of a domestic judgment in regard to consequences.

The question of the effect of divorce upon dower is of especial importance. *Lex rei sitae* governs realty in America. In Georgia and Ohio dower is barred by a divorce when permanent alimony is granted. In Connecticut, Illinois, Indiana, Massachusetts, Maine, Michigan, Missouri and Rhode Island an innocent wife retains dower. In Alabama, Arkansas, Iowa and Montana dower is barred by divorce no matter which spouse was at fault. In New York the innocent wife retains dower, the innocent husband retains curtesy, the guilty wife loses dower, the guilty husband loses curtesy. In America there is no such thing as divorce against or in favor of both parties, as there is in France. Do these provisions of law relating to dower apply to foreign or sister-state divorces or only to domestic divorces? In most states it seems they do apply to all, but not so in New York.

It has been held in New York that section 1156 of the Civil Practice Act, preserving dower to the innocent wife, does not apply to a sister-state judgment. [Monroe County Savings Bank-Yeoman, 195 N. Y. S. 531, (1922); Voke-Platt, 96 N. Y. S. 355, (1905).] The rule is, however, possibly narrower than this, for the court in the Monroe case remarked: "I conclude that the applicant's vested right of dower was divested by a process alien to our procedure, when she procured the marriage to be dissolved completely as to her, without any fault on the part of her spouse, by resorting to a foreign tribunal for relief that could not be had in the judicial forum in the state of the matrimonial domicile." It is possible that dower would be forfeited only in the case of foreign judgment whose validity would not be recognized in New York, but would be preserved to the innocent wife in other cases even where obtained for grounds not known in New York. In Van Blaricum-Larson, 205 N. Y. 355, (1912) the Court of Appeals decided that a divorce obtained by a wife in another state on a ground not recognized in New York did not cause her to lose dower. A divorce obtained by a husband in a sister-state for desertion does not bar the wife's dower in New York. [Vancleef-Burns, 118 N. Y. 549. (1890).] Dower will not vest when the marriage itself is void because one party was still married at the time of the solemnization in view of the invalidity of a foreign or sister-state divorce. In Bell-Little, 204 A. D. 235, (1922), [Affd., 237 N. Y. 519] a Pennsylvania divorce was considered void in New York because obtained by the deserting wife upon constructive service; conseqently she had no dower in her second husband's land in New York.

Concerning personal property, *lex rei sitae* does not necessarily govern the effects of a foreign divorce in an American state. In McGrew-Mutual Life Insurance Company of New York, 137 California 85, (1901) [188 U. S. 291] a Hawaiian divorce between Hawaiians was recognized in California; nevertheless it was not allowed to produce the Hawaiian statutory consequences so far as property in the State was concerned. The Hawaii statute provided that when divorce was decreed for adultery of the wife, the husband should hold her personal estate forever. The wife removed from Hawaii to California during the divorce proceedings. After judgment, the ex-wife brought suit against the defendant insurance company on the ex-husband's death to recover the amount of a policy in her favor. The defendant had already paid the amount to the husband's estate. The court compelled the defendant to pay over again, holding that, the wife being domiciled in California when the judgment was rendered, she was bound by its terms, but she was not bound by the Hawaii statute because by the time the judgment was rendered the wife and her property were beyond the territorial jurisdiction of the statute and the laws of Hawaii could not operate to forfeit property in California. It is not clear whether or not other states would follow the doctrine of the McGrew case.

It is very doubtful if any American court would enjoin an ex-wife from using her ex-husband's name in America after a French divorce. Nor probably would the French three-hundred-day restriction upon remarriage of the woman be given effect.

It is also still an open question in the United States whether or not a French divorce or separation judgment would operate to revoke financial clauses of an earlier American separate maintenance agreement. Possibly the presence or absence of an award of alimony would be taken into consideration in this connection. It is also quite undecided what effect a French divorce would have upon any legacies to a spouse in the other's unrevoked American will as to property in America. Could, for example, an American wife awarded divorce in France claim the benefit in the United States of article 300 of the French Civil Code to retain gifts and other advantages made to her by her husband in an ante-nuptial contract or a separation agreement? Could she claim to be discharged from a release of dower given to him by her, on the theory that he forfeited under article 299, C. C. the advantages derived from her, and release of dower is such an advantage? All these, and many other, questions of vital importance are still unanswered in American law.

In America, judgments date from their entry or from the end of the term of court. It is undecided whether or not the retroactive effect of a French divorce between the parties as to their property would be given effect in the United States. No foreign judgment will receive greater effects in a State than those to which it is entitled in the foreign country where rendered, nor probably greater effect than those enjoyed by a domestic judgment. A French default judgment which has lapsed under article 156 of the Code of Civil Procedure would not be enforceable in America, nor would an interlocutory judgment, nor a judgment still subject to possible appeal or opening of default.

French divorce proceedings even if they do not eventuate in a judgment may produce some effects which would be recognized extraterritorially. For instance, if an American couple enter into a valid separation agreement in the United States and then decide to divorce in France and establish the matrimonial domicile there as a preliminary, this would be an implied revocation of the agreement, in whole or in part. If one of them should cause a bailiff to demand that the other resume marital relations, this too would be a repudiation or abandonment of the separation instrument. If after this the French courts declined jurisdiction, the legal situation of the spouses would require resettlement. A declaration of French domicile in a pleading might later be used as evidence of foreign domicile, in intestacy or testamentary proceedings in America, to govern distribution of the estate. In other words, before spouses resort to France for divorce the consequences should be carefully considered, for the institution of proceedings, even if unsuccessful, is likely to affect their property and personal rights in America.

Chapter XXXIV

CONCLUSION

Napoleon is credited with the remark: "I shall not go down to posterity by the battles I have fought, but by the codes I have given to France." The Civil Code is indeed a magnificent work, in need today of some revision, but still a legal monument. America with the more than forty-eight different civil legislations, cannot afford to criticise the civil law of France. Nevertheless, the French legal system is somewhat defective and particularly is this the fact in matters of divorce and separation.

It will have been observed that the definitions of divorce and separation in the civil law of France and in the common or rather statute law of America and England are quite similar. In respect to the separate domicile of the wife, France follows the English rather than the American rule, and considers that a wife cannot set up another domicile without previous judicial separation. The nature and character of domicile is today in France substantially the same as under the common law. The French law on nationality presents characteristics found elsewhere, though marked by the intense desire of France to add to her citizenship in order to compensate for her low birth rate and war losses. To further this result the principle of unity of nationality within the family has been sacrificed and French citizenship will be restored to wives born French and this even against the wishes of their husbands.

Divorce is not today in France a contractual matter, as it was in Rome and in France during the French Revolution. Separation agreements, even of a nature susceptible of approval in England and America, would be void in France. The invalidity extends for reasons of public policy even to those made by aliens in their own country. With inconsistency, however, France has extended in jurisprudence the scope of the listed grounds for divorce, so that today a married couple really desirous of divorcing can readily create a state of facts enabling them to secure a divorce although no contract to this end may be entered into. A derogatory letter or harsh words will often suffice to create the gross insults for which a court will dissolve the marriage. No less authorities than Planiol and Ripert say this: "Furthermore, the judges have complacently sanctioned divorces by mutual consent in which the legal cause was simulated; the practice of divorce by agreement has extended itself in the large cities, particularly in Paris. An abandonment of the conjugal domicile is simulated, followed by a summons to return which is not obeyed, and the Tribunal pronounces divorce for gross insults; if necessary, an adultery is simulated; more simply they content themselves with the sending of an insulting letter whose terms have been agreed in advance. Agencies have been created to facilitate such dissolutions to couples desirous of breaking their bonds; the divorce industry is more prosperous than the matrimonial agencies." (Planiol and Ripert, *Traité pratique de Droit Civil Français,* 1925, vol. 2, p. 399.) So far as divorce is concerned the influence of the Catholic Church in France is at a low ebb and public opinion is now far from considering marriage indissoluble. The attitude there toward divorce is today much more nearly like that in the United States than it is like that in England.

Whereas in the common law countries evolution in divorce has been from the legislative to the judicial, this has never taken place in France. Divorce by Act of Parliament or legislature is totally unknown in the French Republic, nor was it ever known in the French Kingdom or Empire. The practice of divorce by royal decree, which is still a concurrent remedy with the judicial in various countries, for instance in Denmark, never prevailed in France. Matrimonial causes in France under the *ancien régime* belonged to the ecclesiastical courts. Their power in these matters has passed to the civil courts, though there is a trace of the authority of religious courts still visible in the power conceded to rabbis over alien Jews.

When it comes to the conflict of jurisdictions and conflict of laws, French law differs fundamentally from British and American. The judges of the domicile of the parties are considered the natural judges in the common law, while the judges of the allegiance are considered the natural judges in the civil law. France lays emphasis whenever possible upon *lex nationalis,* England and American upon *lex domicilii* or *lex fori.* The genesis of the French attitude is the nationalistic feeling which swept the country during the Revolution and the Empire. France sought to keep control over her nationals wherever they might be, so she provided in article 3, C. C., that French law should govern their status and capacity everywhere. She endeavored to give them a privileged position in litigation by articles 14 and 15, C. C., which allows a French citizen to sue and be sued in France concerning all *obligations.* For ten years under the Hague Convention France conceded in matrimonial causes concurrent jurisdiction to the courts of the domicile with those of the nationality. This was, however, a departure from the French tradition of the exclusive competence of national courts. Now that the Hague Convention is no longer in force there, the French doctrines in jurisdiction over aliens are unhampered by law or treaty. While the French courts have never gone back to the old exclusive view, nevertheless domicile is today a factor affecting jurisdiction chiefly in relation to possible denial of justice. It is not so much that domicile in France gives French courts jurisdiction as that absence of domicile in the aliens' own country is considered rightly or wrongly to make unavailable their national courts. If there be in fact a remedy before the courts of the allegiance, French courts may decline jurisdiction, although the aliens are domiciled in France, the doctrine of the Hague Convention to the contrary notwithstanding.

A word should also be said about *renvoi* since it now has a material influence in the divorce actions of Americans and English in France. While there is still divergence of views in the common law countries as to whether or not *renvoi* should be accepted, the matter is settled affirmatively in France, though the Tribunal of Boulogne still rebels. French courts will take jurisdiction on *renvoi* to them as courts of the domicile. They frequently apply French internal law as *lex domicilii* on *renvoi* from *lex nationalis*.

The *res* theory of marriage has never obtained in France and no difference is made in the rules of jurisdiction between divorce and separation actions, nor is personal service within the country deemed of especial consequence in actions *in personam*, for all matrimonial actions are personal. French law has never known a French marriage doctrine similar to the English marriage doctrine of Lolley's case. French law, however, for some years went far beyond this and held that the marriage of a French citizen could not be dealt with at all by any foreign court. This ultranationalistic policy has been abandoned, but even today a foreign divorce or separation judgment will be recognized in France only if it dealt with the matter as a French court would have done.

CONCLUSION

An interesting feature of the French law is that a judgment of divorce or separation gives to the French courts perpetual jurisdiction over the parties for the enforcement of its legal consequences, even when both the parties have removed from France in the interval and when no personal service is obtained upon the defendant in the enforcement action. The French law, based upon the Roman law, that the defendant must prove lack of jurisdiction rather than the plaintiff its existence, is also of moment to aliens.

When it comes to the conflict of laws in relation to grounds for the divorce or separation of aliens and their defenses, French law as *lex fori* is combined with *lex nationalis,* sometimes the one sometimes the other receiving preponderance or emphasis. Procedure is not solely a matter of French law. National law is allowed some effect in so far as matters affecting the merits are concerned. This is quite different from the rules of conflict of laws in England and in America, but the same distinction is widely recognized in the other civil law countries. It is also a surprise to note that the qualification of the nature of an act or institution will be decided rather by *lex nationalis* than by *lex fori.* So too, the statutory consequences in France of a French judgment of divorce or separation between aliens will be in principle those of *lex nationalis* of the aliens and not those of France.

In regard to defenses, the rule that recrimination or mutuality of offenses does not prevent divorce or separation, is of importance. An action in France will not necessarily be dismissed or stayed because of the copendency of an action abroad, but this tangible proof that a remedy is available in the country of the allegiance may be considered in the French court's discretion as a reason for declining to retain jurisdiction.

CONCLUSION

When one turns to the position of foreign judgments in France, one finds an unsettled condition which renders it quite impossible to say whether or not France gives reciprocity within the meaning of the Hilton-Guyot case. France is not deliberately or arbitrarily hostile to foreign divorce judgments, nor is her attitude affected by the grant or refusal of reciprocity to French judgments abroad.

The French law of evidence differs from the common law in that especial value is laid by the former upon written, and by the latter upon oral, evidence. No elaborate rules exist in France concerning relevancy and materiality, but this is left to the judge's discretion. No system prevails of cross-examination, no trial by jury in civil actions, no hearing of witnesses in open court or even by the entire bench.

The notable feature of the preliminary French procedure is not the *ex parte* hearing, which is of minor importance; it is the conciliation hearing which is of capital importance. This hearing has no counterpart in English or American practice. The settlement of accessory matters incidentally and orally by the parties before the president at conciliation is also quite without precedent in English and American practice. The French law on the service of process at the district attorney's office and Ministry of Foreign Affairs is deplorable in so far as nonresident aliens are concerned.

That the French court is itself responsible only for the award of a French judgment, not for the *motifs* or *qualités*, *i. e.*, for the opinion and recitals, will also appear significant to common law jurists. Sometime this fact is likely to be invoked before a British or American court in an attempt to discredit these parts of a French judgment. The fact is also of grave consequence, that sometimes a French judgment can be directly attacked and overthrown by a new trial ordered in consequence of a *requête civile* for forgery, fraud or newly discovered decisive evidence within two months after discovery thereof, though this may be years after the judgment apparently became final. The possibility that a French default judgment may have lapsed under article 156, C. C. P., though recorded and ostensibly binding, is likewise of significance.

That divorce or separation may be awarded in favor of and against plaintiff and in favor of and against defendant at the same time and in the same judgment or separately in a later action will be considered novel to English and American readers. What effect in an American state would such a judgment have upon dower?

The French conception that an appeal is a second trial rather than reconsideration of the first trial is not easy to grasp. No record is transmitted by the lower court to the higher. The losing party in the lower court starts a new action before the higher and the case goes to trial all over again but not without reference to the result of the first trial.

Neither in England nor in America is there any provision for the recording of divorce or separation judgments outside of the court records. The system of transcription exists in France because of the elaborate civil status registers in which every important change of status from birth to death is entered.

What should one say concerning the extraterritorial respect for French divorces and separations? The matter is still almost entirely undecided. Gould-Gould is the leading case in America, yet it is not likely to be generally followed, but rather to be limited and distinguished in some other American states and in England. Furthermore, the Gould case, being based upon adultery, is not typical of French divorces. On the whole the prospect that many French divorces will receive recognition in the

British Empire and in the United States is not very promising. The French law of jurisdiction is too broad for the courts of these countries to approve. However, no general or absolute approval or condemnation is possible. Each French judgment must be considered *per se* under the practice which now prevails. This much one can say: the accessory relief of French judgments would probably not be enforceable in England or in America, because it is essentially subject to change or cancellation in France. Revocability ought not to prevent collection of alimony accrued before a change, but nevertheless it is likely that even such alimony would be irrecoverable by action.

Looking at the subject of the divorce and separation of aliens in France from the American and British points of view, one may in closing indicate the following striking features of French law:

1) Jurisdiction over aliens is discretional rather than purely a question of law.

2) Personal service of process is of no greater efficacy than substituted service and there is no constructive service by publication or personal service outside France.

3) Foreign law on grounds and defenses is considered with the French; this is also true of matters of procedure affecting the merits and rules of evidence.

4) Foreign statutory effects will usually be applied to a French judgment between aliens.

5) French default judgments will lapse if not executed within six months, although already recorded.

6) Certain French judgments are not irrevocable until the recourse of new trial has been exhausted, and such recourse is sometimes indefi-

nitely available, *i.e.,* until two months after discovery in the case of forgery, fraud or newly discovered evidence of a decisive character.

7) An action for damages will lie in addition to alimony for breach of the marriage leading to divorce or separation, and such action may be brought even after the judgment.

8) An action will lie for alimony notwithstanding the contrary terms of a settlement and may be brought after the divorce.

9) In order to equalize the statutory effects, the losing party may sue for divorce or separation after a judgment of divorce has been pronounced against him.

10) A judgment or judgments of divorce or separation may exist simultaneously for or against both parties.

11) Recrimination is not a defense in French law.

12) In the court's discretion all evidence—opinion, hearsay, even affidavits and statements made without cross-examination—is available for what it is worth.

13) Agreements which maintain a *de facto* separation are void in France, even though made by aliens outside France and valid according to foreign law.

14) An appeal is a second trial before another court and not a reconsideration of the first one by another court.

The reasons French divorces are popular among aliens are practical and psychological. A French divorce has come to be considered fashionable in some North and South American social circles, and is regarded as having a certain *cachet.* It is popularly deemed superior to a Mexican or Nevada divorce. Until 1927 French divorces could be obtained with celerity and cheapness. Sometimes a few weeks only intervened between the arrival of the aliens and their divorce. At one time a divorce could be obtained for eight hundred dollars. Those days have passed. But there still remain other attractions, particularly the secrecy which surrounds the hearings and the liberality of the grounds for which relief may be obtained. The grounds for divorce in the Civil Code are as generous as in America's most liberal states and far more generous than in England. French courts take jurisdiction readily, although they are becoming more particular in relation to this. Oral testimony is rare and when required is taken privately in chambers. Evidence is not open to public inspection and reporters are excluded. The decision of the court is concisely and discreetly stated. No co-respondents are made parties and any accomplices are usually referred to by initials only. Newspaper reports of the litigation in course are forbidden. Generally nothing whatever appears in the press until after judgment has been rendered and then the mere fact of divorce or separation is announced in the case of Americans in the Paris editions of the New York Herald and the Chicago Tribune, and in the case of the British, in the Daily Mail. French papers rarely concern themselves about the matrimonial troubles of foreigners. In view of these advantages it is probable that France will remain indefinitely a preferred place for the divorce of aliens, although the abnormal rate of resort to French courts by Americans from 1920 to 1927 is not likely to recur.

As Pascal says: "One can see nothing just or unjust that does not change character with change of climate. A difference of three degrees in latitude reverses all jurisprudence."

BIBLIOGRAPHY

(Foreign references, available for consultation at the Author's Law Library at 55 East 65th St., New York City, are marked with an asterisk.)

Books

*Allain: Des effets du jugement de divorce, Paris, 1896

*Andreani: La Condition des étrangers en France et la législation sur la nationalité française, Paris, 1907

*Avid: The Civil Laws of France to the Present Time, London, 1875

*Bentwick: The Law of Domicile in its Relation to Succession and the Doctrine of Renvoi, London, 1911

*Bodington: An Outline of the French Law of Evidence, London, 1904

*Boyer: Petit Formulaire. Suivi de jurisprudence. Procédure en matière de conciliation de divorce et séparation de corps, Paris, 1927

*Cachard: The French Civil Code with the Various Amendments Thereto as in Force on March 15, 1895

*Cannoes: Des rapports du mariage avec la nationalité, Paris, 1900

*Carpentier: Divorce et séparation de corps, 2 vols., Paris, 1899

*Carpentier: Traité théorique et pratique du divorce et de la séparation de corps, 2 vols., Paris, 1894

Carpentier et Frejoneu du Saint: Répertoire général alphabétique du droit français, "Divorce," vol. 17, 1899

*Constant: De l'exécution des jugements étrangers dans les divers pays, 2nd ed., Paris, 1890

Corpus Juris, 'Divorce," Vol. XII, 1917

*Coulon: Le divorce et la séparation de corps, Paris, 1890, 1897, 5 vols.

BIBLIOGRAPHY

*Dalloz: Code de procédure civile, Paris, Editions of 1918 and of 1927

*Dalloz: Nouveau Code Civil, 5 vols., Paris, 1900-1907; Additions au Nouveau Code Civil, ed. 1914

*Degnault: Le Mariage, la séparation de corps et le divorce en Droit International, Paris, 1903

*Despagnet: Précis de Droit International Privé, 5th ed., Paris, 1909

*Donnedieu de Vabres: L'Evolution de la jurisprudence française en matière de conflit des lois, Paris, 1905

*Doyer, de: La Conversion de la séparation de corps en divorce, Paris, 1913

*Eglin, d': Etude sur le contrat de mariage en droit comparé et en droit international, Paris, 1883

*Esmein: Le Mariage en Droit Canonique, 2 vols., Paris, 1891

*Fernaud-Laurent et Dammas: Dictionaire juridique, anglais-français et français-anglais, Paris, 1927

*Foignet: Manuel élémentaire de procédure civile, 5th ed., Paris, 1912

Freeman: A Treatise of the Law of Judgments, 5th ed., 2 vols., New York, 1925

*Fromageot: De la double nationalité des individus et des sociétés, Paris, 1891

*Garcin: Du changement de nationalité entre époux, Paris, 1902

*Garsonnet et Cezar-Bru: Precis de procédure civile, 1911, Paris, 7th ed.

*Goiraud and Thompson: The French Judicial System and Procedure in French Courts, London, 1919

*Groffy: De l'unité de nationalité dans la famille, Paris, 1893

*Hall: The Law and Procedure in Divorce and Matrimonial Causes, London, 1905

BIBLIOGRAPHY

Jacobs: A Treatise on the Law of Domicile, New York, 1887

*Katz: Le Divorce d'accord, Paris, 1912

*Kelly: The French Law of Marriage, Marriage Contracts, Divorce and the Conflict of Laws Arising Therefrom, 2d ed., by Bodington, London, 1895

*Lachau: De la compétence des tribunaux français a l'égard des étrangers en matière civile et commerciale d'après la jurisprudence française, Paris, 1893

*Lachau et Doguin: De l'exécution des jugements étrangers d'après la jurisprudence française avex le texte des principaux arrêts et jugements, Paris, 1889

*Laurent-Bailly: Le Divorce et la séparation de corps en France et à l'étranger, Paris, 1910

*Lehr: Le Mariage, le divorce et la séparation de corps dans les principaux pays civilisés, Paris, 1899

*Loeb: Legal Requirements and Formalities for Marriage of Americans in France, Paris, 1918

*Moreau: Effets internationaux des jugements en matière civile, Paris, 1884

Nelson: A Treatise on the Law of Divorce and Annulment of Marriage, New York, 1895

*Nicolesco: La Condition juridique des enfants après le divorce de leur père et mère en droit français, allemand et roumain, Paris, 1904

*Pellerin: A Digest of Cases Decided in France Relating to Private International Law, London, 1913

*Piérard: Divorce et séparation de corps, 3 vols., Paris. 1927-29

Piggott: Foreign Judgments and Jurisdiction, London, 3 vols., 1908

Piggott: Law and Practice of the Courts of the United Kingdom Relating to Foreign Judgments and Parties Out of the Jurisdiction, London, 2d ed., 1884

BIBLIOGRAPHY

*Pilicier: Le Divorce et la séparation de corps en Droit International Privé, Lausanne, 1887

*Pillet et Niboyet: Manuel de Droit International Privé, Paris, 1925

*Planiol: Traité élémentaire de Droit Civil, 2d. ed., 3 vols., Paris, 1901-1903

Planiol et Ripert: Traité pratique de Droit Civil Français, Paris, 1925, 8 vols.

*Pothier: Introduction à la coutume d'Orleans, Oeuvres de Pothier, by Bugret, 1861, Paris

*Potu: La Question du renvoi en Droit International Privé, Paris, 1913

*Ricaud: Les Régimes matrimoniaux au point de vue du Droit International Privé, Paris, 1886

*Roguin: Traité de Droit Civil Comparé. Le Mariage, Paris, 1904, Le Regime matrimonial, Paris, 1905

*Rosenberg: Ehescheidung und Eheanfechtung, Berlin, 1926

*Rouguet: Des effets du divorce quant à la personne et aux biens des enfants, Paris, 1905

Schouler: A Treatise on the Law of Marriage, Separation and Domestic Relations, New York, 6th ed., 3 vols., 1921

*Vincent et Penaud: Dictionnaire de Droit International Privé, Paris, 1888; Revue de l'Année, 1888 (1889)

*Voland et Beck: Manuel pratique de la condition des étrangers et de la legislation étrangère, Paris, 1914

*Weill: De la notion d'injure grave en matière de divorce et de séparation de corps, Paris, 1906

*Weiss: Manuel de Droit International Privé, Paris, 1914

*Weiss: Traité théorique et pratique de Droit International Privé, 2d ed., 6 vols., Paris, 1907-1913

*Williamson: A French-English Dictionary of Legal Words and Phrases, London, 1911

BIBLIOGRAPHY

Pamphlets and Articles

J. Alexander: Du Mariage en Droit International suivant la jurisprudence anglaise, Journal Clunet, 1881, p. 193

C. F. Beach: The Divorce of American Citizens in France, 9 American Bar Association Journal 26 (1925)

J. C. Beale: Haddock Revisited, 39 Harvard Law Review 417 (1926)

Bioche: Instructions de la chambre des avoués près le tribunal civil de la Seine sur l'application de la loi du 18 avril 1886, Journal de Procédure civile et commerciale, 1886, p. 177

A. Droz: De l'influence de la Convention de la Haye de 1902 sur les questions de divorce en France entre époux de nationalité différente, Journal Clunet, 1907, p. 19

H. Fort Dumanoir: Question pratiques no. 148, Journal Clunet, 1910, p. 841

Féraud-Giraud: De la compétence des tribunaux français pour connaitre des contestations entre époux étrangers, Journal Clunet, 1885, p. 225.375

E. Fortunati: Effets juridiques en Italie des jugements étrangers de divorce, Journal Clunet, 1914, p. 420

C. A. Hereshoff-Bartlett: Napoleon's Divorce, 36 Law Quarterly Review 164 (1920)

A. K. Kuhn: Doctrines of Private International Law in England and America contrasted with those of Continental Europe, 12 Columbia Law Review 44 (1912)

Labbé: Une femme mariée à un Français et judiciairement séparée de corps peut elle se faire naturaliser en pays étranger sans l'autorisation de son mari ou de justice, Journal Clunet, 1875, p. 409

A. Lainé: La Conférence de La Haye relative au Droit International Privé, Journal Clunet, 1895, p. 465

BIBLIOGRAPHY

A. Morillot: De la conversion en divorce d'un régime de séparation de corps consensuel etabli a l'étranger, Journal Clunet, 1922, p. 545

A. J. Peaslee: *Ex Parte* Divorce, 28 Harvard Law Review 457 (1915)

M. A. Pillet: Jurisdiction in Actions between Foreigners, 18 Harvard Law Review 325 (1905)

M. Radin: Domicile in French Divorce, 13 California Law Review 513 (1925)

J. G. Saxe: New York's Recognition of Divorce Decrees of other States and Foreign Countries (1927)

M. Smith: Validity in the United States of French Divorces to Americans, 11 American Bar Association Journal 223 (1925)

Travers: Effets de la dénonciation par la France des Conventions de la Haye de 1902 en matière de mariage, de divorce et de séparation de corps et de tutelle, Journal Clunet, 1914, p. 778

Cases and Briefs. New York Court of Appeals, Gould-Gould, 235 N. Y. 14

Effect of Foreign Divorce on Dower. 2 New York Law Review 481 (1924)

Enlèvement de femme majeure, Journal Clunet, 1887, p. 451

Instructions aux préfets et aux parquets relative à la loi du 10 août 1927 sur la nationalité

*Loi sur la nationalité suivie des décrets et instructions relatifs à l'application de la loi du 10 aout 1927, Journal Officiel, August 14, 1927

INDEX

COLUMBIA UNIVERSITY PRESS
Columbia University
New York

FOREIGN AGENT
OXFORD UNIVERSITY PRESS
HUMPHREY MILFORD
Amen House, London, E. C.

Bei Fragen zur Produktsicherheit wenden Sie sich bitte an:
If you have any questions regarding product safety,
please contact:

Walter de Gruyter GmbH
Genthiner Straße 13
10785 Berlin
productsafety@degruyterbrill.com